Roots To The 92

The debut book by

Andrew Leeder

A journey through the league grounds by a football fan – a tale of what it was like to be there

First published 2016

This paperback edition published 2016

ISBN 1849149488

ISBN 9781849149488

Self-Published using

CompletelyNovel.com

Dedicated to my Dad, Tony Leeder

Contents

Foreword

As a proud ex-Shrimper, I was delighted to be asked to write the Foreword for this book.

I have played at numerous clubs, starting my career at Crusaders in Northern Ireland, then moving to Oldham Athletic as a young 18 year old where I plied my trade before moving to local rivals Bury.

It was at Bury that my career really took off, being chosen for full international honours with Northern Ireland at a time when they boasted two of the world's greatest players in the great George Best and arguably one of the greatest ever goalkeepers in Pat Jennings.

I continued my career with moves to Blackpool and Greek giants Olympiacos, before I made my way to Roots Hall in December 1979 in what was, at the time, a record transfer fee for Southend United of £100,000.

I then spent three of the happiest years of my career at Southend with some great memories, none more so than winning my only medal in professional football for the Division Four Championship, being leading goal scorer and being voted player of the year.

On leaving Southend I had a brief spell - teaming up once again with George Best - at Hong Kong Rangers, before moving back to Bury where I finished my career through injury. In total I played over 400 league games, also making 29 appearances for my country, and scoring over 100 goals along the way.

During my career I have met many supporters, who I always enjoy talking to and spending time with. I feel very privileged to have met some of the people I have encountered during my career, many still in my life as good friends, and it is always great to catch up with them and reminisce about the good old days! I think, sadly, that is what is lacking in today's game, in that players do not seem to have the same rapport with supporters and are not as approachable as back in the day. For me the amount of money that is now in football has ruined our beautiful game and I know many ex-players who are of the same opinion as me!

Having said that I am still working in football, with 20 years' service at Blackpool FC Community Trust this August, working closely with the local community and, as part of my role, helping to inspire young people to reach their aims, goals and full potential. It was through the club that I was put in touch with Andy, who had contacted the ticket office to see if I would be around at the Blackpool v Southend match on 2 April 2016. Unfortunately I was due to be at a family wedding over in Belfast on the day of the match, so I took it upon myself to make contact with Andy to see if he wanted to meet up the day before.

I am so glad that Andy and I got to meet as I didn't realise at the time he had travelled the country visiting all 92 football league clubs and that Blackpool was his final ground, it seemed very fitting that I could meet him here at Blackpool to celebrate him finishing his journey.

I feel honoured that I have been able to be a small part of his 92 grounds quest and I look forward to being able to read this book and hopefully reminisce once again.

With Best Wishes

Derek Spence

Preface

You will quickly gather that I am a Southend fan who wanted to support Chelsea and who also had spells watching Plymouth plus a pair of Bristol's. That is a lot to confess in one sentence.

My aim in writing the book has been for it to be something to which a fan of any club can relate. I have avoided giving match reports – I suspect that even the most dedicated Blue Nose will not be even remotely interested in how dominant they were at corners against Plymouth in 1984. Nor have I sought to provide minute detail of the facilities at Scunthorpe, Sunderland, Oxford, or wherever, there are a host of books and websites that do that adequately enough. Instead, my desire has been to simply describe what it felt like to be there and cover my experiences along the way: to paint a picture as I saw it. For instance, my visit to Ninian Park was to see Cardiff play Notts County, but my hope is that you don't have to be a fan of either club, or even Welsh, to find something to relate to in the memories from my trip there - or any of the grounds I visited.

I cannot avoid the numerous references to Shrimpers or Pilgrims; they are who I was with most of the time. But you didn't have to be a Southend fan at Southampton in 2007 to enjoy the sight of seeing Sponge Bob Square Pants running up and down the aisles as we chanted his theme tune. Nor do you have to be a fully paid up member of the 1980's Green Army to wonder how someone who could so easily have been Prime Minister was frequently found to be standing alone on rain soaked away terraces. And as for being pissed on by Scots standing up in the rafters at Wembley, well, I'm sure anyone will appreciate the delights of that one.

I do admit to enjoying a win against Portsmouth, Colchester and Ipswich more than I perhaps should. But even I can only admire the devotion of Pompey's talismanic top-hatted bell-ringer who has been an entertaining view more than once. And when Colchester turned up at Roots Hall in February this year (2016), watching one of their fans get virtually drowned in cash on a lap of honour after a 40 mile run to raise money for his very ill son was a truly emotional footie moment - it makes me well-up just thinking about it. I am struggling though to think of something to appease Tractor Boys.

I have not loved every ground I have been to. Neither Sixfields nor Priestfield are firm favourites, and as for Stadium:mk, well, other things tend to get in the way of a fair appraisal of that one though it does have comfy seats. I suspect that a Gills fan might think it a tad ironic that I slate their away end (who doesn't?) whilst my beloved Roots Hall is hardly in pristine condition. Beauty though is in the eye of the beholder – we can all maybe agree on that one.

I have set out the book in chronological order, from Roots Hall in March 1971 through to Bloomfield Road in April 2016. At the back of the book you will find a list of the grounds covered in the order they appear in the book.

The chapters are based on broad time periods where there was generally a particular theme to my footie watching. For instance, 'Semper Fidelis' covers my time at Plymouth University when I indulged in all things green.

I have covered all grounds visited when, at the time I was there, they counted for 92 purposes. So, Edgar Street gets a mention as do the likes of Maine Road, Saltergate, Watling Street, etc. Indeed, I notched up 125 grounds in getting to the 92; 23 of them alas are no more and eight are now hosting soccer in the National League or below. One (Twerton Park) exists as it was when I went there as the home of non-league Bath City but no longer having Bristol Rovers as the sitting tenant. Another (Nene Park) still exists but the last person turned the lights out a few years ago. To satisfy the curiosity of anyone getting excited by the rules of all this, I have excluded covering grounds which were the temporary home of a team if they are the true home of another one of the 92, e.g. I saw Charlton as the home team at Selhurst Park, but have covered that abode as the home of their primary dweller, Crystal Palace.

A ground is only prefixed by a number (1/92, 2/92 and so on up to 92/92) if it was one of the 92 at the time I got to Blackpool. I realise that, thanks to West Ham and possibly whoever comes up from the National League, by the time most of you will be reading this my 92 will already be out of date. But my last port, some 45 years after I started, was Bloomfield Road, and a line has to be drawn somewhere, so let it be a tangerine one.

I have included reference to a handful of other key grounds/events visited such as Wembley, the 2006 World Cup in Germany, and the iconic New Writtle Street (the former home of Chelmsford City in case you are struggling to locate that one). They have all been part of my footie watching experience, and act as complimentary supports for the 92 in so many ways.

Completing this book ticks another one off my bucket list as indeed did doing the 92. But it is much more than a 'tick', I have thoroughly enjoyed the experience of recapping all of the memories. I hope you enjoy reading it.

Acknowledgements

There are a few very important people I would like to thank.

First, my pal David Watkins, for passing on his experience of the author process, and providing endless encouragement during the writing of this book.

Second, Derek Spence for agreeing to write the Foreword, an act which is much appreciated and one that followed a very enjoyable pub meet up. Pubs play an important part in the match day experience.

Third, my three sons Jim, Edward and Cameron, who all in their varying ways (and with different levels of enthusiasm) have participated in my footie watching, and who have helped their Dad indulge himself in the ground-hopping ride.

Fourth, my wonderful wife Lizzie, who not only has put up with my quest (and only with minimal fuss), but then helped extensively with the proofreading process.

And finally, my Dad, who first set me on the journey in 1971, helped me to nurture it, and then listened to my tales of it moving far beyond what he would have ever contemplated doing himself.

Introduction

My earliest recollection of footie interest was in the build up to the 1970 FA Cup Final - I was asked in the playground whether I supported Chelsea or Leeds. It would not have been cool to give the honest answer – "no idea" – so I responded with "Chelsea" simply because the name sounded more interesting. My inquisitor, satisfied with the response, bogged off to interrogate some other target and inflict a Chinese burn on anyone who dared to answer "Leeds".

So, I was now a member of the Chelsea fan club – what next? I loved kicking a ball around but had been unceremoniously informed by my seven year old peers that I was crap. So far I had not really taken to the game, instead preferring to ride bikes, pretend I was Davy Crockett, play Lego, annoy my little sister, build camps, light fires and do all the other stuff kids were meant to do in a world untainted by computer games. But now, perhaps, I should show more interest? I obtained a copy of 'Shoot', loved a picture it had of Ian Hutchinson taking a long throw, cut it out, put it on my bedroom wall and informed Dad that I needed a Chelsea kit just like Hutch's.

Dad seemed to have had a bit of a nomadic football interest, his Cambridgeshire roots taking him to the mighty March Town United, graduating from there to his then local league team Peterborough United, next to the Cobblers of Northampton Town (his National Service base) and, on migrating south to the promised land of Essex, whatever footie watching opportunity presented itself. But, if you wanted an "I was there" story, he would be happy to tell you about the time that his Dad had taken him to Stamford Bridge in 1945 with a reputed 120,000 others to see Chelsea take on those nice Ruskies from Moscow Dynamo. This link to my kit request seemed to suffice and, pleased that it might be the start of following his own distinguished footballing career of playing 20 games as centre half for the March British Legion, a Chelsea kit became my eighth birthday present.

I was thrilled. All blue cotton bar white socks, and '11' emblazoned on the back of the shirt - I decided to gloss over a technical detail that Ian Hutchinson had worn '10' at the Cup Final - I now felt like a real footballer. Having a replica kit those days was rare, and simple ownership of one catapulted me to the fringes of non-crap status.

I vividly recall its first outing, a match on the school playing field against the neighbouring catholic junior school mob. My turn came to take part and, resplendent in unblemished blue, on I trotted to the pitch where we were already taking a severe beating. No matter that my shirt was covered with the purple school bib; I was every inch the model FA Cup winner. Told to stay on the wing out of the way, I don't think I touched the ball once, and after then I never troubled the school team selectors. But it didn't matter; I was now a football fan.

Second Home

1/92: ROOTS HALL - Southend United 1 Notts County 0, Division 4, Friday 26 March 1971

By the spring of '71 Dad had decided that I was ready. My Chelsea kit aside, I had purchased my first single, 'Blue is the Colour', and every 'Shoot' pic of the FA Cup holders had found its way on to my bedroom wall. But it was a Friday night. Chelsea played on Saturdays, and here we were getting ready to go to 'the match'. Maybe we were getting an early start.

Our street butted on to the A13, nestled between a resplendent Chevron petrol station and the heavily curtained Kwong Ming Chinese restaurant (it was a dare amongst the kids down our street to go inside – I can't recall anyone ever taking it up). Turn left and you headed to the big lights of London (ok, in true Billy Bragg fashion, you had to experience Pitsea, Basildon and Dagenham first), turn right and it was up Bread & Cheese Hill to Southend, where mods and skinheads regularly kicked the shit out of each other. The Ford Anglia turned right. Bollocks (I probably said something less likely to make Dad turn straight back around and send me to bed).

If not Chelsea, then I would have settled for West Ham – Moore, Hurst, Greaves, Lampard, Brooking, Best (Clyde, not George), they were all playing for The

Hammers that season and some of my mates followed them. However, West Ham was also a left turn, and the Ford Anglia was chugging up Bread & Cheese Hill in second gear aiming for mod hell.

I quickly learned that our destination was Roots Hall, home of the mighty Shrimpers, and that they played in a league 'just' four down from where Chelsea and West Ham graced the beautiful game (ok, Division Four, but Dad was trying hard to sell it to me by not making it sound so naff). 'Our' leading scorer, Dad informed me, was Best (Billy, not George). Notice the use of the word 'our', at the time I didn't realise but I was being sold Southend United by stealth.

I think that any football ground on match night is special – the floodlights seem to convince everyone around that they must go moth-like towards them, though 'everyone' was stretching it a bit as we certainly didn't need to buy tickets in advance. Anyway, add a fine mist to the scene, or better still snow, and the experience becomes magical. Mix in the smell of woodbine and stale burgers, and any dictionary worth its salt has its definition of 'heaven'.

Roots Hall's floodlights stood proud, and still do, showing the way for Dad and me to stride up narrow car-clogged streets to the West Stand, a double-barrelled bicycle shelter to the untrained eye. He gave the gateman 50 new pennies, received change, and once the deep blue paint-encrusted turnstile had just about clicked through under the force of my eight year old muscles, we were in. Before me lay a scene that even today still makes me look twice, the view to the pitch framed by a rectangular entrance inviting you in to experience more of what you could see, hear and smell outside.

In '71 the West Stand was a cavernous terraced shell, and a typical match day would see it populated by pockets of men who, if over 65, stayed where they were, or if under 65 moved in blind hope to whichever end Southend were kicking to. It was only once in that I realised Dad had been carrying something – a milk crate. Try smuggling one of those in to a ground now and you'll get a ten season ban for carrying an offensive weapon, but back then every kid unable to see over the perimeter wall had one. At my adult height now of 6 foot 5 I always think, on what now are sadly rare terrace-days, that a crate would be useful for anyone daft enough to be standing behind me.

Now, I admit to using a little artistic license in my descriptions so far, I want to paint a picture, but the basics are all true – I really did want to support someone else, Dad did drive a Ford Anglia, the whole place smelled weird but evocative, and I did have a milk crate. But I think I'd be stretching it a bit to describe how the match went as I can't recall a thing about it. The records will tell you that Dad and I swelled the attendance to 6,745 and that our slug-balancing winger Terry Johnson scored the only goal of the game. And that will probably do as far as a match report goes – I'm not convinced that readers will be too interested in who crossed to whom, how many shots we had, etc. - I will keep that to a minimum in this book and instead focus on the experience of what it was like to be there.

Anyway, I was hooked, I was now a Shrimper with a guilty interest in Chelsea, and West Ham were consigned to 'the rest', namely all other teams which by definition were clearly inferior. I was informed this by a chant that echoed out from the North Bank – "...we're by far the greatest team, the world has ever seen" – so it must be true.

I've since been to Roots Hall well over 500 times. From living in South Benfleet to Hadleigh (Suffolk), via Hatfield Peverel, Plymouth, Bristol and Colchester, it's been a constant place to return to. I've been there at times when unwell, out of sheer habit, or just when wanting refuge, but I keep going back as more than anything else it provides hope of experiencing something wonderful that you could not ever realistically expect. Would I get that at success-laden Chelsea? Maybe, but at Roots Hall, as all lower-league fans will know, the good times may be less frequent, but when they do come along then ..... well, it can make you go a bit silly.

It seems odd now, but for over 30 years from 1955 Roots Hall was the newest ground on the league circuit. Built on the site of an old rubbish tip, it is testament to a small group of men led by Sid Broomfield, whose miraculous endeavours fashioned a ground that would ultimately hold over 30,000 (once).

Long gone now, but the South Bank was once a massive open terrace. As the designated spot for away fans it often looked comical as a group of 30 or so Exeter, or Lincoln, or Shrewsbury etc. fans stood huddled together in the middle for protection, taking turns like emperor penguins to be on the outside ring, and being surrounded by police protecting them with steely glares towards Southend's finest youth population who were glaring back from the shadows. I often used to think that our strikers would deliberately take aim at unsuspecting lone figures on the South Bank hoping to knock them down like a skittle and earn rapturous applause from the other three sides – it happened too frequently to be just 'chance' surely?

Today, Roots Hall sits proud yet crumbling, waiting for the day when the bulldozers pull down dear old Sid's efforts and replace it with something to match the flats that have sat on most of the old South Bank for the last decade or so. The whole place is held together by minimum compliance on safety regulations, as all investment for years now has been ploughed in to dreams of a shiny new corporate money-spinner on a green field site.

We are fed the line that a new ground is essential for survival, and it is difficult to argue against that, but I do wonder if, with a little more foresight, all the effort and money to date spent on pursuing this dream (which still as I write has no immediate end in sight) would have been better directed to making our main stand more serviceable. Removing the toilet adverts warning of the consequences of sexual disease might even be a start in just making the place appear a little more family friendly – more than once I have heard kids at the ground try and say 'chlamydia' to ask their dad what it was about.

I have taken many folk to Roots Hall - once. They rarely return and I accept it can be an acquired taste (Roots Hall I hope, not a day out with me). Though maybe they should try harder – I did, and quite quickly we were going to nearly every home match as I craved for more of that stale woodbine fix.

A quarter of a century later, first in line amongst my own three boys was Jim, and perhaps over-eager to do the father and son thing, I first took him along when he was only four. For his second match we made a full day of it – fish and chips, ice cream, pier, slots, and then back in to the car to cross Southend and to go to the match. He cried when we got to Roots Hall, but persevered, and now loves the place.

Having all three of my boys there with me at the same time was a moment to treasure (and a rest for my wife) though Edward and Cameron quickly decided it wasn't for them and dug their heels in. At Edward's second game Freddie Eastwood scored inside eight seconds and went on to bag a wonderful hatrick, but the lack of a guarantee that this would happen every time meant

9

his attention was lost. Cameron, to his credit, let me take him to a few away games and we had some great times doing other stuff before and after the match, but finding other attractions in places like Scunthorpe in December to make a more varied day of it is tricky. So sadly I only ultimately managed a one-third son-success rate. Our family hound, Shrimper (if I was a Hartlepool fan I suspect I'd not have had the casting vote on pet naming rights), has yet to make his debut.

Follow a team long enough and you will experience moments that will make you go mad with delirium, cry with joy or despair, be bored beyond belief, laugh out loud, be proud, be frozen, make you sing, feel sick, or just get all warm and tingly. Roots Hall has given me all of this – here are 10 highlights in brief from games I have seen which may jog a few memories for those who were there or for others who have experienced the same at their club:

- Saturday 20 November 1971, Southend 1 Aston Villa 0, FA Cup Round One: Flared trousers and parka pitch invasion by both sets of fans that met in the middle of the pitch and then ran back again. Billy Best, surely blessed with the greatest footie player name ever, ensures that Southend are one of only two clubs to have knocked Villa out of the first round of the FA Cup.
- Friday 20 April 1973 and Saturday 21 April 1973, Southend 5 Port Vale 0, Southend 5 Chesterfield 1, Division Four: Two home games in two days, both

times we score five, Billy Best and Chris Guthrie fill their boots. If only it was always like this .....

- Monday 26 January 1976, Southend 1 Hereford United 3, Division Three: Two days earlier we had beaten Cardiff in a rip-roaring FA Cup tie to make it to the fifth round. But what we really needed was league points in what ultimately proved to be a relegation season, and we now had to play high flying Hereford in a re-arranged match. Southend were awful and it was unbearably cold, but the abiding memory is of the crowd (less than 4,000) who, perhaps buoyed by the cup success or maybe just trying to fight off frostbite, made one hell of a racket throughout. Funny how things like that stay with you.

- Wednesday 10 January 1979, Southend 0 Liverpool 0, FA Cup Round Three: My Geography field trip to the Brecon Beacons had thankfully been postponed due to heavy snow so I didn't have to find an excuse not to go on it (what a tight-fisted college that was, a youth hostel in mid-Wales in January was never going to be 'high-living'). The weather in Essex was equally atrocious, driving snow making John Motson's visit to Roots Hall perched on top of the West Stand something for him to savour. We queued two hours to get in with 31,033 others (in a ground that now has room for less than 12,500). Somehow we held the European Champions to a draw, and if Stuart Parker, clear on goal, had only been more composed.........

11

- Friday 1 April 1988, Southend 3 Wigan Athletic 2, Division Three: Once again the spectre of relegation threatened, and 2-0 down at half-time things didn't look promising in this game either. Then, on comes leading scorer David Crown, lower league journeyman and all-round good-egg, who regularly benefited from Red Card Roy elbowing defenders out of the way so he could nip in and score. But not the rough route this time, sheer class prevailed instead, as having already pulled it back to 2-2 through Ling and Roy, Crowny beats three defenders and smacks in a screamer (say those last four words in a 'Jeremy Clarkson voice' for added effect). Never give up.
- Tuesday 17 February 2004, Southend 1 Colchester United 1, League Trophy Southern Final Second Leg: We were 3-2 up from the first leg and, after 98 years of trying, a debut appearance in a national final beckoned. But our Essex neighbours went one up and it looked as though that would be the half-time score until Drewe Broughton had his moment in the spotlight to fire home the equaliser. I have never, ever, felt as tense as during that second half, Colchester threw everything at us but somehow we held on. Winning a local derby to go to a final – luverly jubberly.
- Saturday 6 May 2006, Southend 1 Bristol City 0, League One: Roots Hall was packed, including 100 Man City fans let in to pay an emotional homage to The Goat in his last professional game. Wayne Gray

broke free to score at the death and send us up as champions. Steve Tilson singing anti-Colchester songs on the tanoy afterwards. A tear was shed.

- Tuesday 7 November 2006 (St Freddy Day), Southend 1 Manchester United 0, League Cup Round Four: Oh that Freddie Eastwood free-kick. Priceless TV footage of Fergie chewing his gum a bit harder as it goes in. Southend's 100% record versus the most prolific trophy winning team ever is still intact to date.

- Saturday 25 August 2007, Southend 1 Millwall 0, League One: For five years the half-time challenge had been to score from distance three goals from four shots over an obstacle between the sticks. The prize was a new car and the sponsor seemed quite content that no one had ever got near. Then someone did it – the image of him running round the pitch going mental as everyone jumped up and down sharing his delight was priceless. And a few weeks later someone did it again. The prize after that was down-graded to a signed match ball.

- Wednesday 14 May 2015, Southend 3 Stevenage 1 (AET), League Two Play-off Semi Final Second Leg: This game saw one of the grittiest performances I have ever seen. Michael Timlin suffered a truly horrific head injury in the first leg yet somehow, wearing protective head gear, played all 120 minutes of the second leg and scored the goal that sealed victory right at the end to give us a Wembley moment we could savour. A true hero.

Long may the memories keep being made. I'll clear the mist from my eyes and now go on a bit of ground hopping ....,

Come To The Shed And We'll Welcome You

2/92 - STAMFORD BRIDGE, Chelsea 3 Wolverhampton Wanderers 1, Division One, Saturday 23 October 1971

A good dozen or so Southend games under my belt, Dad considered I'd been sufficiently indoctrinated not to want to support anyone else, and eased his conscience by setting up a trip to Stamford Bridge. He was now relatively relaxed that, ongoing, I'd remain content with the much cheaper Roots Hall option.

In a wave of further encouragement he had even agreed to change the daily paper delivery to The Sun so I could collect 'Soccerstamps', which became an obsessive challenge to complete an album that he'd later regret as he ferried me around nerdy 'swap clubs' that had sprung up in pursuit of completion and prizes. I didn't win anything but it did further lure me into loving the game, and the album today remains a tattered but treasured possession. And Dad got to look at Page Three every day until Mum eventually sussed that Soccerstamps had ended long ago.

Anyway, this was going to be a big relaxing family day out – take in the sights, a spot of lunch, and then football. Mum, Sis, Dad and I caught an early train in to

Fenchurch Street so we could first go round the Tower of London. A beefeater pointed us to the entrance kiosk, Dad got his wallet out to pay and duly uttered some expletive Sis and I weren't meant to hear. The Chelsea tickets had been left on the dining room table. So off Dad trotted back home whilst the rest of us went to see where naughty folk were once garrotted, meeting Dad back at the same kiosk some three hours later.

We then reverted to 70's stereotype – Mum and Sis went shopping, Dad and I caught the tube to West London. The Bridge loomed large, and people were everywhere even 30 minutes before kick-off (something I was hitherto unused to). The ground looked crumbly but full of character, and I loved the knackered looking two tier stand that sat between the old East Stand and the away fans end, it looked as though it was about to come down (and it did four years later). We had seats (a new experience), and such luxury afforded great views of crowd surges at the Shed End – I wondered how the kids there would ever recover their milk crates.

The match programme foresaw worrying times ahead as the transfer market had exploded with nearly a million pounds being spent that season so far .... across the whole division. It also told of how Jeunesse Hautcharage of Luxembourg had been 'gallant' during their recent 21-0 defeat by Chelsea over two legs in the European Cup Winners Cup. 'A bit crap' was nearer the mark. Chelsea were a stylish outfit back then - Osgood, Hudson and Cooke were the artisans, whilst Webb, Droy and Chopper ensured no opponent went unscathed. The Wolves team sheet was impressive too; Parkes, Parkin and Wagstaffe were their main men in support of the legend they all fed to score, Derek Dougan (I always think that anyone who has the same forename and surname initials must be blessed with a head start in becoming a footballer).

We witnessed a great match, and Dad's appetite was wetted sufficiently for us to return two months later versus Leeds who clogged their way to a 0-0 and Dad never took me to the Bridge again. But I have returned many times myself over the years, and certainly the best was my last visit in January 2009 when Southend turned up to act as FA Cup cannon fodder. Over 6,000 Shrimpers came to witness the mauling, but it never happened. Yes, Chelsea went 1-0 up and should have had a hatful, but the score line stayed at a one goal difference until the 90th minute.

Roared on by the travelling Shrimpers, we won a throw in line with the Chelsea penalty box. Young Johnny Herd, yet to start shaving, threw the ball as far as he could, a Chelsea defender helped it further across the box, and up popped centre-half Peter Clarke to nod the ball home. Type 'Chelsea 1 Southend 1' into YouTube and you should then see a one minute clip from a Shrimper's mobile – it is worth watching as, no matter who you support, it gets across superbly what it is like to experience that last minute unexpected success. If I ever want a 'footie pick-me-up' that clip is where I turn. You can just hear the Chelsea tanoy announcer vainly attempt to enthuse the home support by announcing four minutes of injury time, not that I remember much of it bar having to apologise to the parent of a little kid behind me at the final whistle as I had celebrated the goal throughout those final minutes and I doubt he had seen a thing. His father's answer was pure class – "I don't give a fuck mate", and he carried on dancing with me.

Finally, I do like to look around the surrounding area when visiting a new ground – too often today most 'out of town' prefabricated stadia have little to offer bar maybe an industrial estate with local entrepreneurs inviting you to park your car for a princely sum, and so heading to the club bar is often the only sensible option. But visit Chelsea and you are spoilt for choice.

By all means take a stroll down the Kings Road, or walk down to the relatively recent development of Chelsea Harbour where all those who can now afford a Premiership season ticket moor their yachts, but top of the list in my view is the home of the dead at Brompton Cemetery. Its Victorian mausolea mark in ornate grandeur the final resting place of some 200,000 souls, and it is spooky beyond belief. Add in to that coming out of the Bridge at full time on a cold damp mid-winter evening to walk to Earls Court tube (to dodge the sweaty scrum at the much closer Fulham

Broadway) and your walk will quicken with every stride. Further add in to the mix the concern that a few cheeky little Millwall fans might just be hiding around the corner and the excitement monitor notches up a tad.

One day I must remember to get off at Earls Court in the daylight on the way to the ground – the experience then I'm sure will be more of fascination than fear. But if you like scary thrills, it's far better than paying a score to some student with a fake cockney accent and scar to rattle a chain at you at The London Dungeons.

THE GOLDSTONE GROUND, Brighton & Hove Albion 2 Southend United 0, Division Three, Saturday 7 December 1974

In many ways this was the real start of my 92 odyssey, taking a trip to a footie outpost that wasn't 'main stream'. It was a place where only Brighton or the opposition fans went, not star-searching neutrals. You were only there if you cared about the result.

I was already a seasoned fan, trips to Roots Hall had been regular and I'd tasted the glamour of Chelsea. And I was now knowledgeable of the wider game, having experienced my first TV World Cup where I had learned how to defend a free kick by watching Zaire against Brazil. So, aged 12 and a bit, I was now deemed ready for the 'away experience'.

Dad has never been a footie nomad, he was more content with the less problematic diet of home games, but for some odd reason it seemed Brighton was now to be our destination. Another family trip too, the usual male/female activity split applying. Thankfully the car had been up-graded, we now luxuriated in a 1966 second hand Mark I Ford Cortina with the novelty of four forward gears making the journey seem less like mission control take-off for the entire length. Dartford Tunnel and a selection of A-roads negotiated, Mum and Sis were dumped off in the town centre for a spot of Christmas shopping, and Dad and I headed on to the match.

The Goldstone Ground seemed on a par with Roots Hall, though confusingly with an open terrace along one side (instead of being at an end) and this is where the handful of Shrimpers were housed. As I would learn in the future, it was a policy in keeping with most clubs, who reserved only the very worst area of their home to welcome those who had travelled miles to get there. An oil-crisis fuelled period of inflation had increased the adult admission price to £1.50 whereas juniors and those too old to care were let in for 90 pence.

It was on arrival that I discovered why we were on the south coast – Dad was meeting an old friend who was a Brighton fan and he had brought along his daughter. A girlie at a football match? Well, there was nothing to outlaw her attending, but why wasn't she shopping? I do though recall in my own geeky way taking a liking, and when Jodie Foster hit the screens two years later in 'Freaky Friday' I was instantly reminded of her. But although I searched, she wasn't there when I next went to the Goldstone in 1985, so our distinctly more 'off' than 'on' acquaintance never surfaced again. Jodie Foster too proved to be a bit of a non-starter.

The Seagulls programme had a picture of a dolphin on the front cover. Inside the format was less confusing, and a guide to how to get to the next away game 68 miles away at Watford makes interesting reading now – once leaving Brighton and on the A23 it instructs you to take another 13 different A roads, B roads, un-metalled tracks and possibly a couple of cul-de-sac interludes, to reach the outskirts of Watford. Today you would just use two motorways and then rough it on the A41/A411 for the last couple of miles.

Albion were not blessed with stars and were probably still in remission from the Clough era - Brian had left in the summer to become the long-term hope to replace marmite Don Revie at Leeds United. However, his left-behind sidekick Peter Taylor did still boast the prolific Fred Binney in his line-up, one of those rumbustious 70's forwards who oozed cult status – Warboys and Bannister, McNeill, Friday, Radford et al were all of the same ilk. We had Chris Guthrie to bang in our goals, partnered by Stuart Brace who, in notching up a respectable 43 goals in 122 appearances for Southend never seemed to hit the net from more than two yards out. My abiding memory of our players of that time though is of Willie Coulson, not the most streamlined of players, who puffed his way down the wing until his face got so red he had to be substituted. I always suspected that pasta and yoghurt were not high on his pre-match menu.

The Brighton match was hardly an auspicious start to my away-day travelling. Now, I've seen some bad performances and thankfully I wasn't, at that point in time, sufficiently daft enough to have persuaded Dad to take us via a couple of thousand road changes to the 7-1 defeat at Wrexham later in the season. But losing 2-0 in freezing conditions on an open terrace with two players having been sent off was not the most promising of beginnings.

Also, my Sis had bought some clackers whilst out shopping. It was a long trip back home.

THE BASEBALL GROUND, Derby County 1 Southend United 0, FA Cup Round Five, Saturday 14 February 1976

Making the fifth round of the FA Cup was not a regular event for Southend. But four home ties in a row had seen us make the draw, uniquely with the radio commentary of it played out live on the club tanoy at 5.00pm after the fourth round match, a pulsating 2-1 win over Cardiff. A large proportion of the crowd had stayed behind to hear it: "..... (rustle, click, rustle) .... ball number (whatever) Derby County - football league champions - (rustle, click, rustle) will play ball number (whatever) .... Southend United". The Roots Hall Roar found its voice big time, we were going oop north to take on Archie Gemmill, Charlie George, Kevin Hector, Franny Lee, Colin Todd, Bruce Rioch and .... Roy McFarland.

"Dad, we gotta go, it's vital, forget Brighton, this is different, it's the cup, we are gonna win it and we need to be there every step of the way." By this time we had a Cortina Mark III, sunburst red, black vinyl roof, it looked the bizz, and it was capable of motorway travel. On the day itself we picked up our match day pals, Barry Bond (should've been a footballer) and his son Harvey, and our Chelsea-supporting school chum Copper, and off we went, going up strange roads to a weird smoky world I'd not previously ventured in to. Scarves trailing out of car windows, the M1 was full of Shrimpers in dodgy cars as a reputed 10,000 were making the trip. The hard shoulder was a symphony of spluttering exhausts and boiling radiators. Pulling our scarves back in on arrival the white bits were not so white and smelt of charcoal - the East Midlands still had a manufacturing industry at the time.

We went in to a pub – I suspected Dad was not too familiar with the local hostelries as we found ourselves in a time-warp. High vaulted dark ceilings, brown walls, a 100% smoking elderly male clientele, minimal décor, and stout the beverage of choice; we were stared at as if from Mars. Barry got the drinks in but I was transfixed by the dominos match taking place in what I had always thought to be a somewhat sedate unexcitable pastime, where two shrieking West Indian gentlemen were crashing their tiles down on the table with immense force as they chuckled their way to a crescendo finish. Wow .... was this what they did oop north then? I wanted to stay and witness more, but there was cup history to be made.

I liked the Baseball Ground – it had covered stands on all sides, was big enough to hold circa 40,000 (in days when no one cared much about safety), yet maintained an air of intimacy. But the main feature was the sodden swamp the stands surrounded – seven months in to the season and it was perfect for motocross. Football pitches back then were certainly not the manicured lawns of today (Accrington and Newport aside), but the Baseball Ground truly excelled in mud – no wonder they were champions, no other team could surely have ever got used to playing on it. A few seconds after the final whistle today at the Emirates an army of men with mowers appear to punish any blade of grass that had dared to stretch above the regulation 30 millimetres – at the Baseball Ground an army would have needed caterpillar tracks to make any headway.

I felt a bit out of it at the match; we were seated in a Shrimpers' section along a side and our main travelling support was having a party at one end. Still, it was a thrilling match and one goal from Bruce Rioch settled it. Yet we could have equalised and taken them back to

Roots Hall had McFarland not cleaned the legs out from Stuart Parker when he was clear on goal – it was an act that would have made Chopper Harris blush, yet McFarland didn't even get booked for it. His sticker and Rioch's were ripped out of my 'Soccer Stars' album when I got back home.

Two years later Southend drew Derby away in the cup again, this time in Round Three. A trip up by train on the Southend FA Cup special was our transport of choice this time, fifteen carriages of British Rail's finest 70's slum rolling stock making up our raucous caravan. The massed ranks of coppers that greeted us at Derby ensured we could not return to our favourite pub, it was "Do not pass Go, straight to the ground" only. Sadly it was the same outcome as before, another narrow defeat and heartbreak as the winner was an own goal. McFarland was no longer in the Derby team, clearly he had been upset by my act of defiance after the match two years before.

LAYER ROAD, Colchester United 0 Southend United 1, Division Four, Saturday 19 March 1977

A confession. Roots Hall aside, the tumble down hut known as Layer Road was my favourite ground until it met its demise in 2008. Admittedly, whenever I went Southend won and a victory always aids the away-day experience, but it was not only that. From every pore the old place just oozed ramshackleness (a word unique to Layer Road and not yet in the Oxford Dictionary).

Each stand roof leaked profusely, the away end (until its last few years) boasted planks as terrace steps that aided bouncing, the away end gents frequently flooded (it did not need to rain for this), the main stand had a roofed standing area each side of it romantically named 'Terrace One' and 'Terrace Two', the TV gantry on the main stand roof was one box precariously perched on top of another, the stand opposite had faded adverts on the roof and stanchions designed to block a clear view from any point, and for a period towards the end of its life, there sat in one corner a small tent-like structure to provide away fan covered seating for, ooh, about 50. Yet under lights and packed to the rafters (OK, maybe just packed in the away end), on Essex Derby Day the whole place just buzzed.

I admit to not remembering a thing about the game in 1977 though I would have been there with Dad and he would have ensured we stayed well clear of the regular skirmishes that occurred outside the ground. A nearby home fans pub was one to be avoided unless you wished to experience CS Gas raids or similar jolly's that have since gone down in Shrimper folklore and no doubt been embellished somewhat over the years to become more 'glorious' ('yeah, there were thousands of us in a pitch battle, etc. etc.').

A few Layer Road match memories that I do recall:

- Saturday 4 March 2006, Colchester United 0 Southend United 3, League One: this match was vital as both teams were vying for promotion, but we were 3-0 up at half time. Upon Che Wilson scoring the third, my son Jim cheered so loud his brace spat out of his mouth onto the pitch. A steward picked it up looking as though it was the most disgusting thing he had ever seen at a football ground – I beg to differ.

- Wednesday 29 September 2004, Colchester United 1 Southend United 1 (3-5 on penalties), Football League Trophy Round 1: I arrive at half-time due to train delays coming back from work in London, and cheer Tes Bramble's goal from the A12 as I make my way to the match. Living less than 30 minutes from Layer Road, I lay claim to publishing rights for the little ditty 'last in first back, last in first back' that I sang to myself on the way home. Well, it made me happy anyway.

- Tuesday 24 February 2004, Colchester United 2 Southend United 3, Football League Trophy Southern Final First Leg: when our third went in this bloke next to me, who I had never seen before, hugs me and starts sobbing. Fearing an impromptu snog, or at the very least the need to offer counselling, I force myself away from his clutches and move closer to a policeman for the rest of the match.

- Monday 16 April 1990, Colchester United 0 Southend United 2, League Two: Peter Daley scores our second and all hell breaks loose, more I think in celebration of putting a pretty firm nail in Colchester's league tenure coffin rather than giving a boost to our own promotion push. Any reader will know that derby days are special so it was sad really that we did not then have another for well over a decade.

WEMBLEY STADIUM, England 1 Scotland 2, Home International, Saturday 4 June 1977

OK, not on the 92 trail, but it has to merit mention. I had been to Wembley two years earlier for a schoolboy international (just to be clear, as a spectator, not a player), but the annual battle versus the Jocks in '77 was my debut first class match at the old stadium. It was an occasion like no other, either before or since, and nothing like it will ever happen again.

Dad took me for my 15th birthday treat. An initial memory of the day was that he was smartly dressed for the occasion – add to this that we were England fans amongst a sea of tartan and we stood out like tarts in a nunnery. I do not recall any animosity towards us though, perhaps due in good part to pretty much 100% of our Scottish brethren being completely pissed. Now, we all know that a drunk can get aggressive, but here a general stupor persisted, pierced by bursts of energy diverted exclusively to singing 'Flower of Scotland' and waving a banner remembering a victory in 1314, before then downing more alcohol.

For our £2 lower terrace ticket we were afforded a decent view behind one goal, and though I did spot an

English section or two elsewhere, our area was exclusively Jock. There were 98,000 in Wembley that day, yet it didn't seem packed, I suspect many only got as far as the inner concourse (where the bars were). Gordon McQueen has since reminisced that "When you walked along the tunnel you could not see the crowd, but you could smell the whisky fumes." He was right, and anything alcoholic would seemingly do – in our section there were several communal heaps of lager cans to ensure no one became parched. The drink intake of course had to come out somewhere, and with the toilets over-flowing, any wall sufficed. It rained piss too as a kilted collection got up into the roof rafters and, well, you can guess the rest.

At the final whistle it all went a bit mad, as virtually everyone ran on to the pitch, our section only leaving behind a decent number of comatosed bodies plus Dad and me. "Look oot for ma whiskey for ma will yer" cried one Jock in our direction as he made for the pitch, caring more for his beverage than his mate who was left prostrate across a pile of cans. We just stayed and stared, it was a spectacle beyond belief. I prayed that Bruce Rioch had been trampled in the on-pitch rush.

Over the years I've been to Wembley a few times, and, as with the equally impressive Roots Hall and Layer Road, just referencing one occasion could never do it justice. Whether it is old or new Wembley, it is not really about the building, it is about the fans inside and their response to the day that makes each occasion unique. You may well recognise some of the following highlights from your own experiences:

- Saturday 23 May 1981, England 0 Scotland 1, Home International: Three of us travelled up by coach from Plymouth for this one. A tube strike meant we had to walk from Gloucester Road to Wembley, but after the match, on getting back to the bus station, we still had five hours left until our midnight transport. We entered a pub decked in our England scarves, but not unsurprisingly we found it rammed with partying Jocks who briefly fell silent as we went in. In that tumbleweed pause we wondered whether to leg it, but the party quickly resumed, we were welcomed with open arms, had drinks bought for us continually, and danced the night away to Tenpole Tudor's 'Swords of a Thousand Men' which was played on continuous loop on the jukebox. A top night.

- Wednesday 10 May 1978, Bruges 0 Liverpool 1, European Cup Final: Not a great game, but Wembley reverberating to 'You'll Never Walk Alone' will live forever in the memory. Shivers down the spine stuff.

- Saturday 22 June 1996, England 1 Germany 1, Euro 96 Semi Final: Paul Young only singing the first note as the crowd took over belting out the National Anthem, Baddiel and Skinner dancing to their ditty of the moment, Shearer's early strike, Pearce clenching his fists with sheer gritty passion to urge on the crowd to new heights of noise, that

Gazza miss by millimetres .... and then poor old Southgate turned the power off.

- Saturday 10 April 2010, Aston Villa 0 Chelsea 3, FA Cup Semi Final: Remembered by me simply for the corporate hospitality. It was, well, wow, and we weren't even at the top level. If you are going to watch a boring game at least see it in comfort. A waiter that calls you 'Sir' at a venue where someone has also pissed on you – it is worthy of reflection.

- Saturday 23 May 2015, Southend United 1 Wycombe Wanderers 1 (7-6 pens), League Two Play-off Final: A fourth big final defeat in 11 years loomed until on-loan Piggott swooped in the 122nd minute. Cue pandemonium, with another dose laid on shortly afterwards as the shoot-out was won. Truly wonderful for the Shrimpers, Southgate syndrome for the Chairboys.

PLOUGH LANE, Wimbledon 1 Southend United 3, Division Four, Sunday 22 October 1977

Encouraged by some good early season form, Dad decided it was time we risked another away game, so off to Plough Lane we went, home of the team who were then the league's newest recruits.

Plough Lane lived up to its name, maybe they had the same groundsman as Derby - I certainly suspected it was not the one that tended the tennis courts down the road. But it had everything that a football connoisseur could want, rickety stands on three sides showing moderate signs of decay, a big open terrace for the away fans to get soaked on, and floodlights with 40 watt bulbs. It had though been given a lick of paint to make it compliant with the then less-than-tough football league ground regulations.

Shrimpers had travelled in numbers for this one, and witnessed a win to keep us in the top two. An outstanding memory of that day was the performance of a teenage Paul Clark. He dominated the midfield, directed the play, encouraged those around him as if he was the senior, and capped it all off with a goal. One to watch we thought, but whilst he went on to have an 'ok-ish' playing career, he never really hit the heights of that early promise. However, his career travels did bring him back to Roots Hall as a manager twice, and I often think he might make that a hatrick one day as his passionate yet astute comments now from the BBC Essex commentary box make the game seem so straightforward. Maybe though if he talked in riddles he'd make it a bit further up the football ladder.

3/92 - GRIFFIN PARK, Brentford 1 Southend United 0, Division Four, Saturday 29 October 1977

Stupidly encouraged by the win at Plough Lane, off Dad and I travelled again the following week with the anticipation of another sparkling performance at another basement London club. Except it wasn't that sparkling.

I always think that Griffin Park is the ground most like Roots Hall, compact but showing signs of wear and with limitations to stifle much ambition. I suspect that the current away end stand, in place since the mid-80's, was the inspiration for Southend's own two-tiered Lego structure on the site of the old South Bank terrace at Roots Hall. Griffin Park does though have some good features – planes regularly fly overhead as a distraction if the game gets too dull, plus the well quoted fact of there being a pub on every corner which presents a unique challenge for the pre-match drinker.

It also has for me a romantic memory – it was the first ground I took my wife Lizzie to back in 1988 to see Southend. We had not long been going out together, and with no previous experience of football (aside from being told she was crap at it in a mixed five a side game – we are kindred spirits in so many ways) Lizzie tried her hardest to become interested. But watching Southend lose to a last minute goal in a lifeless game on a bitter January day tests the soul. Off we went over the next couple of years to footie outposts in the Midlands and East Anglia, but it was not long before I got the "You go to the footie, I'll go shopping instead" response to another hot date suggestion. The final straw came at Cambridge in 1990 when I tempted her to an FA Cup Sixth Round tie against Crystal Palace. Two Cambridge fans on the run from the cops after teasing the away support a little too vividly decided to hide behind us with the instruction that we were not to move. Lizzie was petrified and, bar one final day out at

Peterborough later that season for reasons of convenience that was the end of her own footie quest. She is still 81 short of the 92, though I suspect she is not fussed.

Anyway, briefly back to West London in '77. Match report: Southend's display was inept and it was to be another four years until Dad was tempted to go on the road away again.

You can maybe see a theme beginning to develop – it requires a 'special' kind of person to keep going when the game fails to live up to expectations. Like Jose Mourinho, I must be 'special' then.

4/92 - UPTON PARK, West Ham United 3 West Bromwich Albion 3, Division One, Saturday 12 November 1977

My first game without Dad. This had one immediate drawback - he wasn't there to pay. Never mind, I was earning (Southend Evening Echo paper round – still my best ever job to date) and getting in and out of London, entrance money, programme and take-away was significantly less than a fiver.

I went with a couple of mates from our road – both seasoned Hammers. They had been trying to convince me for a while that Upton Park was a more attractive proposition than Roots Hall, and I admit to having been tempted, but loyalty, cost and convenience worked against that. However, I agreed to sample.

Travelling in to London without the parental eye around was liberating. We could annoy fellow passengers, run and go where we wanted, say what we felt like saying, eat from the most gruesome kebab shop we could find, and generally be tiresome adolescents. We got there early to get prime position on a North Bank barrier, and slowly the place began to fill up with East London's youth, all of whom it seemed had a crew cut and an anger problem. Everything and everyone was 'fucking shit' (bar Trevor Brooking who was too nice to earn that accolade), and even when West Ham opened the scoring with a Pop Robson spot-kick we heard "That was a fucking shit penalty he could have missed." When West Brom hit back with two John Wile headers the abuse level reached new heights, with poor old Lawrie Cunningham singled out for some particularly foul stuff.

The game itself was box to box stuff and ended with a share of six goals. But I wasn't impressed, the atmosphere of angst throughout made it a nervy experience, every surge down the terrace seemed to have an element of hate, and the energy spent on self-preservation made it all very tiring. I loved football matches for the banter, dry wit and feeling of there being a bit of an 'edge', but this was taking it to a level well beyond fun. I was glad to get out and go home.

Later that season I did go to Upton Park again, this time with Dad. It was a big game, Arsenal were near the top, West Ham in their traditional relegation dog-fight. We got there a slightly conservative 90 minutes early and took a superb position mid-way along the side of the pitch in the West Stand. Five minutes after kick-off two blind drunk blokes stood directly in front of us and started hurling abuse at Malcolm MacDonald. When Super Mac put Arsenal two up they took the view that they were not having the desired impact on his play and ran on the pitch to confront him. Duly arrested they missed West Ham's fight back, but we got back some degree of comfort.

For an all-together different reason my most recent memory of Upton Park is not a particularly good one either. In August 2004 Southend drew West Ham away in Round One of the League Cup. The match was forgettable (West Ham won 2-0) – Jim had come with me and as he had school the following day I would lose fewer brownie points in taking him if I got him home and into bed before midnight. We made good progress on the trip back.

At that time we had a house with a long sloping drive which led into a narrow lane we shared with our neighbour - I parked the car at the top, jumped out and saw Lizzie coming to the door to greet us. We then both looked back in horror as the car was rolling back from whence it came and gathering pace – with Jim still in it. The car hit a gate and travelled some 50 metres before ending up in a ditch. Luckily Jim was fine though my brownie point score slumped to an all-time low for a few days. For the remaining eight years that we lived there every journey ended with "Dad, have you put the handbrake on?"

5/92 - VICARAGE ROAD, Watford 1 Southend United 1, Division Four, Saturday 15 April 1978

We just had to go to this one – it was relatively local, Watford were top (and had just achieved the points total they needed for promotion), Southend were second (and vying to join them), and .... we might get on the tele as it was the surprise main game choice for Match of the Day (BBC at the time had a policy of occasionally recognising there was life beyond the top division).

Barry and Harvey came with us in our latest 70's collectable, a lurid yellow 2.4 Cortina Mark III estate – it looked like a rather indiscreet mobile home. Having made it to the outskirts of Watford Dad stopped to ask a milkman with a Watford scarf where the ground was, and with a smile he promptly directed us out of town. When we got to Stanmore Dad decided that the information we had received was a tad suspect so we turned around, finally getting to Vicarage Road just before kick-off.

Inside, the place was buzzing. The Shrimpers were on a packed terrace adjacent to a rather sorry looking main stand. Things were getting a little excitable – maybe eager to impress the cameras, those at the back instigated regular surges between the barriers and stuff was flying about a bit – a bottle hit the head of some poor bloke standing right in front of me and eventually the cops waded in to restore order, perhaps as bemused as anyone as to why we were causing so much trouble with the Watford fans segregated some way away from us.

On the pitch a penalty from Southend stalwart Alan Moody secured a point and we went home (avoiding Stanmore and talking to milkmen) to watch it all again on MOTD.

A reminder of the game for the following year was manager Dave Smith appearing in the programme's opening titles. 'The Ciderman' (the name Argyle fans affectionately gave him) was a true gent and the poor treatment he received at the hands of Southend's owners, which led to his departure some years later, was not something for which the club could be proud. Watford I'm sure, would not have acted so callously and I sometimes think 'if only Elton John had been born in Southend ....'

There are a few clubs who had once been considered as rivals or peers to Southend – Wimbledon, Oxford, Northampton, Wigan and Luton have all regularly pitted their wits against Southend, then gone on to enviable success before sinking back down again. Watford were our rivals for a period too, but unlike the others have by and large built on their success with staying power and become known as a credible family club – the Crocodile Rock man is the differentiating factor.

6/92 - WHITE HART LANE, Tottenham Hotspur 1 Manchester United 1, Division One, Saturday 10 March 1979

I'm not sure what to say about this one – I know I went but I honestly have no recollection of it.

I was in the midst of my A level years at Chelmsford, Mum and Dad having decided it was time to move away from my spiritual homeland and re-nest along the Liverpool Street line at Hatfield Peverel. This didn't stop the trips to Roots Hall (the price of my support to the move) but did mean new places and new friends which ultimately led to life taking a different path compared to that had we stayed in South Benfleet. London was just as easy to get to though, and I suspect this game in 1979 was just a trip with college mates to see a big match for a change.

Spurs were the artisans of that era – Ardiles and Villa had been imported from World Cup winners Argentina to provide some class which paid off by Ossie starring in a top 40 hit with Chas 'n' Dave. Hoddle was the master-in-chief, spraying balls all around the park with a creative flair that was only surpassed when Gazza arrived a few years later.

I do recall seeing Spurs take on Manchester United in 1990 – it was the first time I had paid for Dad to go to a game (my birthday present to him – after what was then 19 years of footie watching I figured I owed him at least one match on me). I have never before or since seen one player dominate a match as Gazza did that day. He was just sheer class and cheeky to boot – putting his foot on the ball to stop play and then flicking it past just before old cloggers like Bruce and Pallister got there. You could see him smirking away as he did it, Bruce just went a deeper shade of purple with each dummy he was sold.

White Hart Lane. It's always been an 'OK' ground, gets a good noise going and has a selection of eateries in the High Street outside which seem to 'dare' you to enter. Before a Southend cup tie there once, Jim and I went in to a cafe where a woman with a cat on her lap sat on the floor in the entrance area kneading pizza dough on a piece of wood – random pots and pans were scattered all around her and I suspected that the place might struggle to win any Michelin Stars. I considered walking out, but having just been down the High Street and not spotted anything better I relented to Jim's pizza demands and we stayed without ultimately experiencing any long term effects.

A memory I do have from White Hart Lane was from a Southend visit there in the first leg of a 1989 second round League Cup tie. Being an evening match, many just went straight from work and a fair number of Shrimpers had been tidied up into the traditional away end corner of the ground. The actions of some showed what a 'Jekyll and Hyde' existence folk can lead as the sight of blokes in suits pointing towards the much larger Spurs contingent foolishly singing "You're gonna get your fucking head kicked in" appeared a little odd. The coppers seemed to enjoy it – at the time the away corner had a podium in it on which stood moody looking officials and police pointing at anyone they didn't like much. A fair number of the 'suits' didn't see the full time whistle. Nowadays Spurs have modernised and positioned a white flying saucer above the away fans from which they can presumably zoom in by video in nasal hair detail to anyone who is lip-read as saying anything worse than 'sugar'.

7/92 - BRISBANE ROAD, Orient 0 West Ham United 4, Division 2, Tuesday 1 January 1980

Still in touch with my Hammers mates, we arranged to meet up at Brisbane Road on New Year's Day 1980. West Ham, buoyed on by their ever encouraging home support, had been relegated since I last saw them, and their fans now had to swear at London derbies with Orient rather than Arsenal. Nevertheless, they still turned up in numbers and I stood with them on a packed North Terrace amongst a crowd of nearly 24,000.

It was a walk-over; West Ham won 4-0 with Stuart Pearson bagging a brace. Now, there was a man with a super-cool goal celebration. No running to the corner flag to imitate a chicken, sniffing the touchline or tonguing a team mate for Pearson, he just turned with one arm aloft, clenched his fist and drunk in the adulation. There is a montage of his goals for Manchester United on YouTube; his goal salute is the

41

same every time. Mick Channon's whirly arm was good, and the way George Best and Eric Cantona would often just turn round after scoring and puff out their chest was beautifully arrogant, but for simplistic consistency Pearson wins it for me.

Back to Brisbane Road, another YouTube video worth a look is a grainy 1979 film where the camera just pans around an empty ground to the accompaniment of a haunting but simple piano piece, reflecting perfectly the terrace dominance of a bygone era. I accept and enjoy the relative comfort now of modern stadia, but reminders such as this from a time when all grounds had their own peculiar identity leave a rose-tinted view of the past which do make me regret their passing. Turn up to see Orient at home now and you will experience a much neater affair, oddly with private balconied flats in each corner. One old stand remains though, perhaps only a reminder of days gone by because, for now at least, the money has run out.

Semper Fidelis

8/92 - HOME PARK, Plymouth Argyle 2 Reading 1, Division Three, Tuesday 30 September 1980

I just knew this was gonna be good.

Two months earlier I had experienced the low of receiving my A level results, and to maximise the humiliation Mum and Dad had got to them before me. So, out went a place at Leeds University and in came the reserve of Plymouth Polytechnic who had an Economics/Geography degree course entry requirement of one A-level grade E. It was tough, but I just got in.

Pre M25, Plymouth was a very long way away from Essex (arguably now, excluding midnight to 4 am, it is even longer). But, after an arduous journey, on arrival at my digs I chucked my bags on the bed and headed for The Hoe. It was a gloriously sunny day, all of Plymouth Sound lay out before me and I sat down on the grass staring out towards the glistening blue bay. Wonderful.

Argyle were a league ahead of Southend at the time. Not only that, nine games in and they were perched at the top of Division Three, and three days in to my three year stay at Plymouth I headed to Home Park. Situated high up within a park, on an evening game you headed

43

towards the floodlights but through the dark grassy surrounding lands - meaning that a fair percentage of the crowd arrive with dog shit on their shoes. Not so wonderful.

Back then Home Park had the obligatory open terrace for away fan comfort which had the added feature of facing direct into the rain-soaked prevailing south-westerlies that regularly whip through the city. Joy ...... but hang on, I wasn't an away supporter now, so I opted for the cavernous Lyndhurst Stand which ran along one side (and also housed the vocal home fan element who didn't fancy their own open end much either).

Argyle's form had attracted over 11,000 that evening - they weren't disappointed as their team bossed it with a win to remain unbeaten. It was their signature tune played as the teams entered the pitch that did it for me though – 'Semper Fidelis' (Latin for 'always faithful') blasted out from the knackered tanoy on a scratchy record – it instantly stirred up a homely image of days gone by and made you feel this was a good traditional club. All was wonderful again.

I went on to see many matches at Home Park and they became my adopted 'second club' as, outside of holiday periods, Roots Hall was not within normal budgetary range on a student grant. I made regular trips to Devon too for a few years after leaving as I ended up for a period living only 'just up the road' in Bristol. Away trips were also a good way of staying in touch, with the well populated Plymouth Argyle Supporters London Branch (PASLB) providing a great 'family feel' to regular social gatherings both before and after matches. I recall one year when PASLB returned to the renowned Manningtree Railway Station Bar which they had nominated as their pub of the year from the season before. A presentation to the bemused landlord on the way to a game at Ipswich had been arranged, with the press involved too. The bar at that time had a maximum capacity of about 30 if no one was carrying a beer gut – about 100 turned up and caused chaos.

At Home Park I have witnessed promotions, rip-roaring Devon derbies, and more than anywhere else, games lashed by the incoming rain. I have even seen Ian Gillan of Deep Purple come on to the pitch a tad worse for wear in a charity match and suddenly spark in to life, beat three defenders and smack in an unstoppable shot from 30 yards, before being carried off a minute later with exhaustion.

But the outstanding memory has to be an FA Cup sixth round clash versus Derby County in 1984. Somehow over 34,000 were allowed in that day, the place was rammed. Our little group had made it to somewhere in the middle of the Lyndhurst, from which there was then no hope of moving. The game was a tense 0-0, though on the hour mark a Gordon Staniforth shot that hit the post and rolled along the line nearly won it for Argyle.

That strike was too much for one poor bloke in front of us as the rumour went round that someone in front of us 'needed a shit'. There was no chance of making the bogs from where he was stood and all of a sudden we were pressed backwards as room was made for him to squat. Not long after another shot went close, the crowd swayed forward, and his little terrace oasis gap was closed. We checked our shoes on the way out as well as on the way in that day.

Clean footwear or not, still wonderful.

9/92 - PORTMAN ROAD, Ipswich Town 1 Aston Villa 0, FA Cup Round Three, Saturday 3 January 1981

Home for Christmas, Dad and I decided it was about time we paid a visit a few miles up the A12 to Portman Road. We were hearing great things about our new Suffolk neighbours - Burley, Butcher and Brazil bringing some British guts and passion to the fare on offer whilst Thijssen and Muhren added panache and programme team sheet spelling mistakes.

Uniquely there was no uncovered terrace, away fans being housed in a pen in a corner of the North Stand. A couple of seasons later I spent a somewhat excitable time in that pen with Chelsea fans – it was far too packed, there was a hell of a racket and there were too many folk in it looking for a fight wanting to get back at the baiting farmers rattling the cage from the other side. It was not a nice place to be.

Portman Road was, and still can be, an atmospheric ground when there are a decent number in and things are going well - the four stands keep in the noise. Back in the early 80's sublime football brought success upon success. We certainly enjoyed that game in 1981, the football on offer was of a high standard and I recall at least for a minute or two Dad and I wondering if we should sample more of it instead of the diet of 'thump and hope' that we had been used to at Roots Hall. It was a short-lived lapse; we came out acknowledging that our fate was tied to less artisanal surroundings.

Spinning forward a bit, for 15 years from 1998 I worked in Ipswich. The locals seemed to find it odd that there was a Southend fan amongst them and I had to fight my corner in footie debates which, for a period of relative success for the Shrimpers and Ipswich under-achievement in the middle of the last decade, became quite enjoyable.

This culminated one day in March in 2007 when Southend visited Portman Road. I had been setting myself for up for a likely fall, leading the banter, exchanging bets and generally stirring the pot – I probably deserved to be taken down a peg or two. Over 2,000 Shrimpers were at Portman Road that day, my 'Suffolk Shrimpers' flag facing the home support as added wind-up. But against the odds we won 2-0, and never has an away win felt so good (or such a relief). Celebration donuts were on the office boardroom table for 80 first thing on Monday, with two allocated for

Ipswich season ticket holders. My popularity took another dive.

10/92 - ST JAMES PARK, Exeter City 3 Leicester City 1, FA Cup Round Four, Wednesday 28 January 1981

A few of us decided that an unofficial geography field trip to Devon's second city would be a good investment, so a day exploring watering holes capped off by a cup replay was arranged. I travelled with a Cardiff fan, a Bristol City fan and a Tranmere Rovers fan – none of us could ever be accused of following glamour clubs and we all instantly felt at home at the real St James Park. It had 'character', an estate agent label which can often correctly be interpreted as 'needing some attention'.

Both ends open to the elements, the side opposite the rickety main stand had a grass bank in front of it and the floodlights were little more than streetlamps. But the piece-de-resistance was a holey net strung up along one side of the main stand attached to some of those streetlamps to stop wayward shots going on to the railway line. They clearly were not very confident of the shooting in these parts – the net was immense. Both the ten-steps-deep away end and the main stand survive intact today with little changed, a clear sign of some hard times during the past 35 years.

One thing I loved about footie in the 80's was that you could turn up to virtually any game on the day without a ticket and pay on the gate to get in. No pre-planning

48

months in advance, or having to become a member of some scheme to qualify for the opportunity to buy tickets, or having an arranged marriage with a season ticket holder, or taking out a mortgage to get into the corporate area. Nope, none of that palaver was needed, just wash (though that was not necessary either) and go. And I'm not sure if Exeter City has a corporate area anyway.

St James Park (Exeter style) apparently had room for about 15,000 - at least that number squeezed in for the Leicester game and pay on the day it was. There was a drawback - the turnstile set-up was geared for about 10,000 less, the queues enormous, and after a day in Exeter hostelries well, we were 'relieved' once we finally got in.

It was a terrific match, with local favourite Tony Kellow bagging a hatrick. We loved it so much that when Exeter drew at the other St James' Park in Round Four we turned up for the replay for a carbon copy day. Defeat at Spurs in the quarter final sadly put an end to our Exeter field trips, but long live stadiums like the real St James Park.

PLAINMOOR, Torquay United 2 Tranmere Rovers 1, Division Four, Sunday 1 March 1981

Brian was a Tranny (he still is) and insistent on some company for a trip to see his team at Torquay. Fine, but it was Sunday, students did even less on a Sunday, and a trip to the English Riviera involved quite a bit of effort. We did it though, and in return for a pint agreed to be Trannies for the day which increased the away turn out significantly.

Torquay were experimenting, in a bid to boost attendances above a season average of 2,282 'Sunday soccer' was heralded as the saviour. In his programme notes the manager, Mike Green, tried out some logic: "Peterborough had 28,000 watch them play Manchester City in the Cup, of whom 8,000 were City fans. Against us less than 5,000, so there were 15,000 potential fans who stayed away on a fine afternoon for a top of the table game featuring two of the League's finest scorers ...." Hmmm, not sure Sunday soccer is ever going to be the answer to that one, but they were desperate to try anything. An extra 364 turned up, including us four, so it was not a resounding success.

Mr Green was on a bit of a rant-fest in his notes; maybe he wanted a lie in on a Sunday too and was miffed at having his routine disturbed. On he moaned: "I am still shaken that a player of Bruce Rioch's calibre cannot put on at least 500 on our gate. That goal he scored in our last home game was worth the admission money on its own." What? Rioch at Torquay? Result, it's an intimate ground, I might have the chance to chastise him for his lucky winner in '76 and of his team-mate's callous tackle. I then read on: "As you are no doubt aware Bruce has now signed a long-term contract with Seattle Sounders." Bollocks, he must have heard I was coming along today.

Plainmoor was a bit of a dump back in 1980. The open away terrace had narrow crumbling steps, the main stand had two different roofed sections with terracing in front of a miserly collection of seats, and the opposite side and home end were partially covered terraces so had less 'garden' growing on them. A sickly peeling yellow paint was plastered over anything in rotting wood. 'Development opportunity' would be the Devonian estate agent's line.

Visit Plainmoor today and you will enjoy a much smarter affair, but it's still a 'real' stadium. They should be congratulated on making much needed changes without buying a set of pre-packed concrete slabs and a cordless screwdriver.

What about the match back in 1981? Well, we didn't have much to cheer other than taking comfort in only having about 30 miles to get home rather than the handful of real Trannies who had not far short of 300 miles to travel.

I did have a more memorable visit to Plainmoor at the end of that season. Southend were having a great year and secured promotion with a 3-0 win at Torquay in their penultimate game of the season. Around 200 Shrimpers swelled the end of season Torquay party to just over 1,700, the Sunday experiment had been dropped in favour of the odd old habit of 7.30 pm on a Saturday night. I wonder if Derek Spence remembers who chaired him off the pitch that evening?

51

HIGHBURY, Arsenal 2 Aston Villa 0, Division One, Saturday 2 May 1981

Enthused by sealing promotion at Torquay I just had to be at Roots Hall for the promotion party the following Friday evening against Rochdale, so on the day I set off at first light to hitch home.

Back then hitching was common place and I never usually had any problems. Often there would be a few fellow hitchers standing by the roadside – if any were female then it was a hopeless task competing so you just stood back until they got a lift and then tried to look more normal than the other blokes left behind with you.

Anyway, on the Friday all went fine until I got to Heston Services on the M4 just outside London. Standing by the garage slipway I flipped my sign over from 'London' to 'Chelmsford' and waited – I was not kicking my heels for long. A van stopped and the middle-aged driver said he was going to East London - pleased that this would take me through most of the capital I hopped in. All hair and glasses, he seemed to be a little quirky but the conversation flowed and we were soon travelling along the Embankment. It was then it started. "Wanker" he shouted into a mic (wired up to an outside speaker) at this bloke on a zebra crossing in front. The poor pedestrian looked around startled wondering whether this term of endearment was meant for him, and to make his day as he just stood there trying to figure things out he upset an

52

impatient motorist on the opposite carriageway who wanted him to move.

Hair Bear cracked up and looked round to me to see how impressed I had been - I admit to having had a little chuckle. Suitably encouraged, Hair Bear proceeded to greet other pedestrians and cyclists for the next hour as we made our way towards Romford – I became embarrassed by it all and slunk lower and lower in my seat hoping to stay out of external view, but he was like a dog with a new toy and just kept going. It got a little scary at one stage in the stop-start traffic of Stratford High Street as one youth took exception to being called "Tosser" and started to bang on the side of the van when the traffic lights were on red. Eventually, and after making sure that there was no Benny Hill line of irate Londoners chasing us, I made my excuses and got out earlier than scheduled. I wonder what age Hair Bear lived to.

I still made it to Hatfield Peverel in good time, met up with Dad and off we went to the party. It was OK, but I'd been at the real deal the previous week and it all seemed a bit like arriving at a student bash when the only drink left was the home brew. In need of some further footie stimulation I decided to go to Highbury the following day.

It was too short notice to go with anyone else so for the first time I travelled on my tod to a game. Not that I was alone – over 57,000 squeezed in to Highbury that day. Again, pay on the day and I get lucky – shortly after I squeezed in to the North Bank the 'ground full' signs went up. It was a huge match – if Villa won they would be league champions for the first time in 70 years, if they lost then it all depended on how Ipswich got on at Middlesbrough.

Arsenal too needed to win to secure a place in next season's UEFA Cup (you know, that cup which clubs make a huge effort to qualify for and then field a team of reserves in the first round and go out to a bunch of fishermen from the Faroes).

I stood at a top corner of the North Bank but it was like being on a tidal wave, and going with the flow was safer than resisting. Somehow by the end of the match I was in the middle. Anyone below average height would not have seen a thing bar jackets and armpits, but the crowd volume level permeated all. For some reason Pele appeared for a lap of honour before kick-off and received a rapturous greeting from all four sides – for the next hour though it was mostly the Gunners fans who made the noise as Terry O'Neill's men dominated. Ipswich were also one-up at Ayresome Park. Villa, and their fans, slumped in to a nervous state of inertia.

Then, with nothing of note happening on the pitch, some 20,000 Villans at the Clock End went mental as news filtered through that Bozo Jankovic had equalised for Boro. Not long after the Serb scored a second and the Clock End boogied again. Villa seemed content thereafter to rely on Boro and their luck held out to spark even more amazing scenes at the end with both sets of fans happy. For Villa their long wait for another title made their joy very special. I felt lucky to be there.

FELLOWS PARK, Walsall 0 Southend United 1, Division Three, Saturday 29 August 1981

I had ended the 1980/81 season with its biggest game at the mighty Highbury. To kick things off for 1981/82 the slightly less glamorous and sparsely populated Fellows Park called.

Dad had a business contact who was a Walsall fan (Dad always moved in high circles) so that was all the excuse we needed to see how the Shrimpers might fare now they were a league higher up. For a change we travelled to Southend to get the single supporters' coach – a dilapidated relic reserved especially for football supporters. The journey seemed to take forever but we were safely delivered and met up with Dad's mate. This meant we had to sit in the stands rather than enjoy the August sunshine on the away terrace – I told myself that open away ends were more atmospheric when the sleet was driving straight at you anyway.

My abiding memory of Fellows Park is that the stand we were in had so many stanchions I spent the whole game swaying around trying to follow the play – it was knackering. Oh, and that the Chairman had clearly got a vast amount of red paint on the cheap as everything was painted in it, even one of the roofs had been red-washed to help advertise some local brew.

Southend scored the only goal to win and it was a nice day out, but I can't really find anything else to say about a middle of the road lower league ground in the middle of England. Fellows Park will no doubt hold romantic memories for the older Walsall fan, but I suspect most of its other visitor's will, like me, struggle to recall, bar a bit of stanchion neck ache, having ever been too energised by the place.

RECREATION GROUND, Chesterfield 1 Southend United 2, Division Three, Saturday 17 October 1981

Saturday. No parties lined up, no bands on in the Union Bar, TV put under the stairs due to it being known the licence spotter van was on the prowl, and the usual Plymouth forecast of 'peeing down' set in for the weekend. There was now't else for it, time for a day trip to Chesterfield.

No other takers for this one (I wasn't surprised, it was a bit 'specialist'), so I travelled alone. Five hours on the train there, six back, all for 90 minutes of footie. Mmmm, too much ale during Freshers Week had probably rotted some brain cells. Still, I was out of the Plymouth rain.

Saltergate was an 'ok' type of ground – the traditional three covered sides staring at one open end. This away end though had a special feature; as long as you were at least of average height you could take a pee in the gents and see over the wall to carry on watching the game. So the tall away fans gave a commentary to the shorties and not a moment of action was lost. Archibald Leitch could not have designed it better.

Chesterfield were top going in to the game so an away win was a surprise. Further, the small huddle of Shrimpers wondered whether they had witnessed the birth of something important. Danny Greaves, son of Jimmy, was making his Southend debut and scored the winner. Hail the new messiah who would no doubt lead us to the promised-land before being flogged to Juventus for millions. Well, not quite, he played 53 times in three years before going on to Cambridge United, Chelmsford City and having a spell as manager of Witham Town. Oh well.

If a trip up to Chesterfield from Plymouth is long, a trip back on the same day is longer, especially 1980's style. It was just relentless, hour after hour of clickety-clack, screaming babies, moaning old men (not me of course, I was only 19 back then), stale buffet offerings, jealous looks at folk getting off before you, more clickety-clack, unflushed toilets, snorers, empty cans of Kestrel rolling down the aisles .... However, it did afford me the opportunity to meet a rare breed of people, special folk who took a day trip out of Cornwall to see their team 'oop north' every week.

Pasty makers or tin miners by day (I stereotype for effect), these driven souls spend their weekends on trains for that 90 minute buzz. Not for them the excitement of Bodmin Town or Liskeard Athletic, or even a trip across the Tamar to see the mighty Argyle, it's just not enough, they have to travel ..... and travel more. I met Manchester United fans, West Brom fans, Sheffield Wednesday fans, Bolton fans, and even a fellow Southend fan (though he got off at Taunton – lightweight). I got back to Plymouth at around 11.30 pm, but these nomadic folk still had an hour or two to go, and then probably a long horse ride back to their mine (I stereotype again – apologies). I engaged some in conversation but it was not inspiring, talk seemed limited to how far their next trip was, Star Wars, and different types of rolling stock, and they had a bit of a far-away look in their eyes. May the force be with them.

11/92 - ASHTON GATE, Bristol City 0 Southend United 2, Division Three, Saturday 14 November 1981

A no brainer - a Southend away game only 130 miles up the road. Just around the corner in West Country language.

An added bonus was that I had a travelling companion, my mate Simon who was a Bristol City fan, plus we were staying over for the weekend at his parents' meaning we got that longed-for desire every away-from-home student craves seven weeks into a term - properly cooked food.

We met up with Simon's friends before the match – a good bunch who stood together every home match and with whom four years later during a stint living in

Bristol I would end up adding to their group for a short while. In many ways they epitomised what football is all about, a real togetherness where sometimes you will experience despair, other times you will feel so good, but as one you always support each other and your team. To this day a few of them still meet up every game and watch from the same place albeit from seated comfort.

However, I was not part of the group yet, and on the way to the ground we went our separate ways, me turning off alone to the away end and its obligatory 'open to the elements comfort'. Ashton Gate seemed to be relatively large, with the circa 6,000 on the day failing miserably to fill its vast swathes of terrace and seats, and with just a few Shrimpers huddled together in a corner pen for warmth and safety. In the next pen a group of West Country lads inaccurately informed us that we were Cockney scum, and we retorted with a ditty about shooting a red robin. Yes, football is about togetherness, but usually only within your own clan.

Recent developments to Ashton Gate have seen it morph in to a very swish stadium – back in 1981 it looked as though it wanted to be something half-decent but that the planners had messed up a bit. The main stand had a disproportionately large terrace in front of the seats, the opposite (and back then relatively recent) Dolman Stand appeared to have been set at the wrong angle as the front row of seats were still several feet up from pitch level, the away terrace was a jungle of red barriers, and the home end had numbers painted on each stanchion as if they were there for some weird kind of target points game. Yet, for all that, it looked imposing. That day though Southend weren't impressed, and a 2-0 Shrimpers win made my host a little less chipper for the rest of the weekend, but thankfully it did not impact on his Mum's great cooking.

At the time of my mid-eighties Bristol stint Simon had stayed local to his roots so I instantly had someone to go to see a game with, but it was during a fallow period for City and by and large I recall that there was nothing worth recalling from my 30 plus visits to Ashton Gate over three seasons. Apart that was from the violence.

At a time when hooliganism was at a height and causing Maggie and her glove puppet Colin to flap without real effect, at Ashton Gate there always seemed to be an undercurrent of hate. Maybe it was because that was just where I happened to be at the peak of those dark footie days, but every game had its skirmish, inside or out.

Once when standing outside the ground I happened to be near a group who were actively plotting the best way to attack some Chester City fans (a more benign and sparse group of individuals with no axe to grind you could ever wish to meet). Another time, Argyle served up a larger and arguably more 'rival' target, and both before and after the game it was outside the ground where trouble kept flaring up. I witnessed a car being rocked and windows smashed just because a green scarf inside had been spotted – the family were terrified but the police were nowhere to be seen, content perhaps that they had the inside of the ground marshalled like Stalag 17. Something like this happened every game.

My personal eye-witness account of physical football violence over the years has thankfully been rare, but still today the issue is on a light simmer waiting for an opportunity to boil up. It will perhaps never fully go away, but the TV money that has poured in since Sky came on board has been the true antidote – the Football Association know that Mr & Mrs Sky Subscriber will not cough up to see pitch battles every week so the money has been channelled into making things safer. Vested interests and all that.

Care though needs to be taken in not making the experience too benign, padded seats everywhere in the ground might be kind on the bum but they can cause spectator drowsiness. Lessons from some of our European friends and the orchestrated rhythmic chanting look fun, and maybe we need to get on that bandwagon?

EDGAR STREET, Hereford United 3 Southend United 1, FA Cup Round One, Saturday 21 November 1981

In 2006, BBC 5 Live's 606 programme invited listeners to submit a brief story 'about the passion, drama, agony or ecstasy of the beautiful game'. A 1981 trip to Edgar Street was my entry. There was a 300 words limit and my offering was as follows:

'A Southend fan washed up in Plymouth in 1981, our ball had come out of the hat after Hereford's. So off I went to Edgar Street, once host to a glorious 70's FA Cup parka pitch invasion, for a nice relaxing day trip and the start of our annual forlorn assault on Wembley. I left my digs at 6.30 am for the seven mile cycle ride to the train station. One mile in I had a puncture, ran back home to dump the bike, and then hitched a lift to Plymouth centre. Train caught just in time, three changes and five hours later I was in Hereford. We lost 3-1. About turn for the train ride back, but British Rail was in meltdown. Changes this time had to be made at Newport, Bristol Parkway, Bristol Temple Meads, Taunton, Exeter St David's and Newton Abbot, arriving back in Plymouth around 1.00 am. It was peeing down (I mean, really peeing down, Plymouth style), the last bus had gone, no stranger wanted to give a drenched inadequately clothed young adult a lift, and so I walked. An hour or so later, about one mile away from the end, a cop car pulled up and asked where I had been. I told them my story and submitted a soggy programme as Exhibit A. They took the piss, told me that they were on the look-out for a peeping tom but believed my unique alibi and desire just to get home rather than peep at Tom or anyone, declined to give me a lift up the steep hill before me, suggested I support a better team, and sped off laughing. I eventually got back some 20 hours after leaving. Never mind, there's always next year I thought.'

12/92 - FRATTON PARK, Portsmouth 0 Southend United 0, Division Three, Saturday 30 January 1982

Funds had got a bit low towards the end of the previous term but I now had a part-time job in the Student Union bar and was feeling sufficiently flush to afford another away day, this time 'just' along the south coast at Portsmouth.

Have you ever tried the journey by train from Plymouth to Pompey? On the map it looks easy enough, by train it's a different matter. Five hours if you are lucky, and the Hereford experience had scarred me sufficiently to be cautious, so it was another early start.

Fratton Park back in 1982 was a traditional looking ground and not too much has changed since. The locals were passionate yet unfriendly, and everything about the place seemed to say 'get out quick'. Then add to the mix that it was a dark January day, a biting northerly wind blowing on another open terrace, a thoroughly forgettable 0-0 draw, the not unrealistic feeling that there were folk waiting outside to jump at you from the shadows, and the prospect of a long lonely train trip back. I looked on it as some kind of character building test and wondered whether the Duke of Edinburgh Award might take it up as an activity.

Pompey has never been a place I have warmed to. I can't fault the loyalty and support they get from their fans, and love him or loathe him the fanaticism shown by John Portsmouth Football Club Westwood is quite remarkable. I once watched the man dance on top of the roofs of the executive boxes at Ipswich for virtually the whole game, the police unable to get him off due to fears that the roof would collapse. It was true entertainment Keystone Cops style. But the harshness of my first experience of Fratton Park has stayed with me and I was not overly enthusiastic when, on retiring to the Isle of Wight for an 18 year period, Dad became a Pompey regular. Ipswich aside, a Southend win against Pompey is now something I enjoy more than most when it happens.

My last visit to Fratton Park was indeed one of those occasions. We've all had times when getting to a game has been a bit fraught – well, 26 November 2013 fell in to that bracket. Things had started so smoothly too: drive to Shenfield, train in to London for a meeting which I made sure ended early, back to Shenfield, change clothes in the car trying to stay out of sight of any weirdo manning the security cameras, and I was on the M25 by 3.00 pm. Loads of time for a leisurely drive and a pint before the game, watch the match, then a short hop to Chichester to stay in a comfy hotel (as long as I could get Lenny Henry out of the bed) before a meeting there the next day.

It all started to go wrong on the A3 – the Hindhead Tunnel is a great improvement on the bottle neck that traditionally used to hold up traffic for hours in that location before, but when an accident occurs in it everything comes to a grinding halt for a very long time. One hour to kick-off and I was still north of the thing, but eventually I turned off and, along with many others, played Wacky Races along some one-track roads to eventually get through and arrive at the ground at 8.15 pm. Pompey were already one-up, and listening to the locally biased commentary had made the journey even more agonising.

Then there was nowhere to park, so ultimately I drove to the main gate and here it was where my luck changed as I found a reasonable steward who took pity on me and let me in to park next to the team bus. A second result was getting in the ground – the ticket office was in the process of closing but outside another late running Shrimper had just arrived and had missed meeting his mate to hand him a free ticket, so he gave it to me. Togetherness is within the clan.

Inside, the place was buzzing. Pompey fans, unused to winning at the time, were making plenty of noise, but Shrimpers had travelled in numbers and, with Fratton Park now affording the luxury of an away end roof, the din being made was terrific. But then another set-back – one of our subs gets sent off for knocking the head off a Pompey player after only just entering the pitch, and with 15 minutes to go the odds were firmly against us.

Now, we all know that the predictable thing about football is that it can be unpredictable, and on 76 minutes the ten men equalised. Jubilation turns in to delirium a few minutes later as Big Bad Barry Corr stoops to head home the winner. Lovely stuff.

EASTVILLE, Bristol Rovers 2 Southend United 1, Division 3, Saturday 27 February 1982

Another of those 'just up the road' trips, and with the bar job supplying the cash and good form putting Southend up to fourth, it just had to be done. No weekender with home cooking this time though, Simon was firmly 'City only' and didn't even bother to respond to my suggestion that a trip in to enemy territory would be good reconnaissance.

I've mentioned before that YouTube is a good source for seeing what some grounds used to be like. Well, type 'Bristol Rovers Eastville' into the search box and you won't be disappointed. The 1:32 minute film takes you back to a day (this time in 1979) when football grounds were oh so different, and the haunting tune that accompanies every film in that series seems to have a mild whistling wind blowing through its pan of Eastville.

Three years on from '79 and, bar a fire in the South Stand, there had not been any ground improvement work. It remained a beast of a place with huge covered stands assembled in a pick 'n' mix fashion around parts of three sides, and the away end, well, you know what that will be.

The place trebled-up as a greyhound and a speedway stadium, so the spectator was a little remote from the action, but the sheer variety of its structures made it a fascinating monument to a sporting life. The main stand had a ludicrous double-storey narrow box on the roof, the Tote End roof was dedicated to greyhound racing scores, Hofmeister Bear adverts ('for great lager follow the bear' was the logical claim) were everywhere, a giant gasholder loomed in the background, and the place even at one time had flower beds behind the goals. They don't make them like that anymore.

Despite the challenges of travel I was beginning to get the away bug, as at least on the pitch things had always seemed to go well (until this game – optimism has usually proved over-rated when following Southend). When we scored to put us in the lead I jumped out of the small dancing throng of Shrimpers to take a picture. It shows the fans celebrations with a disproportionate number of bored on-looking coppers on the fringe – a great memory of terrace life back then. I failed to take a picture of the disconsolate faces as Rovers scored twice to win it.

During my Bristol days I went to Eastville quite a few times and if I had to pick out a favourite of grounds now long gone the old home of the Gas Heads would win it hands-down. Sadly it closed to football in 1986 and Rovers ended up having a prolonged holiday in Bath.

My drive in to work until early 1988 took me down the M32, and it was on those trips that I witnessed the slow decay of a place that had once housed nearly 40,000. Today a giant IKEA store is on the site – it is so huge it probably has a bigger capacity. I wonder if it has any football ghosts?

THE DEN, Millwall 1 Southend United 1, Division Three, Monday 12 April 1982

It was a time of war – Argentina had just marched in to the Falklands. Back in Plymouth the naval dockyard had been a tad busy, and by 12 April a taskforce was already on its way. Maggie was in her pomp and had temporarily forgotten about other troubles including what to do about the growing issue of naughty folk at footie matches. Maybe then it was an ideal time to go to The Den whilst the nation's mind was on much more important things – slip in and out and hope everything would be low key. There was nothing riding on the game – Southend's form had slumped and both teams were firmly entrenched in mid-table. Interest in the game was minimal (only 3,025 bothered to turn up). Conditions were perfect.

Back in Essex for the Easter break, I took a short train ride to Liverpool Street then a quick tube to New Cross Gate, and I was in the tropical surroundings of Cold Blow Lane. Lovely. I was on my own, Dad had made his

68

excuses – "That's the last place I wanna go to, good luck" he voiced with parental concern.

It was on arrival that things went a little awry – pleased to get that far without incident I just went to the first turnstile I saw, paid and went in .... straight into the home end. Bollocks. Loyalty to the cause had triumphed over common sense so I was sporting a Southend scarf, though thankfully both club's colours were similar.

I looked around – in a stadium that had once held 48,000, and this game not exactly packing them in, any new arrival was immediately noticed and examined by the locals for recognisable features: crew cut, DM's, scar, bomber jacket, knuckle tattoo etc. I stuck out like an Eskimo in the Sahara and looked about as comfortable.

I started to chew gum to 'look hard' but felt that wasn't helping and thankfully spotted a copper to whom I explained that I'd rather be elsewhere. He said he felt the same but agreed to take me round to my small band of fellow Shrimpers, so I got to enjoy being marched around the perimeter of the pitch by the police (just the kind of high-profile trip I had been trying to avoid). The away fans were housed in a yellow cage, security not comfort being the objective. The whole place was like some indestructible fortress – Hitler had bombed it 40 years before without much success.

The game was a 1-1 draw ensuring mid-table obscurity for both teams and lack of interest for conflict – great for the trip home which was uneventful.

I know that The Den had a somewhat dodgy reputation and my limited memory of the place might have been tarnished by this. But reputation can go before you and Millwall suffered from that whether fairly or unfairly. I now had the treasured Den badge though, and ticked it off the list - there was now no need to ever go back.

ELM PARK, Reading 0 Southend United 2, Division Three, Saturday 24 April 1982

Another match with nothing riding on it, but the fixture gods had set it up so that I had a game to go to en-route back to Plymouth at the end of the Easter break. This meant train travel rather than the thumb as I thought it would be pushing it a bit to expect any driver to wait for me whilst I went to the match.

A side-effect was that I had a packed rucksack with me, mostly made up of contraband raided from Mum and Dad's fridge to help eke out next term's food budget. Not ideal for taking to a match but I left myself with no option after dismissing the Reading station left-luggage area as undesirable. But match security 1982-style consisted of coppers looking for known hooligans based on iron filing images (the nearest thing back then to e-fit). I wasn't on that radar so was let in without even a cursory glance, the only challenge being to squeeze through the turnstile with a bulging rucksack. If only the Reading burger bar had a can opener there was a tin of rice pudding I could now have for a snack.

Elm Park was standard fare for lower league soccer – lots of terrace, one seating side, and only the sides covered. At the risk of offending the Royals (sorry Ma'am), Elm Park had no outstanding features whatsoever, it was one of those places which just oozed nothing-ness.

At one time they did have the enigmatic Robin Friday, but he had left in 1976 for Cardiff before retiring as a slightly jaded 25 year old – any player though who has had a single called 'The man don't give a fuck' (Super Furry Animals) dedicated to them deserves mention. In his oh too short a life he made George Best look like a monk whilst still playing with immense skill and panache.

The main man on the block in 1982 was Kerry Dixon, but our defenders had him in their pocket as the Shrimpers ran out 2-0 winners to silence the silent home support in the massive 2,840 crowd.

It felt a bit weird at Reading station after the match – about 100 celebrating Shrimpers were on the platform waiting for the next London-bound train. I took over the west-bound platform.

As a final aside on Elm Park, this was where I learned never to sing the away team winning ditty 'Jingle Bells' until after the final whistle. In December '85 I went to see an in-form Argyle and they were cruising at 3-0 with some of their football just being a sheer joy, passes being spread all over the pitch and one-touch stuff coming-off Brazilian style. With 20 minutes to go up went the cry "Jingle bells, jingle bells, jingle all the way, oh what fun it is to see Argyle win away." Argyle lost 4-3.

13/92 - HILLSBOROUGH, Sheffield Wednesday 2 Norwich City 1, Division Two, Saturday 15 May 1982

One of my Economics lecturers, Nick, had been getting progressively chirpier as the season drew to a close. His team, Norwich City, had just kept on winning since February and, from nowhere, now found themselves facing the last game of the season needing only a point to return to Division One.

I couldn't work up the enthusiasm to hitch home that weekend to see a Burnley promotion party at Roots Hall – nothing worse in my view than witnessing the opposition celebrating what your team had unsuccessfully strove for over the previous 45 games. On the other hand, being a neutral at another promotion party had some appeal, so I put the idea to Nick about a little day trip to Hillsborough - it couldn't do my course work rating any harm either. He was impressed and plans were made.

So, I found myself taking a 550 mile round train trip to a game in which I had no real interest. It proved to be a great day. The journey was fun – Nick was good company and there were the usual Cornish nomads on the move to various parts of the country for their final season fling to wonder at. Sheffield was awash with Canaries and we joined a reported 10,000 of them at the Leppings Lane End. 'Colourful' doesn't do it justice – everyone seemed to have a dozen yellow and green balloons and when the teams entered the pitch they all got released, it taking well into the first half before they ceased being a nuisance on the pitch. Where was 'Pop' Robson when you really needed him?

Wednesday were a bit miffed by it all and in no mood to play a bit-part. Three points for a win had been introduced that season – had the old system been in place they would have entered the match needing a win to go up, but instead lay fifth with nothing to play for. The introduction of play-offs was still a few seasons away – if they had known that they would have been double-miffed. But manager Jack Charlton wasn't one to roll over and have his tummy tickled, and the Owls went 1-0 up – if Leicester could now win at lowly Shrewsbury then the Canaries big day out would fall flat. It was all still in the balance with just five minutes left when Keith Bertschin rose to nod home and we all went ballistic. Funny how you can get caught up in someone else's joy.

The Owls were now well and truly pissed off. It should have been them jumping up and down but the wrong bird was now having all the fun. The home fans were getting excitable and itching to get on the pitch – one was already as the ball fell to Mel Sterland on the wing with the clock ticking past 90 minutes. Sterland swung over a first time beauty, the errant fan thought it was for him and dived to head it in but Gary Bannister just got there first and it was Wednesday's turn to go mental. Hundreds of fans streamed on to the pitch and it took several coppers and some energetic gesticulating from Big Jack to get them off again. I suspect a Mr A J Hamil from Wolverhampton, referee, was cacking himself at this point – the fan in the box must have distracted the defence but the programme notes said that the he had a wife and family to support and he perhaps took the view that owls, unlike canaries, were carnivorous.

There was barely time to kick-off before Mr Hamil legged it to the dressing room for all he was worth and the fans came pouring back on. It was a surreal situation – Wednesday fans taunting us yet all this time we still had no news of the result from Gay Meadow. When it finally came, 0-0, it was our turn to get happy again, and the Wednesday fans sloped off the pitch to find good positions to hide until stray Canaries started to fly out. They had a long wait – Kenny Brown brought the players on to the pitch and a proper celebration was held.

We eventually got back into Plymouth at a silly hour, Cornish nomad noses pressed against the windows wondering what they would do in the summer as we disembarked. I had thoroughly enjoyed being a Canary for a day.

It is of course impossible to mention Hillsborough without referencing the tragic events of 15 April 1989. I consider it would be disrespectful not to. Any footie fan of that era can recall where they were when the news came through – I had been enjoying a bit of sunshine in the garden with Lizzie in our first house together in Colchester and had popped indoors to get a drink and catch up on the scores. The news was just starting to filter through, and after sitting there a bit numb, I wandered back out.

My neighbour was in his garden just over the fence and, without thinking to say why, I just enquired if he had seen what had happened – he asked me to keep quiet as he wanted to avoid knowing the score until watching it on Match of the Day that evening. I remember insisting he switched on the news and in he went a bit bemused. We didn't see each other for the rest of the day, both glued to the TV and radio as the reports got worse and worse.

My words on it all are irrelevant, but for a book with football grounds at its heart it would be churlish or even insulting to say nothing. I was not there, I did not know anyone who was there, I was not a Liverpool fan, but a love of the game is a common unshakeable bond.

In retrospect it may seem inappropriate to have any rosy view of what grounds and the management of them could be like pre-Hillsborough. Games I have already mentioned – Southend v Liverpool 1979, Arsenal v Aston Villa 1981, Plymouth v Derby 1984 – could just have easily turned in to a similar scenario. The Leppings Lane end had also been packed behind those fences on Norwich's 1982 promotion day. Hillsborough on 15 April 1989 changed things forever. RIP the 96.

14/92 - CRAVEN COTTAGE, Fulham 4 Southend United 2, League Cup Round One Second Leg, Tuesday 14 September 1982

Still on my summer break, and hot-footing it from my holiday job as the world's tallest Little Chef chef in 1982 (well at my height it has to be a reasonable bet and it's difficult to disprove so I'm claiming that one), an evening appointment at The Cottage was on the menu.

A friend from Chelmsford joined me – Rob's modest target at the time was to see every football league team and Fulham would provide another tick in that box. He was also a rare breed of person as Dad and I had taken him to Roots Hall more than once – for most just once was sufficient. Even rarer, he is now a Chelmsford City lifetime season ticket holder, an affliction for which there is no known treatment.

Anyway, we were now in post-war Britain – Maggie 1 Galtieri 0. All seemed well in the world and a new sense of optimism was emerging as we got to Fulham on a warm late summer's evening. A couple of pints alongside the riverbank watching the trendies of Kensington and Chelsea strut by. Playing spot the car without a personalised number plate. Walking by local renaissance-style architecture. Admiring the Archibald Leitch Grade II listed Johnny Haynes Stand and its adjoining corner cottage. All very pleasant.

Not therefore the environment we were expecting to view one of the most mindless solo acts of 'supporter passion' I've ever seen. We get to half-time, Southend were not exactly playing well, and one of our 'fans' takes exception to things. Staggering across the away terrace steps he makes it to Cottage Corner and promptly insults and then gobs on players as they go in for their half-time cuppa. All hell breaks loose and several coppers are required to carry the offender out. There really are some charming folk in the world, and that's sadly all I remember the game for.

There was a very different aura about the place on my only other visit (to date) some 15 years later. The Princess of Wales had just died and the nation had been in mourning. When Fulham hosted Plymouth on 9 September 1997 the funeral had taken place and I had popped in to the grounds of Kensington Palace on the way to the game to witness the sea of tributes. Mohamed Al-Fayed, who had only purchased Fulham

FC that summer, walked out in to the middle of the pitch before kick-off to pay tribute to Diana and his son Dodi who of course had died with her. It all made for a very surreal atmosphere for a football match. No one gobbed on anyone that day.

MAINE ROAD, Manchester City 3 Coventry City 2, Division One, Saturday 2 October 1982

The start of my final year of studies at Plymouth so time to get a trip in with the nomads and experience another day in the hands of British Rail. Manchester was about as far as you could get for a footie game without investing in a weekender, and to escape the Plymouth drizzle I decided to head for the sunshine city.

It was a bread and butter Division One match, the two teams went into it in mid-table but, bereft of any big stars, it was to be a season of struggle for both. The home Sky Blues had Daddy Bond as manager and Baby Bond as centre half, the away Sky Blues had Dave Sexton in a post-Chelsea snooze as their chief and a hairy Gerry Francis ageing quickly as skipper. But in one of those rash last-minute decision moments the game appealed, so off I went.

It was worth it as back then Maine Road was a sight to behold. The ground loomed large amongst a sea of back-to-back Coronation Streets. It really was a fabulous example of the inner-city football gathering place, just oozing matchstick men and matchstick cats and dogs. You could be fairly sure that everyone for streets around was one of The Citizens. Turnstile operation had to be slick, day-trippers from Plymouth and away fans aside, virtually everyone else only had to leave their house 15 minutes before kick-off to get there.

The game itself was good entertainment, as was the trip back with a collection of nomads breaking out into community sing-song until stamina sapped at around about Taunton.

Later that year one of the City's got relegated and one finished fourth from bottom. It was the men from Maine Road who suffered the drop thanks to a last-gasper from Raddy Antic. That goal saw Luton leap frog both City's to safety and give rise to one of those classic football images - a beige suited David Pleat doing a middle-aged 'Tardelli' to plonk a smacker on his goal scorer. I have no great feeling for Luton, nor any wish to wear a beige suit (though I'll own up to having one once), nor any desire for kissing Raddy Antic, but watching the video clip of that moment again is a bit of a goose-bumper.

SOMERTON PARK, Newport County 1 Southend United 1, Division Four, Saturday 23 October 1982

Superlatives can be easy to dish out, especially in football circles, but none in my view can be more earned than those aimed in the direction of Tommy Tynan. Yes, he had the head start in life granted by his parents of same-letter initials, but prolonged brilliance has to be earned.

Going nowhere with Liverpool, the scousers loaned him out to Swansea in 1975 and from there until 1992 with nine clubs he scored 259 times in 646 games. I witnessed a fair few of those goals, none better than the 10 in nine games spell he notched to help Argyle to promotion at the tail end of the 1985/86 season. The man is considered a cult hero by both Argyle and Newport fans, and his record over shorter spells at Swansea, Sheffield Wednesday, Rotherham and Torquay was none too shabby either.

Tommy was in the Newport side back in 1982 with a young up and coming John Aldridge, and together they had formed a destructive partnership. Newport were on the up, fourth in the league and having the previous season reached the quarter finals of the European Cup Winners Cup when 18,000 had crammed in to Somerton Park to witness a narrow defeat to Carl Zeiss.

Quite how Somerton Park coped with 18,000 I don't know. The place was crumbling back in 1982 and had the remnants of a disused speedway track hugging the pitch for added visual mess. There was a lot of gently-stepped terracing which was losing a battle with vegetation, and the stands were a real mish-mash affair coated in a thick amber paint. Back then it might have been called a bit of a dump, today it's another now long-gone 'proper stadium' home for the footie fan to get all nostalgic about.

Newport ended the season in fourth, missing out on promotion due to some dire end of season form. That was as good as it got for County. Relegated from Division Three in 1987 and bottom of Division Four in 1988, the days of European glory counted for nothing as in 1989 they went out of business. Bit of a bad run that.

As with Wimbledon and Aldershot, their rise back from the ashes since is a testament to the herculean effort and loyalty of a small group of fans – respect to them all.

15/92 – ANFIELD, Liverpool 3 Brighton & Hove Albion 1, Division One, Saturday 30 October 1982

Tranny Brian had reached the grand old age of 21 and a Birkenhead knees-up had been arranged. I had dropped the bar job in my final year at Plymouth to concentrate on studies – the real impact of this was to reduce funds and I couldn't afford the opulence of British Rail two weeks running, so it was time to pull the thumb out again.

Two of us set off to meet up with Brian in his homeland, but hitching together proved to be a mistake. Folk were reluctant to stop for a male duet and my mate Steve declined to put on a dress in the hope of increasing interest, so it proved to be hard going, only slow-moving lorry drivers agreeing to stop. Six hours in and we had only got as far as Birmingham, so we agreed to split up and that made all the difference as we both made it to Birkenhead in time for evening pub opening. Brian's Mum directed us to a local where we found the birthday boy already three-parts cut, so we had some catching up to do. I'm not sure what happened after that.

I woke up the next day in a house strewn with comatosed bodies. It just did not seem right to travel north and not take in a new ground, but with the exception of Brian's Mum no one was sufficiently alive to contemplate moving. I therefore ferried across the Mersey alone to have a Kop experience – it was a bit choppy and no one batted an eyelid as I vomited over the side. 'Life goes on day after day' they probably all thought.

Mr Marsden went on to warble "People they rush everywhere, each with their own secret care." How true, it took a while before I could get someone to give me directions to Anfield which, when it came, helpfully consisted of "Follow that bloke with the red and white scarf." I had no idea of where Anfield was so pursued this chap incognito - as I was still wrestling with the contents of my stomach I was not really feeling up to striking up any conversation with him. I got a bit concerned when he hopped on a bus which I duly managed to do too - what if he was just off to, say, a train-spotters conference? No matter how exciting that might be I hadn't travelled all the way up for getting aroused by carriage numbers. However, assurance came with the conductor being happy with my request for "Anfield return" and soon I was to see a few others in club colours heading Lowry-like to their mecca.

The presence of Stanley Park made the approach look a little less like an urban jungle than Maine Road, but Anfield still loomed high over surrounding terrace rows. Outside the ground looked impressive – my penchant for stereotyping meant I was anticipating a massed swaying throng all singing 'She Loves You' once inside, but instead the Kop was almost silent. I found out that there was a good reason for this – there was still about 90 minutes to kick-off. Bugger. Going to a game half-awake had a number of drawbacks.

I choose my own crash barrier and settled down to read the programme – one advert claimed: "Niagara gets you fit and keeps you fit, read what Bob Paisley says about Niagara". I looked at the picture of Uncle Bob and decided not to bother. Elsewhere there was an article bemoaning falling attendances – Liverpool were winning everything back then with a team full of legends. From 1 to 11 their team sheet for the day read 'Grobbelaar, Neal, Kennedy, Thompson, Whelan, Hansen, Dalglish, Lee, Rush, Lawrenson and Souness. Every one of them remains an Anfield icon, yet still they were not packing them in. Today it's a major exercise to secure a massively over-priced ticket to see the likes of Bogdan, Randall, Can, Allen and Origi, not exactly names that trip off the tongue. Perhaps that's a point too easily made, and you could argue that fitness and skill-wise the Liverpool team of today would wipe the floor with those weighty names from the past. I think that's a point worth exploring, just not in this book though – leave it for the bar.

Now, getting to a game early and choosing a good spot to stand doesn't mean that it will prove to be a good choice. Ten minutes to kick-off all was fine and relatively comfy, come kick-off it was not. Folk joined me on the barrier and it soon became clear that I was not meant to be there – my new terrace chums had probably stood on 'their spot' for years and viewed they had earned that residency through years of devotion. The Kop was special and it was theirs, not mine. I was trespassing and, though not asked to move, I was not exactly made to feel welcome. Not quite the Kop experience I was hoping for. I was not in a state fit for any debate either, and got the distinct impression that if I opened my mouth my delightfully smooth southern tones would not endear me to anyone. So I just meekly bogged off to a quieter part of the Kop to see out the inevitable home win.

It was all a bit of a let-down – I had seen those wonderful nights of European glory on the TV in front of a swaying mass of Beatles haircuts but all I got was a nudge out of the way and a quick rendition of Gerry's other hit as it approached full time. I went back to Brian's – his Mum told me they were all in the pub.

16/92 - LOFTUS ROAD, Queens Park Rangers 2 Newcastle United 0, Division Two, Saturday 15 January 1983

We went to this one just to see what all the fuss was about. For just over a year a plastic carpet had covered the Loftus Road pitch and folk had been moaning. It hadn't exactly led to the start QPR had hoped (Luton had done them 2-1 and promptly went off to order their own veg stall cover) and a first season finish of 5th in Division 2 implied that the plastic hadn't been fantastic.

Back then Loftus Road had an intriguing approach as the main route in to the ground passed White City, a monster of an old stadium which had once hosted the Olympics and a World Cup game. But it was on the decline and in '83 was just home to speedway until the bulldozers trashed it two years later. Loftus Road was on the up though – a refurb had been finished in '81 and it was now a trim all-covered ground which, bar the subsequent move back to grass and change to all-seater, has remained much the same since.

Before Tel became 'El' he was a bit of a crafty cockney. He allowed visiting teams to train on the pitch before a game and then (I think this is where I am meant to insert the word 'allegedly') dampened it somewhat just before the game so it played completely differently. Whatever, something was working - 82/83 was to finally be QPR's season and they went in to the match against Newcastle sitting in second.

The ball bounced around all over the place – it was interesting rather than entertaining, and made some players look dafter than they might otherwise have been. QPR won 2-0 with a couple of goals from John Gregory, but it was their next home meeting with Newcastle on 22 September 1984 that sticks in the memory. I was at a bit of a loose end that day and decided to see a match in London. Travelling in to Liverpool Street I flipped a coin – if it was heads I would see West Ham v Notts Forest (which ended 0-0). It was tails so I found myself back at Loftus Road when, at kick-off, the scoreboard oddly announced that it was already QPR 2 Newcastle 6.

Big Jack was now in charge of the visitors and, having conceded 10 goals in the previous three games, he took steps to tighten his defence for this one. The defence was hardly needed in the first half as Waddle and Beardsley ran riot to put the Toon 4-0 up.

Tel was now El so that old pundit Alan Mullery was now in charge of QPR – his half-time team talk must have been interesting. Whatever he said though it seemed to work as QPR pulled three back only then for Waddle to bag another and give the points to Newcastle .... until QPR scored twice to make it 5-5 at the end. Wow. I doubt if I will ever see another game quite like that.

Big Jack wasn't impressed – he was quoted as saying after the match "People are asking me where I intend to start with the problems, but I just don't know. It will take years to put it right." He was not wrong there.

17/92 - ABBEY STADIUM, Cambridge United 1 Sheffield Wednesday 2, FA Cup Round Five, Saturday 19 February 1983

I'd hitched back from Plymouth the previous day to catch a Southend Friday night fixture at Roots Hall for part one of a quick footie feast. Part two was a trip up to Cambridge with my mate Rob to see the imaginatively nicknamed 'U's' in the fifth round of the FA Cup.

Rob at the time drove a Lada which was possibly the worst car in the world. It was a beige box perched on four bald tyres ('racing slicks'), and when the engine fired up its hairdryer tones completed the embarrassment. It had four doors but was so under-powered Rob discouraged passenger numbers in excess of one. On the way to Cambridge we had to pull in to a layby when it rained as the windscreen wipers had failed. On the way back the brakes got stuck in the 'on' position so we fastened the tow rope (a multi-purpose piece of kit) on to the brake pedal to pull it up after every braking. The smell of burning rubber was almost over-powering by the end of the trip. It was not a babe magnet, but there again watching footie in the 1980's at stadiums like The Abbey was not necessarily putting you in the right place for plentiful female company – the flat caps had gone but football watching at the time remained a bastion of male dominance.

The Abbey Stadium back in '83 was much like it is now – 'compact'. It was a tad more rustic back then though - an open away terrace turned the corner to allow away fans to also share part of one side so that a few of the away following could huddle under roofed luxury and enjoy looking at their soaked mates. Wednesday turned up in numbers and swelled the gate to nearly 11,000 so most got wet, but they all went home happy as Big Jack (him again – I was not stalking) scared them in to winning in one of those typical ding-dong cup ties.

I like the Abbey, not least because I'm usually there with the away support and in around 10 visits have never seen Cambridge win. Say what you like, football is a results game.

NEW WRITTLE STREET, Chelmsford City 3 Corby Town 1, Southern League, Monday 4 April 1983

In addition to the league grounds visited I have added to this book Wembley, the Millennium Stadium, the Nou Camp and a couple of overseas international trips. There is though one more monument to football that I need to cover outside of the 92 trail – New Writtle Street.

It was a place I first got to know in the late 70's as the host venue for sixth form college parties. The dimly lit social club that ran under most of the main stand was a perfect venue for 16 to 18 year olds to discover alcohol, as no matter how ill-treated the place was the partying never spoilt the decor. It was also the kind of venue that Arthur Daley would have loved, and many real-life impersonators seemed to frequent it.

Not a venue on the same circuit as Earls Court and the Royal Albert Hall, it still attracted acts, albeit not of particularly high quality. A stage of sorts nestled between doors to the ladies and gents toilets, and this could be distracting. On one occasion we were watching some fifth-rate comedian rattle through his set – "Right folks, who wants to hear 20 Irish jokes?" Before anyone could answer he was already on the third and a couple of minutes later he was on to 20 Scottish jokes, and so on, no race was safe, we just listened in silence trying to keep up with it all. Mid-way through one collection of 20 a chap in the audience walked past him to the gents – our star turn looked up startled and enquired "Oi, where the fuck do you think you're going?" "I'm gonna have a piss before the comedian comes on" came the reply. For the first time that night we all collapsed laughing, the comedian never recovered, stuttering to the end of his latest 20 before retiring to the bar.

I had been going to New Writtle Street for over four years before I actually went to a game there – on about the 50th time of Rob asking I finally succumbed and attended a Chelmsford match in 1983, something I still repeat every so often when Rob catches me out with the more attractive headline of some accompanying social event (with a match being hidden in the small print).

Chelmsford is one of those 'what might have been' clubs. Big enough to support a team of higher standing, back in the late 60's and throughout the 70's they were something of a non-league power house, but never got past the closed-shop of league clubs when applying for full membership. Eventually this took its toll and they fell away into an all too familiar self-fulfilling story of spiralling debt and failing form. I attended a few games at New Writtle Street in its last couple of years of existence up to 1997 where the fans were always passionate for the cause. In one of the last games a bloke streaked on to the pitch with nothing but a sign saying 'Save Our City' covering his trophy cabinet. I don't think he was even arrested – in the end he just came off resigned to the inevitability of the club having to find a home elsewhere as debts needed to be paid. 'Loser' by Beck was a favoured number on the jukebox at the time. The city of Chelmsford has I feel ultimately been the loser though, by allowing the club at its heart having no choice but to move out of town to survive. It took nine years until they could return, but home now is a soulless athletics stadium. Watching a game over an eight lane track just doesn't work.

THE MANOR GROUND, Oxford United 2 Wigan Athletic 0, Division Three, Saturday 23 April 1983

What goes well together? Spot the odd one out: fish and chips, Cagney and Lacey, apple pie and custard, retirement and seaside, two football clubs that loathe each other. Got it? Well, Mr Robert Maxwell failed the test at the back end of the 82/83 season.

Oxford and Reading at the time both rested in football's third tier, the former being a bit more successful on the pitch, but off it both were cash-strapped. Maxwell was Chairman of Oxford and widely acknowledged as having saved them from bankruptcy in '82. He also had a minor shares interest in local rivals Reading, a penchant for a mad idea, and an un-erring ability to get what he wanted no matter what the consequences were. Now, if you were a sane individual with no knowledge of football then maybe the idea of merging two struggling neighbouring clubs to make one big and better one would make sense. But football is not rational. It is driven by emotion.

Maxwell's plan was to marry the two rivals and base their love nest somewhere in between like the footballing hotbed of Didcot. There was even a name for this warped embryo – Thames Valley Royals. He was not exactly sensitive in announcing matters – news leaked out on a Saturday afternoon as both teams were about to play their respective league matches. Antagonism of the fans aside, consider how the players and other employees must have felt – a combined workforce of around 100 or so mortgage-payers would have been a tad distracted and worried about their futures.

Fan reaction was almost completely anti, perversely uniting the two rival groups in their violent opposition of being united. After a week of hyped media interest, all was set for the coming Saturday – a mass protest by Oxford fans at the Manor Ground, leaving Reading supporters rallying to do likewise before their next home match a week later.

I was sucked in by the media hype and, with nothing else to do, journeyed across to the Manor Ground for the demo. The atmosphere was one of pure hatred towards the very thought of merger, and I sat with 2,000 others (approximately one half of the crowd) on the pitch before the game eventually was allowed to kick-off some 30 minutes late. I didn't do anything pretentious like claiming Shrimper Solidarność with my Oxford brothers (I lacked the Lech Walesa tash to carry off anything like that), I just joined in. It was my Greenham Common moment.

To this day I don't really know what spurred me on sufficiently to travel over 100 miles to do it other than it just felt right. Oh, and the Manor Ground was another one I could then tick off the list – at that stage I had no concerted thoughts of doing the 92 in any specific timeframe, it was just an interest to follow when the opportunity presented itself.

Oxford's bosom of rest was one of the more quirky footie homes, with three stands along just one side, an away end that tapered off to a small seated hut, and its situation in the leafy suburb of Headington. The whole place looked as though it had just evolved gradually over the years with a series of small scale DIY additions, which it probably had.

Anyway, in the end the Thames Valley Royals idea floundered thanks in no small measure to the efforts of a small group of Reading folk. Would TVR have prospered had the notion had public support? Hindsight tells you not, the waters around the Canary Islands in 1991 would probably just have had bigger ripples.

Have Oxford and Reading prospered since '83? In many ways they have, I certainly recall thinking in the mid/late eighties that Oxford fans were having fun and, despite some dark times, like Reading they went on to experience the top flight. Above all though they have maintained their own community identity which brings pleasure to those within it and that is what matters in the end. [Note to self: do not get too carried away with such prophecies in the rest of this book, it could be perceived as having grand designs on becoming some kind of footie-version of Kevin McCloud.]

She Had A Wheelbarrow The Front Wheel Went Round

18/92 - SELHURST PARK, Crystal Palace 1 Sheffield Wednesday 0, Division Two, Saturday 26 November 1983

Life immediately after Plymouth involved a harsh reality – I needed a job.

I got one pretty quickly, working as barman at a big pub in Chelmsford. Jolly nice it was too, money in the pocket, good social life, home living comforts at Mum and Dad's, do what I want when I wanted (well, mostly), and new Fords to drive most evenings (Dad had a ludicrously quick turnaround on his company cars). But though it was never said, I was conscious that a bar job was not the anticipated parental desire after three years of studying for a degree.

Eventually something else did turn up – in the wonderful world of insurance. Actually it was a bit more exotic than that, it was insured pensions. Mmmm, I don't recall anyone ever standing up at school saying "When I grow up I wanna be in pensions". But it was a 'proper job', it included the (never fulfilled) promise of 'graduate training', and there was the interesting target of moving to their Bristol HQ after gaining a year of regional office experience. In the end it was a path to serve me well for some 31 years.

More immediately, and cash-rich, a football bonanza now presented itself. Home games, away games, other games, and if my guard was down, Chelmsford City games. For the next new footie experience Rob and I decided on a trip to the Palace. Rob's choice of car had not improved so I borrowed Dad's latest Ford for the trip, a 2.8 Granada Ghia. Driving round the streets of South London trying to find the ground I felt like Arthur Daley (I wasn't quick enough for The Sweeny) – I just needed a camel coat for me and a bomber jacket for Rob.

Now, if you fancy a challenge and have not yet been to Selhurst Park, get in the car and try and find the place. No cheating, you are in 1983 so ditch the Sat Nav and all mobile communications. For added difficulty take Rob as your map reader. South London is just one huge jungle of concrete with no distinguishing features. We got to Croydon at about 2.00 pm - Selhurst Park is two miles away. Taking in to account local parking restrictions, Croydon is about the nearest you can get. We eventually got in to the ground shortly after kick-off – I have passed an hour in more relaxing ways.

Anyway, we were in, and stood on the Holmesdale Terrace. For me one of the all-time classic footie images is of that terrace in 1979 when Palace secured promotion against Burnley – there were over 50,000 in the ground that day and the Holmesdale end must have absorbed the majority, it was just a sea of humanity. Where did they all go? Perhaps there was no parking permit police state back then. There were just over 11,000 at Selhurst for our game four years later, maybe the rest were still driving around outside in circles looking for somewhere to park.

I do like Selhurst – today it is a more modern affair but still has old saggy bits. And the atmosphere generated by the fans comes across really well on the box; it makes me want to go again. But next time it will be by train.

19/92 - THE VALLEY, Charlton Athletic 0 Watford 2, FA Cup Round Four, Saturday 28 January 1984

At the time I had one London ground left to visit. It was time to go in to The Valley - any excuse to play those great Skids rifts.

Charlton were in turmoil. Years of under-achieving and a decaying monster of a ground had taken their toll – it felt like it was a case of 'see them whilst they were still around'. Indeed, later that year the club went in to administration and re-formed as Charlton Athletic (1984) Limited. A year on from that and they were forced to move out of The Valley, moving to Selhurst Park for six years until their parking permit was revoked and they got in bed with West Ham for a year until an emotional return to a revamped Valley a year later.

Back in 1984 The Valley was monumental. Dad had told me of how his father had taken him there in the 1940's to stand on a packed East Terrace to watch the then FA Cup holders. I took up the pilgrimage to return to the same spot – it was awesome. Row upon row of terrace steps reaching towards the clouds, it was a tribute to crash barrier construction, and it was ringed by a matching perimeter fence. If you stood at the top and a programme seller walked by on the side of the pitch he'd be on the opposite side of the ground by the time you made it down the steps to buy from him.

Charlton that day fielded two of the iconic lower-league strikers of that era – Ronnie Moore and Derek Hales. But they didn't get a sniff as Watford eased through and ultimately got all the way to the final where Elton held hands with Renate. On a misty February afternoon the defeat added to a feeling of gloom around the place – old men stood remembering, dads stood worrying, young men stood getting angry.

As I left I took one last look behind me, I just had a feeling that it was a view that would not be there much longer. 'Ahoy, ahoy, boy man and soldier' the Skids rallying cry proclaimed ……… I did not know it at the time, but thanks in no small part to fan power this wonderful place would rise again.

97

20/92 - THE HAWTHORNS, West Bromwich Albion 0 Plymouth Argyle 1, FA Cup Round Five, Saturday 18 February 1984

My first Argyle away trip, I had travelled up on the snappily titled Plymouth Argyle Supporters London Branch FA Cup Away Day Special, a couple of designated Green Army coaches tacked on to a Euston 125 to Brum. Expectations low, spirits high, this was just going to be a damn good day out to end the cup run on, a run which had started of all places at Southend (hmmmm). I learnt a new song on the way up:

She had a wheelbarrow the front wheel went round

She had a wheelbarrow the front wheel went round

She had a wheelbarrow the front wheel went round

She had a wheelbarrow the front wheel went round

It relied upon variance of tone to make it sound vaguely poetic. So, new chart topper committed to memory, the trip up passed quickly, unlike the queue into the ground as 5,000 Argyle fans became increasing frustrated at the miserly number of turnstiles open. Once inside it was bedlam, the Green Army was in buoyant mood but there wasn't really any room to be buoyant – we were all wedged into one small corner whilst all other areas of The Hawthorns had room a-plenty. Does that sound sadly familiar? It was certainly dangerous. What made it worse were police incorrectly interpreting terrace sways and people wanting to get more space as folk causing trouble, and one or two sorties in to the crowd to make ejections of incorrectly identified troublemakers only made things more scary. I couldn't really tell you what the rest of the stadium was like, self-preservation was the focus.

Just before kick-off an excitable tanoy man announced "Ladies and gentlemen, show your appreciation for our new management duo, Johnny Giles and Nobby Stiles". The crowd seemed happy enough with their new rhyming couplet, and we suspected from our corner of the ground that their new charges would be eager to show their masters how many they could score against lower league opposition.

But when the great Tommy Tynan poked in a Staniforth cross in the first half it all went manic and never really calmed down after that. Argyle deserved their win and, after their big entrance, the Baggies new management duo sloped off to a chorus of boos – what a difference 90 minutes can make.

The journey home was one beautiful long sing-song about garden equipment.

21/92 - THE CITY GROUND, Notts Forest 3 Sunderland 1, Division One, Saturday 1 September 1984

A farewell weekender with my regional office insurance office chums before my Bristol adventure.

Football, cricket and a few jars – luverly jubberly. Footie was the trailer for the main event, an Essex match against Derbyshire where an Essex win would secure the John Player League title.

First though to The City Ground, the hyped attraction being the sight of still a relatively rare breed back then - an overseas player. Cloughie's pre-season capture was none other than .... Johnny Metgod. Who? Well, he had been signed from Real Madrid, but beyond that his CV listed DWS Amsterdam, Harlem and AZ 67 Alkmaar as his clubs. Not exactly a European Butter Mountain of football hot-beds. And he was a defender. And he looked about 90. But scroll forward a couple of years to witness one of the most brutal goals ever seen, a 35 yard free-kick howitzer that simply blitzed through a West Ham defence ducking out of the way for safety, capped off with a memorable celebratory salute. Yes, he hung around for a few years, played a bit of international football, won a gong or two at the end of his playing days with Feynoord, and turned his hand to coaching. But as much as William Roache is a tad typecast, Johnny is one of those players who will also only be remembered for one thing. YouTube him now for a reminder of his glory moment (Johnny, not Willy).

We stood at the Trent End to watch the game, back then a terrace with a low covered roof that afforded great acoustics – cough loud enough and those at the opposite end would look round startled. We were amongst a crowd of less than 16,000, so just as well the sound projected. The travelling Wearsiders were made to feel like outcasts, herded together in a corner pen on the opposite open terrace, with the obligatory group of home support forgoing relative comforts elsewhere in the stadium for the opportunity of staring and pointing at the away following from an adjoining pen. The garment of choice for those in both pens was a Pringle jumper, worn as the top garment in the blazing Summer sun just as it would be in the January ice. I always marvelled at its all-weather qualities.

A brief match report: the away Pringles told the home Pringles 'You're gonna get your fucking head kicked in'. The home Pringles told the away Pringles 'There's gonna be a nasty accident'. Brian jumped up and down on the touchline gesticulating in no particular direction. Johnny got out his Dutch/English dictionary to try and make sense of it all. Forest won 3-1.

Match done, a night in Nottingham followed, and then a cricket match which (please forgive me) I will now describe a little. Unlike the City Ground the day before, Derby's County Ground was packed, mostly with travelling Essex men up for some sunshine, refreshment and to witness another trophy win. It was just glorious. Halcyon days for Essex CCC – silverware a-plenty came the way of Captain Fletcher and his merry band. Gooch and McEwan slogged majestically, Foster and Lever swung both ways, and Pringle did whatever he felt like doing. Like his namesake knitwear range, Del Boy Pringle liked to stand out in a crowd and the fans knew it – a banner held aloft by the travelling Essex contingent proclaimed 'Pringle is a Poser', and Del Boy, like the good sport he was, duly obliged by standing by it for perhaps longer than needed.

Derbyshire went in to the game rock-bottom but were in no mood to give the Essex men a happy ending and amassed a respectable 215 from their 40 overs. In reply Gooch and Fletcher top-scored, but with one ball to go and one wicket left Essex were one run behind. Stuart Turner, the distinctly quieter man of Essex's all-rounder duo, swung his bat and memorably slogged a six. We ran on the pitch and I stood next to Fletch as he is interviewed by the BBC, I suspect it was one of his proudest moments.

Back now to those gentile times at 1980's footie grounds, I won't mention that relaxing, sunny, seated, exciting, beer-consuming cricket rubbish again.

22/92 - ST ANDREWS, Birmingham City 4 Plymouth Argyle 1, Milk Cup Round Two, Tuesday 26 September 1984

I always think I am cheating a bit in counting St Andrews as a ground visited. This is because what exists now is on a different planet to the cavernous crumbling edifice I experienced in 1984.

St Andrews was certainly imposing in George Orwell's 1984 – huge deep stands on all sides which on an evening game such as this stretched back into the gloom to give the impression they had no end. I suspect the place looked impressive when full – for Argyle's visit in an early round Milk Cup tie it was very sparsely populated. Every rusty metal railing, paint-peeled stanchion, weed-ridden step and crumbling concrete wall was on view where the light was bright enough to see. When new owner David Gold arrived in the early 1990's he was quoted as being more than a little shocked at what he saw, and I suspect that the odd well-publicised riot or two that had taken place since my visit had done little to improve the general ambiance. An enormous clock in one corner was certainly a stand-out feature; it looked as though it had been designed for pilots passing overhead to check if they had got the timing right for their approach to the local airport.

What exists now is a well thought out, modern, yet unique design which looks neat despite retaining the old but polished up main stand, and it comes across on the TV as still being atmospheric. I really must go again, though hopefully the travel experience will be better than what it was back on that September mid-eighties night. I was staying over at my friend Chris's house in Dartford and, like me as an ex-Plymouth student, he had remained keen on all things green. Pre-kids, his car of choice back then was an old MG – luverly jubberly, a treat to a ride in a sports car to see a match, it certainly beat hitching or the delights of the rail network.

We got there fine, witnessed the not un-expected defeat, and were on the outskirts of Brum coming home when Chris tried to change out of third gear. It wouldn't budge, and with AA membership considered to be an unnecessary luxury we drove the remainder of the circa 150 mile journey in a grumbling car. Mostly this was at 45 mph on the M6/M1, which is a tad dangerous when everything moves along at a much faster pace. The regular prospect of being smacked up the arse by a juggernaut relieved the boredom of the slow progress.

23/92 - THE PRIESTFIELD STADIUM, Gillingham 3 Plymouth Argyle 3, Division Three, Wednesday 2 October 1984

Mmmm, Gillingham. At the risk of upsetting any Gills fan (a risk worth taking), not the most enticing of places to visit. From Essex it appears tantalisingly close, a short river-hop, but via conventional road it takes forever, especially if the Dartford crossing is in its usual tailback-induced coma. Every journey there is forgettable because you immediately desire to erase it from the memory bank.

Then, when you do get there, well, let's just say that it's a bit of a let-down. The popular image of Kent is one of rolling green fields, hop-pickers toiling in the sunshine, majestic castles, exquisite gardens, gentle seaside towns, white cliffs, and the quaint streets of God's HQ in the UK. Gillingham misses out on all of that.

Also, from an away fan's perspective, Priestfield is one of the few grounds in the last 40 years to have actually got worse. For over a decade now visiting supporters have had to endure an ugly scaffold structure with seats bolted on, all open to the elements, and its temporary nature does little to make you feel safe in anything more than a mild breeze. Before, albeit open and terraced, at least you had the security of being on terra firma. The away end is named after dear old Brian Moore, presumably because, like the great man himself, it has nothing up top to keep it warm.

So, having alienated every Gillingham fan, what can I do to try and put matters right? Well, each time having forgotten the previous trip, I am frequently tempted to return on the basis of it either being a 'local' derby, a match where there is something at stake, or to view old players I once cheered who Gillingham always seem to nick. Then when I do go, I typically suffer. After the usual frustrating journey it either pisses down or I see the team I support get stuffed, or both – 8-1, 5-0, 4-1, a couple of 3-0's, whether it's the Shrimpers or the Green Army the outcome is the same.

Only once in about ten visits have I witnessed victory, and then I had to sit with the home support because I went along with a Gillingham fan mate. Yes, my first visit was it seems a six goal thriller, but I cannot recall anything of the game – at a guess I suspect Argyle would have been three up with five minutes left.

105

Let's move on to the next ground, it's all getting a bit depressing.

24/92 - KENILWORTH ROAD, Luton Town 3 Watford 2, Division One, Saturday 20 October 1984

What better way to change the mood a little than to think about Luton. It's cool for cats.

Everything about the place makes you want to smile - Lorraine Chase singing about its airport, hats, Vauxhall Viva's, Monty Panesar, carnival costumes, a team that plays in a steward's kit, and Eric Morecambe. OK, it has in its time been voted as 'the worst place to live in the UK' and 'dirtiest town in Britain', but let's gloss over that. Just drive as fast as you can through the surrounding sprawl, park up somewhere where there's an above average chance your car will still be broadly intact at the end of the game, and walk through the alleyways to the ground.

There's no one quite like Grandma, nor Kenilworth Road. Like a novelty tune with an annoying chorus, Kenilworth Road's quirkiness makes you want to look as long as no one else sees you doing it.

The away fan has the delight of entering the ground through a gap in the surrounding terrace houses, going to the loo below someone's house, and walking up a gangway taking you above house backyards (which have yet to see a visit from Mr Titchmarsh) so you can admire their washing or old discarded fridge.

On entering the footballing arena, you are then, to the left, afforded a view through a festival of stanchions to what can best be described as a series of double glazing showrooms. If you can then take your eyes off those there are two main stands on the opposite side and one seated construction at the home end to enjoy, all decked out in a 'matching' blue and orange. There's nowhere else quite like it.

My first trip to Luton back in '84 was for a game against near neighbours Watford in the top flight (that's not a typing error, it was a regular top-flight fixture back then). Pre-Tardelli dancing David Pleat versus pre-turnip labelled Graham Taylor. Bring Me Sunshine Eric Morecambe v Yellow Brick Road Elton John. Curly top Ricky Hill v even curlier top Wilf Rostron. TV host Nick Owen v ...... I'll stop now on the basis your interest might be starting to wane. What counts is that it was a match that mattered, the tiny ground was atmospheric (it was pre-double glazing box days, they came after Millwall dismantled the old Bobbers Stand the following year), and Luton edged a five goal thriller.

Long may bananas Kenilworth Road reign and the sensible corporate money-spinner stay on the drawing board.

THE RECREATION GROUND, Aldershot Town 6 Southend United 2, Division Four, Wednesday 24 October 1984

You win the FA Cup, European Cup Winners Cup, World Cup, grace Wembley countless times, achieve 108 caps for your country, are named Footballer of the Year, win the BBC Sports Personality of the Year Award, appear in an ad with your wife about drinking down your local and .... you manage Southend to a 6-2 defeat at Aldershot in Division Four.

I saw none of the late, great, Bobby Moore's greatest triumphs, but I was one of the 1,824 at the Recreation Ground back in October 1984. It certainly wasn't great, Southend were unbelievably cack in the 84/85 season, and only avoided applying for re-election by winning their final game. Poor Sir Bob really had been sold a pup, no money to get players in, home gates averaging less than 2,000, a chairman who four days prior to the Aldershot game had been arrested, money mysteriously leaking out of the club .... it wasn't easy.

Now, Aldershot is a fine club who win my complete admiration for coming back from the dead, but getting stuffed at the Recreation Ground can be a bit of a low point. I have had a few even lower moments watching Southend – losing at Aylesbury in the FA Cup with the chap on the tanoy singing "Oh when the Ducks, oh when the Ducks, oh when the Ducks go steaming in" springs to mind – but 24 October 1984 ranks quite highly as not being one of the best.

First of all, if you have to enter what appears to be a park to get in to see a match then it does tend to mean you are not going to be watching a game of the highest quality. Then there is one end of the ground that just does not exist aside from some advertising hoardings. On your way in you are treated to a birds-eye view of a dreary 60's office block towering over the main stand (and it doesn't need to tower very high to tower over). The club shop resembles a toilet block from the outside. There is the distraction of trains running right alongside the ground. And despite a low fan base there always did seem to be a high percentage of squaddie wannabe's lurking around wanting to further spoil your day. Lovely.

However, as long as it is dark enough for floodlights, Aldershot's little home has some appeal – despite the lack of bodies usually in it the low stand roofing helps to project what sound is made, and though an interior designer might scoff, the red and blue colour scheme works quite well. Indeed, I'd go far enough to commend the Recreation Ground as an exhibit for the Tate Modern under the title 'Never Mind the Jackson Pollock's here's The Recreation Ground'. Why not? There are weirder ideas already in that place.

But I digress. Match report: Southend get stuffed, another ground done (which no longer counts), we go home.

THE VETCH FIELD, Swansea City 0 Plymouth Argyle 2, Division Four, Saturday 1 December 1984

I'm now ensconced in Bristol, so West Country jaunts can again move to the top of the social diary. Swansea is west, indeed it's very west, and not fancying a long drive down the M4 on a cold wet day in my newly acquired second-hand turd yellow Ford Fiesta (Dad wanted his company cars back) I opt for British Rail. This also afforded the opportunity of sinking some Brains at the London Supporters Branch pub meeting place.

There's something quite comforting about walking in to a strange pub in a strange town and seeing it full of familiar faces. I wasn't betrayed by my accent and manners, I was already wearing the right clothes (it was full of Argyle). The London lot are a friendly bunch, and at a time when Maggie was starting to swing her handbag in aimless fashion about the hooligan problem, this little group represented everything that was still good about the game. The beers flowed, but I needed to maintain some sense of decorum – the new Argyle manager and ex-Shrimper David Smith had invited me to say 'hello.' It followed a brief letter I had sent congratulating him on his new appointment. As a Southend fan that also followed Argyle, I considered myself sad enough to be qualified to honour him with this important welcome. When I eventually got through the Vetch Field secret police before the game to shake his hand he acknowledged my unique insanity with two match tickets – Smiffy is a true gent.

As a little aside, and to try and dispel any thoughts you might have that I am some serial geek who annoys football folk with letters they would prefer not to receive, I have written just three others in my time (to date):

- Tommy Gibb 1977: actually it was my Dad who wrote this one, but it was about me. Mr Gibb, a hardened old pro who had made his name at Newcastle in the Chopper Harris role, was winding up lower league strikers by winding down his football career with Hartlepool. With 10 minutes to go at Roots Hall, Hartlepool were 1-0 down and searching for an equaliser. The ball was booted off the pitch for a Hartlepool throw and it came straight to me – Mr Gibb comes for it and I throw it straight over his head (I don't recall that it was deliberate, I was just crap at throwing). Well, Mr Gibb was none too pleased, told me I was a "fucking wanker" and goes to get the ball. The West Stand erupts behind me (as much as 500 old men and a few kids can erupt), informs Mr Gibb he is not very nice, and Dad the next day writes to Hartlepool to protest. In fairness we receive a humble apology back, though the author had the last laugh as Hartlepool went on to equalise from that throw.
- Colin Murphy 1993: this was a gloriously odd time. Southend were in the middle of a six year spell in

111

the second tier of English football, but the fans were getting complacent – after a lifetime of lower-league fodder we now wanted to go one further and feast at the top table. The messiah David Webb had fallen out with the Chairman and bogged off – upset by this we get Colin Murphy to take us forward to the Promised Land. Now, perhaps I might be guilty of the odd extended sentence, but Mr Murphy just didn't know when to stop. No one could make head or tail of what he was on about and his programme notes left you struggling for breath. His tactics, too, were baffling – after one match of long balls to an inexperienced diminutive lone striker I felt I had to protest and put pen to paper asking for an explanation. Not expecting a reply (I was quite rude), I got one and true to form it ran to a couple of pages and made no sense bar making one telling remark – "Please remember that it was me who signed Stanley Collymore." Murphy got sacked a couple of weeks later, Collymore kept us up and went on to earn Southend circa £3 million in transfer fees. OK, I'll give him that one.

- Peter Taylor 1993: Murphy gone, Fry went from hero to zero in a manic year when Karen Brady tantalised him with exotic Birmingham fruits, and in next came local lad Peter Taylor. Pete, who had started his footballing career at Southend, was a flying winger who had then moved on to better things at Palace, Spurs and England (cue iconic image flashback of Taylor, red and blue sash on his front, number 11 on his back, curling in an FA Cup stunner at Stamford Bridge in '76 and turning away to celebrate). In the early 90's he turned up at Standard Life as a consultant who made the most of his talents (which I suspect were not insurance related) by reeling him out at football matches against broker firms with whom they were trying to ingratiate themselves. It was a policy (no pun intended) that seemed to work – my office at the time (back in Essex) would usually struggle to put out a Subbuteo team, but dangle an ex-England international in front of us and we were suddenly over-subscribed. I organised the team so was a cert for the starting line-up, decided to mark Mr Taylor who then scored a hatrick inside ten minutes, before I subbed myself in shame. A few months later, clearly inspired by this, he turns up as Southend manager. Another letter wings its way to Roots Hall and he sends me a lovely reply apologising for the nutmegs etc. I give up letter writing after that, it only seems to end with some form of embarrassment.

Where was I? Ah, Swansea. Apologies to any Jack who had expectantly thumbed forward to this part of the book ready to get all misty-eyed about their beloved Vetch only to read about a bunch of old letters. Well, my summary of The Vetch is that it was .... a bit worn. Oddly, Stevie Wonder had played there earlier in the year (a concert, not in the Swansea midfield) – I suspect he hadn't been too fussed about the aesthetics, but anyone could tell that it was a ground on the way out, albeit the end proved to be lingering.

A meteoric rise up the leagues in the late 70's only led to everything marching back down the hill in the mid-'80's. By the time of Argyle's visit things were not looking good, and not just because Gerry Francis had turned up to flaunt his ageing perm. The programme for the game on the fixtures page had a column for 'league position' – just one answer of '20th' was inserted in September, the editor had become too despondent after that.

The Argyle fans were housed in the West Terrace behind one goal to witness more woe being piled on a lacklustre Swansea. The rear part of the stand we were in was seated but closed, left to decay until it was built over in later years. Opposite was one of the weirdest stands to be found in the Football League, a relatively new two-tiered affair with narrow terracing below and seats above. However, it only spanned just over one-half of that end of the ground, hinting of un-finished business. It also featured a floodlight leaning over a corner towards the pitch, looking like it was just about to un-balance the whole structure.

The rest of the ground carried on the mish-mash theme – the place certainly had character but needed either massive investment or putting out of its misery. Ray Charles might have liked it though.

25/92 - DEAN COURT, AFC Bournemouth 1 Plymouth Argyle 0, Division Three, Saturday 26 January 1985

"We wanna stay here, we wanna stay hereeeeeeeeeeee, Bournemouth's so lovely, we wanna stay here." A nice take on a popular footie ditty by some visiting fans recently to Dean Court (OK, now known as the Vitality Stadium).

Bournemouth back in '85 was still as alluring as it is today – wide open spaces, long sandy beaches, blue sea and affluent housing. Pensioner heaven. Dean Court was a tad different – a bit rough around the edges, dark stands, lots of terracing and a crumbly open away end, but nice enough for the lower leagues. They had attracted some pensioners too – Bill Rafferty and John Beck were well past their sell-by date, but were cornerstones of a Cherries team plodding along in their traditional Division Three comfort zone.

Argyle had brought a fair few as ever along the South Coast, and amongst their number on the away terrace was old Father Time himself, The Right Honourable Michael Mackintosh Foot MP. Back then he was a familiar figure at Argyle matches, walking alone (in later years he did have someone with him to hold him up) to support the team he loved. For someone who had seen so much and who had fought a failed election campaign to attempt to become Prime Minister, it always seemed incongruous to see him on the terraces at a football match. Today any high-profile minister might be well advised to just sit with the nobs in the Directors Box, but I suspect Mr Foot might have told them where to get off on that one. Whenever I saw him I never knew whether to feel proud that someone as steeped in history such as him stood and cheered with us, or worried that some harm might come to him, or just sad that he often seemed alone when, had his party not been in such a mess at the time of the 1983 general election, he could have just as easily that day been waving his CND badge at Reagan in the Whitehouse.

That's about it really. I hadn't made it to the pre-match pub, the journey was uneventful, I travelled alone, Argyle lost in a dull game, Bournemouth sea front on a cold January day held no appeal for a visit, and I went straight back home.

Dean Court today is still compact, but much smarter. The pitch has been turned 90 degrees, but in case some Smart Alec claims that it is not the same ground that it was back in '85 so no longer counting in its old form for 92 purposes, I have been back since the re-shuffle. I have the 'It took me nearly two hours to get out of Bournemouth's club car park after the match' badge to prove it.

NINIAN PARK, Cardiff City 1 Notts County 4, Division Four, Sunday 17 March 1985

Bob Marley concerts, Jehovah Witness rallies, show jumping, boxing matches, football internationals, defeating the great Real Madrid, Rugby Union, Rugby

League, American Football (ugh), cup finals (well, Welsh ones) and the death of Jock Stein in the away dugout. Ninian Park has seen it all. I suspect though that Cardiff v Notts County on an early spring day in 1985 will not make the highlights list for any reminiscing Bluebird.

Going into the match Cardiff had one team below them in Division Two – Notts County. Form had been consistently bad, win one lose three, and attendances were sinking. Less than 4,500 had attended the last home match, and in a bid to attract some new punters a switch to a Sunday for the Notts game had been set up – it was not a roaring success, my attendance swelled the crowd to 3,631.

But it worked for me, a quick trip across the bridge and another ground bagged instead of polishing my turd yellow Fiesta singing 'Root-de-doo-de-doo, a-root-de-doot-de doy di, a-root-de doot de dum, a-ree-de-dee-de-doo dee' or doing something equally pointless.

Ninian Park seemed to have a fetish for roof adverts – the stands were covered with them to catch the passing air traffic which was no doubt pleased to be reminded of the need for bread, steel and rum. The whole place appeared cavernous, especially with only a handful of us in it, and somewhat dreary too. It needed people to fill the Bob Bank and virtually empty open away terrace to give it some oomph, but folk had lost interest. The Cardiff defence had given up too – shipping four goals to a forward line that had scored significantly less than a goal a game in their preceding 30 matches.

It was almost pitiful at the end, no booing, just silence as I stood alone on the Bob Bank watching the outwardly contended but privately tormented figure of Justin Fashanu walk towards the handful of Magpies to acknowledge their dedication. Notts County had now leap-frogged Cardiff in the league table but it proved to be in vain, they were relegated at the end of the season along with their hosts from that March day.

Job done though, it was time to drive back home, then close my eyes and drift away for the remainder of a lazy Sunday afternoon.

26/92 - THE COUNTY GROUND, Swindon Town 2 Southend United 0, Division Four, Saturday 6 April 1985

I am a little bit superstitious and one thing that often seems to ring true is the old saying 'things come in threes'. With this in mind I really do not want to go to the County Ground ever again.

After my first visit back in 1985 I had just got on to the M4 to drive back to Bristol and a car sped past me, hit what must have been an oil patch and smacked in to the central reservation, span round, just missed the front of my car and came to a rest on the hard shoulder. I stopped along with a couple of other cars to check if they were ok which remarkably they were, but it could all easily have been so much worse (for them and me).

Two years later I went to see Argyle play at Swindon. A local derby of sorts (in Argyle terms) and both teams riding high in the second tier, a decent crowd was attracted with Argyle travelling in numbers. It was the height of the hooligan era and you could feel the tension at the ground – rumours then spread that there had been some trouble outside before the game and sadly this resulted in an Argyle fan dying from injuries sustained in a fight. It was a bit of a shaker when I learnt of it afterwards – I had walked to the ground alone wearing an Argyle scarf, and though I have never looked for trouble it could have just as easily been me that had been targeted just for wearing the wrong colours.

So, daft as it might seem, I won't go again. From a TV view perspective the County Ground now compared to 1985 doesn't appear to have changed too much anyway – forced by the Hillsborough aftermath, seats have just been bolted on where terraces once prevailed. The key change has come along the TV gantry side where there used to exist a somewhat unique (that I am aware of) roofed two-tiered terrace stand. I recall that back in 1985 the top half had been closed due to it being deemed unsafe – presumably the club officials were not concerned about those who dared stand on the bottom half.

May the Argyle fan that lost his life RIP – I never knew him but I do think of him from time to time.

PRENTON PARK, Tranmere Rovers 2 Southend United 0, Division Four, Friday 26 April 1985

Have you ever been to an away game to forget? For me it was Tranmere away on a Friday night in April 1985. Southend were really poor that year (again), attendances were often less than 2,000, the match programme was made of what looked to be low grade toilet paper (unused), and Trevor Whymark was in the team earning some pennies before his knees gave up completely. League form was appalling, and a win at Prenton Park became vital to stave off an embarrassing re-election application.

Being in Bristol, Tranmere away seemed almost local. And my old Uni mate and Tranny fan Brian was up there, so a few beers and a match together seemed like a good idea. Wrong.

The car wouldn't start. No problem, I caught the bus to the bottom of the M32 and started hitching. Not a bad trip up, I recall about three lifts got me there and that the drivers weren't too odd. Getting to the Wirral in good time I knock on Brian's door (his Mum's) only to be told that he had got an interview in Oxford that day and had naffed-off down south for a few days. Life before mobile phones was a mess.

Never mind, his Mum welcomed me in, made me some dinner and then set me off to walk to the ground via a recommended pub. "You'll find Brian's brother Frank in there; he'll buy you a pint." Pub found I enter a depressing scene, plenty of folk around but mostly all sitting apart cuddling a lonesome pint in what was a soul-less dump. Through the smoky haze I try to spot Brian's brother, realising that I actually didn't know what he looked like. I buy my own pint and stare into it - blue, red and white Southend knitted scarf aside I thought it seemed safest to try and blend in and copy everyone else. No one called Frank declared themselves, but I didn't want to risk rejection and ask anyone either. I spotted a juke box and thought about trying to liven the place up with a tune. I remember being really tempted to play "Winner Takes It All" by Abba but thought better of it, and instead just supped up and left. I wonder if that pub is still there and if so whether anyone inside has moved.

The ground wasn't far and easy to spot with the floodlights glaring - just as well as if I'd tried to follow the crowd I suspect I'd have been more likely to end up at the local chippy. Just 1,072 entered Prenton Park that night. Away fans (around a couple of dozen I think) were housed on a side terrace. But that's about all I can remember of the game or the ground, I know we were dire, we often were then, and lived up to expectations by losing 2-0.

Coming out of Prenton Park, not knowing anyone and deciding it would be healthier for the spirit to stay out of the pubs, I go back to Brian's. His Mum had forgotten I was staying that night and had gone to bed. I manage to wake her up, and several others in the street too, by shouting through the letter box, and am given a sofa for the night.

Tea and toast in the morning, Frank was levered out of his pit by his Mum and instructed to drive me to a suitable hitching-point off the M53. Probably still full of Newcastle Brown Ale, a chain-smoking Frank beckons me to follow as he staggers to his car and duly obliges with the lift, made in total silence aside from the clanking of a loose exhaust and his fag-induced coughing fits. Some four hours later, about 28 hours after setting off, I get back to Bristol.

What a waste of time. Brian told me afterwards that I should have stood in the Cow Sheds for the ultimate fan experience – being a visiting fan aside it didn't sound too enticing; perhaps like the local pubs it was an acquired taste.

27/92 - GOODISON PARK, Everton 3 Norwich City 0, Division One, Saturday 27 April 1985

Four new grounds in six weeks, perhaps I needed to broaden my social life. However, this trip involved a stop-off on the way back to see another old Uni mate and he hated football, so some limited social skills outside of the world of tribal chanting, violence and decaying monoliths were being maintained.

Now, as much as I do not want to go to the County Ground again, I would be delighted to find myself back at Goodison Park. If I had to design a football stadium it would look like Everton's home. Ringed by houses with real people in them and a park rather than faceless warehouses, it looms proudly over its surroundings. The stands are big and blue and, to a large extent now, modernised, but retain an identity which says 'there is no place quite like this'. I even love the stanchions that still exist in parts of the ground – I am used to these at Roots Hall, their existence keeps you moving on cold days as you sway from side to side to follow the play. For that authentic home-watching footie experience I often think that a stanchion blocking the telly view in the middle of the living room would work well – my better-half begs to differ so I suspect that if I am to keep my life goals attainable I will have to delete that one from the bucket list.

The only downside to Goodison is that, on arriving (I have been back a couple of times since and it is the same), you are descended upon by local 11 year old entrepreneurs wanting to 'look after your car'. Failure to agree risks new go-faster stripes being added. On my first visit, much as I thought this might improve the look of my Fiesta, I succumbed to the request and paid across the requested fee. On my second visit I thought I would remove this financial transaction from the day's expenses by parking in a proper car park, but the little buggers had infiltrated there too so I ended up paying twice for the privilege of parking. On my third trip I decided to drive by where I was going to park then zoom in to the space and leave as fast as I could when the coast was clear – it worked, I was too quick for the aspiring Lord Sugars, but I did spend the whole game worrying (needlessly as it turned out) whether my car would still be intact when I got back to it.

Any Toffee will tell you that the 84/85 season was the bizz. They had won the FA Cup the season before (though it should have been Argyle's cup), and followed that up by winning the European Cup Winners' Cup and the First Division crown. There is a goal from that time that sticks in the memory – it was against Sunderland just three weeks before my visit. Paul Bracewell volleys a pass from the half-way line to Trevor Steven on the opposite wing, he controls it sublimely, beat his marker and lashes one in from a narrow angle. It was a goal that just oozed confidence and, much like buying an album because you have heard one great track (I've done that a few times, not always with great results), on the back of seeing John Motson describe that goal on Match of the Day I decided to go and see the champions-elect.

Well, there were no crackers scored against Norwich, instead I witnessed one of those games where there was only ever going to be one winner and it was as if both teams knew that before the kick-off. But I did get to experience something even more predictable – the Z Cars theme tune. Semper Fidelis aside, that has to be the most iconic tune for any team to come out to. Played loudly on the tanoy, it blocks out the sound of keys being scraped against the sides of cars where any owner has failed to cough up the appropriate fee.

28/92 - FIELD MILL, Mansfield Town 3 Southend United 0, Division Four, Saturday 28 September 1985

Saturday 28 September 1985 was a bit of an embarrassment.

Encouraged by an eight game unbeaten start to the 85/86 campaign which saw Southend sitting at the top of Division Four, I decided to risk the Fiesta on a day trip from Bristol to Mansfield. The 957 cc's performed admirably and I was parked up in good time, which for Mansfield in the mid-80's (or probably any time during the last 100 years) meant being there within five minutes of kick-off.

Field Mill today has some bright yellow seats, and if you ignore the condemned stand running along one side it looks quite tidy. Back in 1985 it was drab, mostly terraced, and if memory serves me correctly, the stand that is condemned today was condemned back then.

The away terrace was open and very sparsely populated by Shrimpers – despite the recent good form the away following was not great at that time. I chose my crash barrier (we all could have one each) and watched Southend stroll out with an air of confidence. Ten minutes later we were 2-0 down and playing woefully. A few Shrimpers gathered together to vent their annoyance and then I noticed a fist fly, then another, and before long there was a full scale brawl. The nearest Mansfield fan must have been 50 yards away. Stewards then police joined the fray and a good number of Shrimpers were ejected from the ground. I have no idea what the argument was about – I didn't dare ask for fear of it sparking off again. There were only around 20 of us left afterwards and we watched the rest of an inept performance in silence.

Ugh, my last Southend away day at Tranmere had been miserable and before that it had been dire and nearly much worse at Swindon. I was in need of some enlightenment elsewhere.

29/92 - VILLA PARK, Aston Villa 1 Manchester United 3, Division One, Saturday 14 December 1985

A Bristol work colleague was a Bishop's Stortford fan. I thought I had it rough. Anyway, he persuaded me it would be a great day out to see his team at relatively local Cheltenham Town in the Third Round of the FA Trophy. It ended 0-0.

I had gone on the basis he would then go with me to a match of my choice. If I had been feeling vindictive I could have opted for Torquay v Southend, but I wasn't in to self-harm so ultimately opted for a bit of glamour at Villa Park. Being the 80's it was pay-on-the-day, easy-peasey, so off we went to experience some top-flight quality at a ground which would have too many bodies for half of them to be arrested no matter how effective the police were.

I had been there 18 months previously for the FA Cup semi-final between Argyle and Watford, but to be 'purist' (or anorak) I considered I needed to see the resident hosts play on their own turf for it to count for 92 purposes. Back in '84 I had stood opposite the Holte End feeling somewhat out of a party where green had met yellow in canary-style harmony, this time I made sure that I was on it. The rest of Villa Park stretched out impressively before us, voluminous old stands either side, and a modern looking Witton End straight ahead (complete with smoky-glassed executive boxes declaring that the corporate era was ready and waiting if only folk would stop rioting). Outside, Villa Park was magnificent too, a tribute to red bricks. This was (and still is) a great footie ground.

Big Ron was in town, jangling his bracelet, sporting December shades, chewing gum and walking with a swagger. Liam Gallagher incarnate. Ron's team had won the first ten games of the season, and although they had stuttered since they were still top, with a young Mark Hughes scoring for fun and an even younger Norman Whiteside just bossing it.

Villa in contrast were, bar a couple of blips, doing what post-WWII Villa did best, nothing much. The locals were revolting, less than 15,000 had turned up for the last home game against Spurs, but United were still box-office and nearly doubled the gate. The Reds won efficiently, subduing the Holte End for most of the match so doing nothing to make up for my semi-final blues. Big Ron walked off the pitch like John Wayne.

TWERTON PARK, Bristol Rovers 0 Mansfield Town 0, Division Three, Saturday 13 September 1986

I'd been having a bit of a footie holiday, the odd Argyle or Southend home game, but had cut out trips to lands far far away in the interest of paying a newly acquired mortgage and car loan.

I was now a member of the debt-ridden economy. Life didn't feel like Maggie's loadsa money world to me, but I did have a flat with a twin tub, and a go-faster Mk III red Escort with twin spotlights to woo the chicks back to see my dancing washing machine. It wasn't a roaring success, but I did like a car that could get up the A38 hills to Plymouth without changing down to second.

I could afford a local trip though. Bristol Rovers were in dire straits and had to find a more affordable abode. No Bristol twin tub for them though, City didn't like them, so instead it was off for a bit of posh at Bath. Bath is beautiful – Georgian crescents of houses crafted from limestone, tree-lined walk-ways, ancient preserved buildings, Roman monuments, romantic bridges, theatres, art galleries, two universities and sweeping parks, all set amongst the steeply rising hills of the Avon valley. Then there is Twerton Park – a 'back to basics' ground that was now on my doorstep.

Beggars can't be choosers, Rovers needed a home and Bath City welcomed the extra cash. It was only gonna be a temporary thing anyway (which lasted 10 years), and the Gas Heads were a loyal bunch who wouldn't mind a few extra miles every fortnight (to their great credit they stayed with it – average attendances remained fairly constant throughout their Bathing adventure). An advert in the programme for the Mansfield game for lottery ticket sellers paints a picture regarding the perilous position of Rovers finances at the time: "Wanted, full time Sales Representatives, hours = to suit, pay = nothing."

Twerton Park was not luxurious – lots of terracing, and stands heavily featuring stanchions to prop up the aging structures. Rovers ended up spending (thanks to grants) over a million pounds upgrading the facilities to get it up to league standard – 'we'll have some of that' the Bath Board must have thought. Bristol City remained unfriendly – their fans damaged the tarted-up main stand in 1990 in an arson attack.

Amongst all of the historical sites Bath had to offer, in 1986 there was another monument to a past era to appreciate – Gerry Francis, fresh from a three-game season at Pompey. Mullet getting madder the more out of fashion it became, we watched him walk around the

129

middle of the park against Mansfield as fast as his growing stature would let him. Incidentally, you might like to know that Gerry's hair now has its own Twitter page.

Not discouraged by a dull 0-0 on my first visit, I ended up going to Twerton Park a few times until I left Bristol in 1988 – it was always a friendly place, and the views of the houses of Bath clinging to the surrounding hillsides were a welcome distraction whenever the action became a little dull.

30/92 - EWOOD PARK, Blackburn Rovers 1 Plymouth Argyle 2, Division Two, Tuesday 30 September 1986

I've come up with a few implausible suggestions to get a footie match in over the years. A friend (who I'd best leave as anonymous for a reason that will become obvious) was travelling from London to the West Country. A fellow Argyle second-club man, I knew he would be keen to see the Pilgrims if an opportunity presented itself, so I suggested he stop off in Bristol with me overnight and we travel up to Blackburn for a night out – it was kind of on the way for him I argued. Without any hesitation he agreed, with the proviso he could leave his wife in my flat whilst we went out. Class.

So off we went, a 200 mile each way trip, catching up on footie and past times as we drove whilst his wife had the company of my twin tub for the evening.

Ewood Park back in 1985 was a mixture of the old and the new, but mostly the old. After a fire at one end, the club had recently put in some executive boxes and the match programme proudly boasted about its 'glass lounge' where you could eat a delicious one-course meal and binge out on biscuits at half-time.

Elsewhere it was not so sumptuous - the wooden Riverside Stand had failed a safety check and the rest of the ground looked a bit grim. An old chimney towered behind one end to give the place an added Victorian feel. Like so many grounds of the time it was in a trap - tired and in need of substantial investment, but with dwindling crowds and the games dire image insufficient money was coming in. Patching on a glass lounge with a one course meal was not really enough, it was very much in need of a touch of 'arte et labore'. At that time a fairy godmother miracle was required - Ewood Park today is proof that sometimes wishes do come true.

The 5,300 in the ground that evening did not exactly test the capacity of the non-condemned parts, most areas were silent as Argyle stylishly controlled matters and the echoing noise created from a small platoon of the Green Army that evening is a memory that has stayed with me. The wheelbarrow song is always better if not many are listening.

We bombed back down an empty M6/M5 thoroughly satisfied with our evening. I suspected that my friend had a few brownie points to make up though.

131

GAY MEADOW, Shrewsbury Town 1 Plymouth Argyle 1, Division Two, Saturday 8 November 1986

Football in the 80's could give you grim Ewood Park one day and quaint Gay Meadow the next. The contrast could not have been greater.

It was not that Gay Meadow was blessed with comfy facilities - it didn't even have a glass lounge - but it did look lovely.

Surrounded by trees, it had a river on one side for the boating fraternity and railway tracks on the other for train spotters. Like Twerton Park, it afforded pleasant views of the town on surrounding hills, with sights of an abbey and a castle completing the vista. The added twist was the boat owner who retrieved balls from the river - his nautical skills were often in heavy demand.

Gay Meadow at the time was a happy field. Think of Shrewsbury Town and you probably think of a team in the lower leagues, but in 1986 they were in danger of becoming an established football powerhouse, being in the midst of a ten year spell in the second tier. At the time too they were also on their way to the quarter finals of the League Cup, and the previous season had upset Middlesbrough by relegating them (which had led to a number of Smoggies filling the local courts due to getting a tad upset). Unless you count Steve Ogrizovic, Gerry Daly or Bernard McNally, that period of success was not exactly on the back of importing-in household names, so it is to their eternal credit that they achieved what they did.

I had always thought that the Gay Meadow designer (though I suspect the term 'design' is used rather loosely here) had a somewhat sadistic nature – all of the stand roofs were far too short to cover the fans below so, on rainy days, there was a tendency for everyone to disappear to the shadows. My visit in November 1986 was one of those days, though standing on the open away terrace the only option was a soaking. By the end of the match Michael Foot's hair was a complete mess.

Gay Meadow bit the dust in 2007, victim not of real financial necessity but of a desire to achieve a bit more. I suppose if Shrewsbury Town ever regularly challenge Barcelona for European trophies the move will have been justified.

31/92 - OAKWELL, Barnsley 2 Plymouth Argyle 0, Division Two, Saturday 5 September 1987

Ee by gum, am guin down t'pit, Dickie Bird, Michael Parkinson, Grimethorpe Colliery Brass Band, Kes, flat caps, black puddin', ferrets, Arthur Scargill, Charlie Williams, Harry Worth, Seth Armstrong .... I'm off t' Barnsley cock. Well, that's got the stereotyping out of the way in a Norwegian commentator rap kind of way - I apologise if I have offended anyone who owns up to loving Barnsley (or Norwegian commentators).

It was time for another away-day train trip with the London Branch, which meant a stop-over in London first. A new season and early optimism – Argyle were top of Division Two and Barnsley second. It was the match of the day between the big two – Leeds, Birmingham, Stoke, Manchester City, Crystal Palace, Aston Villa, West Brom and the mighty Shrewsbury could only admire from below. A few of us travelled up from Kings Cross, which would swell the attendance to 4,163.

I had been to a few places north of Watford by 1986, but Barnsley did seem to have a charm all of its own. Admittedly the approaches to towns do not always reserve their finest for the sides of railway tracks, but Barnsley looked like a place going downhill fast. Derelict warehouses, copious quantities of wasteland, defunct chimneys, rows of dilapidated back-to-back terrace housing, all with the occasional 1960's architectural horror thrown in for good measure. It was great – I would never have experienced this within the confines of Southend, Plymouth or Bristol. Going to places you would never otherwise remotely contemplate is one of the joys of ground-hopping.

Oakwell was a similar joy, and stuck in an Archibald Leitch time warp it was fascinating. Today the old West Stand is the only part of Oakwell that remains from the 1980's, and back then with a massive terrace in front of the rear seated area it looked even odder than it does today. The away fans were seated in it for Argyle's visit, it being deemed not worthwhile opening up the vast open away terrace for the London Branch and a bus load of Green Army from Devon. Opposite us was a large covered terrace sporting on its roof an advert for John Smiths Bitter (whose own adverts of two old flat cap farts drinking in The Three Ferrets did little to shed my stereotype image-painting). This just left to our right the Ponty End, outside which the Barnsley hardcore tied up their whippets (apologies again).

The game was a close fought draw, enabling us to have sing-songs about being top of the league on the train ride back to London. Make hay whilst the sun shines as it is unlikely to stay out forever, you never know when you might have to go to Barnsley again.

Working It Out

THE DELL, Southampton 2 Coventry City 2, Division One, Monday 26 December 1988

Life was starting to take a different path. I was now living in Colchester with my missus-to-be and a decent-sized mortgage, the net result in footie terms being a few more trips to a now closer Roots Hall, but fewer trips to new exotic faraway lands like Barnsley.

Going to games on a whim was no longer appropriate. I had responsibilities, and things needed to be justified and earned. Tactical skills in determining this had to be sharp. "I'm not going to the footie today, think I'll give it a rest and save the pennies, what shall we do instead?" So off we'd go for a walk somewhere whilst I'd keep an eye and ear out for trying to find how Southend were getting on at some northern outpost I'd never had the intention of going to anyway. Lizzie meanwhile, much smarter than me, would be fully aware of my juvenile attempts at point-scoring but let me think I had got a result. It's a game of life played out across the land.

A trip to The Dell though was an opportunistic treat thanks to spending Christmas with new family-to-be members in nearby Gosport, me offering a morning of shopping for bargains at the sales in Southampton in exchange for a chance to view the silky skills of Matt Le

Tis in the afternoon. Deal secured and, after a morning of looking for imported bargains, off we went to see a Saints team made up of 100% Englishmen.

The Dell had been a ground I'd wanted to visit for some time; it always seemed to have so much to offer. Tightly packed crowds, great atmosphere, Mick Channon whirling his arm, Saints teams over-flowing with players who had 'been there seen it done it' yet entertained with skill and passion (George, Ball, Keegan, Armstrong, Osgood, Golac, Paine, MacDougall, Peach, Montgomery, Rodrigues, Davies ....), moderate success at the top level, and all backed by a stability the envy of everyone (back in '88 Chris Nicholl was only Southampton's third manager in 33 years). Alphabetically Southend came straight after Southampton, but that was usually as close as the two clubs ever got.

The Dell didn't disappoint for our Boxing Day trip. It was an entertaining 2-2 draw, Le-Tis dominated, three Wallace's on the same side played blinders, Ogrizovic and Flowers flew all over the place to keep the score down, Speedie annoyed, Kilcline was brutal, Houchen huffed and puffed, I got to stand on the lop-sided Milton Road terrace, and 16,008 of us went home happy. All for just £8.80 in today's terms (£3.50 back in 1988) – a proper bargain and it wasn't even in the sale.

32/92 - CARROW ROAD, Norwich City 1 Coventry City 2, Division One, Saturday 14 January 1989

Brian the Tranny fan was visiting. Safe in the knowledge no one else would know him in Colchester, he took an unofficial day off from work and drove down to see us in glorious Essex. He did well to make it – transport was a Datsun Cherry which had seen better days and with a star feature, due to the doors being dented and permanently rusted shut, of having entry/exit via the Starsky & Hutch method. This was fine when parked up at home, but did tend to make folks stare and laugh when out and about, particularly if you went arse over tit.

Drinks and a good catch-up aside, a double footie-fest was on offer – Tranmere away at Colchester on the Friday night followed by getting Carrow Road ticked off the list on the Saturday. We enjoyed Layer Road – the Trannies won 3-2 and we were virtually the only two in the away end. This, however, ultimately led to a bit of an issue. At the time Saint & Greavsie had a habit of featuring the Friday night games on their Saturday lunchtime programme. Both Brian and I were clearly visible on the screen as Saint described the goals going in at the away end, and initially Brian was pleased with this national recognition for being a loyal away Tranny. At least that was until his boss called him in to his office on the following Monday to question his ability to travel from his sick-bed to watch a football match some 250 miles away on a cold Friday evening when he had been unable to attend work. Sometimes TV fame has its disadvantages.

Anyway, Carrow Road. The Datsun was left outside our Colchester house, Lizzie agreeing to keep an eye out for it being decorated with 'Police Aware' stickers, and instead I drove slowly up to Norwich on the A140, famed for tractor-traffic with no passing spaces. Coventry were again the opposition, in a game which half-way through the season had a 'top flight top of the table clash' billing. Millwall were third – it was proving to be an odd season.

Carrow Road has for a long time always been neat and tidy and, to the un-trained eye, always looked much the same. Stands on all four sides, by 1988 it even had a touch of the 'modern look' about it with a new stand along one side replacing one that had burnt down in 1984 thanks to someone apparently leaving on a three-barred electric fire overnight. I expect the new heating system was made a little more sophisticated in the new build. Yes, there was still some terracing back in '88, but it sported the luxury of roofing – farmers got wet enough during the week so shelter was demanded for their fortnightly footie respite.

Back in '88 we did not enjoy any luxurious catering – re-constituted hot dog in slime from an un-hygienic looking portable stall served by unwashed hands used to wipe a winter dripping nose was the standard favourite for the masses at Carrow Road at the time, as it was everywhere else. Visit today though and Delia's delights will tantalise your taste buds, and if you get to enjoy one of the hospitality suites that run underneath most of the stands you can expect some proper fine-dining. On a visit a couple of years back we entered at one end of the ground and seemed to walk around at least half of it before getting to our swish dining room destination, our journey taking us through a maze of different areas where the varying depth of the carpet pile was an indicator as to the price of the menu. It was very nice, but I do find being called 'sir' by a waiter at a football ground a little strange. "You'll find the ketchup darling on the side of the van" is my usual experience.

Back briefly to 1988 when we watched the 'Speedie Show'. The little man hustled and harried all game long, tapped in Coventry's equaliser and then delightfully chipped Bryan Gunn to score the winner. I'd put Mr Speedie in the same bracket as folk like Billy Bremner, Joey Barton and Franck Ribery – someone most will love to hate but who, given the choice, you'd want in your team if above all else you just wanted to win by any means (ok, maybe not Mr Ribery).

WATLING STREET, Maidstone United 3 Southend United 0, Division Four, Saturday 31 March 1990

This is a sorry tale, and one I feel I now need to seek absolution for in a confession. It is my entry for the Simon Mayo BBC Radio 2 Drive Time regular programme slot along those lines.

Maidstone United had been in existence since 1897. For most of that period they had bumbled along in non-league circles not offending anyone, achieving the odd success such as winning the Stutchbury Fuels Challenge Cup in 1987. Then, all of a sudden in the late '80's, they gather some momentum, and in 1989 gain promotion to the Football League. In anticipation of this move to greatness they sold their old ground and moved in bed with Dartford FC, throwing cash at the place to get it up to standard. Watling Street was tidy but unspectacular, its key feature being a main stand that covered no more than half of one side and sported two floodlights which stood directly in front of it to block the view. The rest, from what I can recall, was open terracing.

Southend were on a roll and challenging for promotion, Maidstone were plodding along doing their best to remain incognito, so a short hop into Kent to bag a new ground and three points was the order of the day. Arriving quite early I parked in a street close by and strolled to the ground, peering through a gate to a car park next to the away end to check things out. Leaning against the gate it opened so I walked in to get a better view, and before I knew it I was standing on the terrace. Forming the opinion that I had paid enough to the game of football over the years, I just stayed where I was, grateful to Maidstone for saving me a fiver. I did buy a programme, and in a sudden pang of guilt, a Maidstone United club raffle ticket.

Perhaps in divine retribution, Southend hardly had a kick all game and lost 3-0 in a woeful match. Maidstone finished fifth that year, but that was as good as it got. By the start of the 92/93 season, riddled with debt, they went into bankruptcy, not even the sale of their Watling Street ground improvements to hosts Dartford FC for circa £500,000 being enough to save them. Indeed, that purchase cost their fellow Kent buddies dear too, as it pushed their debt too far and they ended up both having to sell off Watling Street to developers and withdraw from the Southern League. Maybe if I'd only paid my entrance money things might have been different ....

33/92 - LONDON ROAD, Peterborough United 1 Southend United 2, Division Four, Friday 4 May 1990

After relegation the year before, the yo-yo history of Southend United was set for another twist, this time in the right direction. A win was needed to secure automatic promotion – Peterborough required victory to secure a play-off spot for that old slug-balancer and half-asleep pundit Mark Lawrenson. Everything was set up for a nail-biting day.

Judging that Lizzie's enthusiasm for football was on the wane I thought a promotion party might re-kindle some interest and it tied in with visiting relatives, so I had her company for this one. We also had a stroke of luck on the way in as we were handed two free tickets by a club official who was simply looking to off-load

142

them to anyone he could find. Though mindful of the match outcome last time I had got in for free, we accepted the tickets. This had both a benefit and a down-side – it meant we had a nice seat in the main stand which Lizzie preferred to bouncing up and down on the terrace, but also meant we were seated with the Posh folk.

London Road in 1990 was a little bit like the old Goldstone Ground – an open terrace running along one side facing three covered stands, with the only seats being where we were at the back of the main stand. All very basic, but perfectly adequate for a club which appeared to be at home with lower-league life. Like many grounds though, post-Hillsborough its days of seat-frugality would be numbered (albeit the Posh held out longer than most).

David Webb had started to assemble a decent squad which could play some good stuff as well as fight for the cause. Red Card Roy was on the way out, he could not be relied upon to stay on the pitch before he ran out of puff and was subbed, and in had come the likes of Ian Benjamin and 'Ooh Andy Ansah' to support goal machine David Crown. Around 1,500 Shrimpers had made the trip, all bar the two of us jumping around in the Moys End as Crowny banged in a brace.

I felt somewhat annoyed with myself this time for getting in for free – perhaps it was further just-deserts for my Maidstone deception. All I wanted to do was join in with the away fans singing, but instead I had to just sit there listening to old men moaning about another season of lost opportunities. The Posh did pull one back to make a bit of a fight of it, but Southend held on and the players partied on the pitch. Lizzie and I were about the only ones left as they came off and I could hold back no longer, waving my scarf and shouting out my appreciation. My reward came – lofted arm salutes waved back at me from the pitch albeit they were probably thinking some nutter had been let out for a few hours. I suspected Lizzie had similar thoughts too – it remains the last football match she attended.

FILBERT STREET, Leicester City 3 Plymouth Argyle 1, Division Two, Saturday 2 February 1991

Two notable events took place for my visit to Filbert Street.

First, and it was on the cards, Lizzie, although joining the trip up (from our then new and still current residency in Hadleigh, Suffolk), decided that an afternoon of shopping was more fun than standing in the pouring rain watching football, so left me with my London Branch friends to seek out the delights of Leicester High Street.

Second was the opportunity to sample for the last time a pint which cost less than £1. Average beer prices at the time were already some 25 pence higher, but ever canny for a cheap drinking opportunity the London Branch had snuffled out a back-street boozer which had yet to catch up with the world economy. The place was a dump but this was of secondary importance, it was completely rammed with the Green Army taking advantage of the yester-year prices, and I suspect that not all made it to the match.

Like many grounds at the time, Filbert Street was counting down time until improvement plans could be finalised, though for me, used to less salubrious surroundings, it was already impressive. Stands on all four sides with the corners covered in, the quirky North Stand was my favourite with its executive boxes forming a roof for those seated below. It also brings back memories of Barry Davies bawling "Weller .... Oh yes, what a smashing goal. From the corner a real cracker from Keith Weller" in a 1975 commentary as the iconic Leicester winger volleyed one in from a corner at that end. Any football memory can lead to others, so as a quick aside what about the following commentator descriptions of other great goals from the '70's:

- "Right out of the book, and on the first line too": Barry Davies describing Ernie Hunt's free kick set-piece combo with Willie Carr for Coventry against Everton in 1970.
- "Beautiful, absolutely beautiful": Barry Davies eulogizing about George Best's chip over Pat Jennings in 1971.
- "Big John Hughes, moving forward, breathing the chance, and giving it the hammer": Barry Davies

again, simply salivating over John Hughes's pile-driver for Palace v Sheffield United in 1971.

- "1-0, and only players like Osgood take goals like that, a really superb volley, you don't blame goalkeepers, you congratulate the scorer": David Coleman on a wonder goal from Peter Osgood at Stamford Bridge when Arsenal were the visitors in 1973.

- "What a goal, they do not come better, it went in like a shank, to say that Laurie Sivell had never saw it is really not enough": David Coleman commentating at Portman Road in 1974 when a delirious Emlyn Hughes went mental after volleying one in.

- "Well taken by Walsh .... Davies is on the far side .... Ainscow's coming square, that's the ball, that's a good try .... oh what a goal, oh what a goal to decide it surely": Barry Davies on Blackpool's Mickey Walsh superb 1975 goal of the season (and for me, if you combine it with Bazza's wonderful tones, the greatest goal anywhere of all time by miles).

- "McDonald, good try, oh what a goal, what a brilliant goal, magnificent, and with the right foot too. It sends that lot into ecstasy, and leaves Siddall wondering where it came from": Barry Davies describing the second of two corkers from Supermac in an FA Cup thriller at Burnden Park in 1976.

- "And McDonald bites the hand that used to feed him": John Motson on Supermac, this time scoring for Arsenal against his old club later in 1976.

- "Here's Jones, oh yes, what about that, what about that, and look what it means, just listen to what it means": Barry Davies on a vital Chris Jones strike for Spurs at the end of the 1977 season.

Hmm, it must be the thought of cheap beer making me go all sentimental. Back to Filbert Street. Those of Green Army who were sober enough to gain entry were placed in a terraced pen, but we had little to cheer as Leicester rallied under their new caretaker boss to win easily. We should have stayed in the pub.

UNDERHILL, Barnet 5 Tiverton Town 1, FA Cup Round One, Thursday 14 November 1991

Ticket tout Flashman v an often over-enthusiastic Fry, a kind of Sumo/Weeble love-hate match. Lots of noise had been coming from the direction of the North London suburb of Barnet, so it was time to see what all the fuss was about.

Barnet had just been promoted to the Football League, and for a small club they appeared to generate a disproportionate amount of publicity. Mostly this was due to a chairman/manager duo who were gazing into each other's eyes one minute then slagging each other off the next (Fry claims Flashman sacked him on eight occasions, only to kiss and make up each time). Scroll forward to 1993 and Barry Fry had a volatile sojourn at Southend – one minute we were patting his bald head as he did a lap of honour after saving us from relegation, then less than a year later he was the subject of voodoo doll-like hatred as he returned to Roots Hall with his latest declared love of all things Brady and Birmingham. To this day I'm not sure what to think of the guy – it probably depends on what kind of reflective mood I'm in.

Barnet in their debut Division Four season were on fire (no, not an Underhill insurance scam), they were banging in goals for fun and, after losing their first match 4-7, had started to get some defensive qualities too. Rob, used to non-league life with Chelmsford, was my guide for this one and we made our way through the endless streets of shops that North London seems to specialise in (just how do they all stay in business?) to park within a couple of hundred yards of the ground, though with it still out of sight. Underhill existed in a dip and failed really to catch the eye until you were directly outside and faced with its lurid amber paint. Inside it was homely enough, two open terraced ends and two low-slung stands running along the sides, but hemmed in on three sides by London suburbia it was never going to become anything more than a half-decent non-league ground.

Barnet won the game at a canter, showing their Great Mills League opponents they were the big boys now. Despite the open terracing a reasonable noise was created, helped by both home and away fans being housed in the low-roofed terrace stand along one side.

Indeed, until its demise in 2013 I experienced some cracking atmospheres at Underhill, mostly with Shrimpers who always travelled the short distance there in numbers, falling every time for the publicity saying it was not far away which though true failed to take into account that it usually took at least an hour to travel the last three miles.

Indeed, the suburban traffic jams once caused me to miss out on getting in to Underhill (the only time that has happened to me anywhere). At the end of the 2000/01 season Barnet played Torquay – it was billed as the 'game of death', as whoever lost would be relegated to the Football League dumping zone of the Conference.

Intrigued, I interested a car load of work colleagues to join me to witness this macabre affair (as actuaries they flourished on predicting death), and we set off in good time only, after turning off the M25, to sit in traffic and get more and more fed up. Still, we had allowed plenty of time, and parked up about an hour before kick-off only to find chaos all around as seemingly thousands of others had the same black-curiosity as us. Queuing went out of the window, it was just a scrum, and had it just been me I might have stood a chance. But in trying to keep my merry band together we lacked penetrative thrust and, after several failed attempts, the 'ground full' signs went up.

We turned for home, leaving 5,523 to witness a five goal thriller in the sunshine complete with streakers, missed penalties and own goals – and Football League death for Barnet.

34/92 - VALE PARK, Port Vale 2 Exeter City 1, League Trophy Southern Area Final First Leg, Tuesday 16 March 1993

For me this was a landmark game. I'd been to matches courtesy of work before, but it had always been with others when, usually suited and booted at some corporate hospitality affair, I needed to either act as the perfect host or as the engaging guest. Both roles were tricky. This time I was going on my own to a meeting in Liverpool, and searching the fixture lists noticed that Port Vale were at home the night before – the Potteries being a hitherto unexplored territory. I persuaded the boss that travelling part-way up the night before and staying in a B&B made sound business sense. Self-indulgent luxury was secured.

There was good interest in this game – not only did it afford the opportunity of a trip to Wembley for the winner but, to enthuse the locals, in the previous round Vale had beaten neighbours Stoke at the Victoria Ground in front of 22,000. They were up for this one, which I could sense on the way in from my B&B, and not one to shy away from striking up conversation with strangers I walked in with a bunch of lads who still seemed to be on a high from that Stoke win. They suggested I viewed the game from the then recently seated Railway Paddock so that I could "enjoy the view of the fabulous Lorne Street Stand".

Lorne Street certainly was a wonder from a bygone era. Running the length of one side of the pitch, it primarily consisted of a narrow seated area at the back under a patchwork corrugated roof, fronted by a large terrace strewn with black crash barriers. But the real joy was the collection of boxes on its roof – I think there were at least five, all different in appearance and presumably serving some media-related or pigeon-loft purpose. To complete the hotchpotch picture, a separate disabled stand sat alongside in one corner. Sadly today Vale Park is much more uniform in appearance.

Vale won an exciting cup tie, went on to win the second leg, and then beat Stockport in the final. It was their first trophy since 1959 – I suspect the locals celebrated that one. I had enjoyed it all too and walked back to my B&B wondering how I could arrange more meetings around footie games – it was certainly a cost-effective way of progressing my 92 quest and, as a minor by-product, gave added motivation for attaining my work appraisal aim to 'look for opportunities by creative thinking'.

35/92 - THE NEW DEN, Millwall 3 Southend United 1, Division One, Saturday 13 August 1994

My first new ground since the birth of my first son Jim, but he was only 15 months old and an away day at Millwall somehow didn't seem appropriate for his football debut. So I took Rob instead – he was over 30 and just about old enough.

Rob had upgraded his Lada fearing an MOT test on a car with a rope attached to the brake pedal might be touch and go, though his latest carriage looked no more reliable so I drove. We should have taken the train. Arriving early we managed to park up close to the ground, but I was nervous – the immediate environment was not that savoury. We had parked under a dark railway bridge next to a derelict house/wasteland combo, old caravan and bent railings. Close by was a pub which screamed 'don't go in'. An elderly gent, cloth cap and wizened face, walked by and gave us a wry smile – he knew we were outsiders. I thought about turning round and parking somewhere that looked safer, but the drive in suggested I'd need to go a fair distance. So I pointlessly checked too many times that the car was locked and we walked the short distance to the ground.

The New Den (back in '94 it was still 'new') loomed large. It was like some unimaginative giant Lego construction – four identical looking stands decked out in blue with the odd yellow bit to break up the monotony. Lego clearly didn't provide rounded bits for the corners – it seemed to be a missed opportunity as the gaps gave the place a 'chilly' feel even in August – perhaps it was a deliberate homage to days gone by at Cold Blow Lane.

The new ground was meant to be a new start. But the programme notes provided a reminder that at the end of the previous season Millwall had hosted Derby in a play-off semi-final with their fans rioting when things on the pitch didn't go their way. Two pitch invasions during play, lengthy stoppages, Derby players assaulted, racist abuse forcing Derby to sub their black players – it wasn't good, and the game we were at was the first one since that evening. Not for the first time I thought of my car.

The atmosphere inside was a little tense - perhaps understandably the numbers of police in attendance were way out of proportion to the occasion, and it felt like every fan shout was rewarded with a direct stare from scowling coppers. Millwall fans sang their anthem 'No one likes us', something it was hard to disagree with. I thought of my car again.

The season before at Millwall's first competitive match in their new home, Southend had stuffed the Lions 4-1 - it had been screened live so back then I had chosen to save the pennies and watch it on the box. A season later a game featuring Millwall was no longer considered to be appropriate viewing before the 9pm watershed, and Southend were not exactly a big box office draw, so the only way to view was to be there.

This time Millwall got it right on the pitch and won easily – the Southend players, probably wishing they were still on holiday in Benidorm rather than being at Millwall, did little to enthuse. With the game a bit of a bore and the stadium not exactly interesting I resorted to counting policemen as some kind of distraction therapy to try and avoid thinking about my car.

153

The final whistle came as a relief and we rushed for the exit, only to come to a grinding halt, our way blocked by rows of coppers. "Away fans are asked to stay behind after the game for a short period" announced the tanoy man – it implied we might have a choice but there wasn't one. And it wasn't 'a short period' either – it was close on 30 minutes after the game had finished before we were let out. "Train on the left, coaches on the right" a copper blurted out from behind a megaphone. I asked one of his colleagues what those who had come by car were meant to do – he gave me a Captain Mainwaring 'you stupid boy' look and just waved us on.

When we got to the car it was in a right state – it was virtually obliterated in pigeon shit. Those little feathered rats clearly had a bit of a thing going on in the rafters of the bridge above and had seemingly pooped out every last bit of waste kebab for streets around on my previously blue Escort.

I now twigged why, when virtually every other non-restricted space around the ground had been used, this one had been free. Still, a side benefit was that no one had been tempted to fire-bomb or steal the car – any self-respecting hoodie probably didn't fancy going anywhere near it.

So, another ground done, but it had been a crap day.

36/92 - ELLAND ROAD, Leeds United 2 Leicester City 1, Premier League, Monday 24 October 1994

I was starting a six-venue tour for work giving talks to a client's employees about their pension scheme. A total of 27 different sessions saying exactly the same thing – I reckon I peaked at about session number eight. A few of the employees didn't exactly motivate me to reach pension perfection, some just seemed to attend as it gave them an hour away from the daily grind and afforded the opportunity to grab 40 winks, one even had the audacity to wear headphones throughout. I did get a few 'I've got this friend' questions from one guy which raised a smile amongst those still compos-mentis in the audience who knew that the inquisitor didn't have any friends.

However, for my first three days I was running another more rewarding tour in tandem – a footie fest at Leeds, Liverpool and Wolves. Two new grounds and a revisit to see my mates on the Kop. 'Always look for opportunities' the bosses preached at work - I thought I had excelled this time.

Staying overnight on the outskirts of Leeds, I stopped for a pre-match drink at a country pub. I immediately struck up a football conversation with a Leeds fan having a beer, we got on great and he suggested we meet up after the game and go to his club. Hmmm, initially I wasn't totally sure about that, but if you drew an e-fit of a likely axe-wielding mass-murdering pervert this chap didn't appear to be it, so I agreed.

To Elland Road for my debut match in the then still new, bright and shiny Premier League. It was the Sky Sports 'Monday Match', I was looking forward to the large blow-up wrestlers Sky had invented for the half-time entertainment in their inaugural season, but sadly I learned they had been dropped – they had decided that the UK really wasn't yet ready for such a spectacle. Instead we just had the occasional wave from old Hairy Hands Keys in the 'Sky Box' to look out for.

Elland Road looked massive - four huge stands with the corners filled in. Some bits were a little dated but you could just tell it would create a good atmosphere. The match tried its best to quieten things, Leeds just edging an uninspiring game, but the home support still rallied to chant their inventive 'Leeds, Leeds, Leeds' ditty.

I have since been to Elland Road a couple of times as an away fan – at the time hemmed in one corner, you were made to feel decidedly uneasy by the vocal locals on either side who show support wonderfully for their team. Maybe that's why not many neutrals like Leeds much, the volume their fans create can make you feel a resentful second best with your own efforts. But watch a 70's video of Leeds on the pitch lunging studs-up at opponents with Revie on the side lines being full of protective arrogance and it does give you cause to be a bit happier than usual if you beat them.

Anyway, afterwards I returned to my pre-match pub, met up with my new found mate and off we pop down to his club. It was 'Wheeltappers and Shunters' revisited, a real-life working men's social watering-hole where on a Monday night at nearly 11 pm after 'Bingo Fest' an Elvis impersonator was going full pelt on stage. He was in the middle of murdering 'Don't Be Cruel' when we arrived which seemed to be a tad ironic, and just like the Leeds fans his volume was impressive. It was difficult to talk above the high-octane crooning but it was certainly memorable, and I left at around midnight anticipating that 'It's Now or Never' might be his final encore (he had already done three).

37/92 - MOLINEUX, Wolverhampton Wanderers 2 Nottingham Forest 3, League Cup Round Four, Wednesday 26 October 1994

My third night of footie in a row, it certainly beat the lonely life of being stuck in a hotel room night after night trying to avoid opening the mini-bar knowing it would be a difficult conversation to cover the cost when submitting the expenses claim.

I was anticipating Molineux to be the highlight of my tour - it didn't disappoint. At the time it was one of the, if not the, most modern grounds in the country. It had risen out of the ashes of a complete mess a decade before when, with half of the ground closed and one stand a ludicrous distance from the pitch, its fall in to disrepair mirrored the clubs on-the-field experience. But in just under four years Sir Jack Hayward invested millions to turn it round, and a shiny gold masterpiece now gleamed before me.

Outside it was an explosion of brindle bricks and striking paving arrangements (the nerdy landscaper in me rising to the appreciative fore there), whilst inside it just shined. OK, back then the corners weren't filled in, but unlike Millwall that didn't seem to matter – the gold glow kept you warm. Every stand had a name – John Ireland (now Steve Bull), Jack Harris (now Jack Haywood), Billy Wright and Stan Cullis. I chose Mr Wright, the one-club-man Wolves legend, the first player to 100 England caps, 1952 Footballer of the Year, winner of three First Division championship medals and an FA Cup, Commander of the Order of the British Empire, and one of 42 people to have appeared on This Is Your Life twice (I looked that last one up). Billy had passed away just the month before and a good way of honouring him seemed to be by sitting on him.

I loved the pre-match build up in the ground. The PA announcer knew his stuff, the song choice was spot-on and the Wolves mascot danced up and down the aisles of a stand behind one of the goals as the home fans joined in with some rhythmic chanting. It even seemed to work that the away fans were allowed the bottom tier of a stand along the side as it helped to goad the home support at both ends in an 'all-round Dolby stereo' kind of way. A very respectable 28,000 turned up for what was only a Third Round League Cup tie – it all made for a cracking atmosphere.

Another reason for wanting to be at the game was to check on the progress of Stan the Man. During the last two-thirds of the 92/93 season Mr Collymore had transformed Southend's fortunes, playing a robust and fast-running style that scared defenders witless and in doing so saved the club from relegation. After just 30 games (15 goals), Frank Clark (a less than impressive slug-balancer) had seen sufficient to pay £2 million for him plus success based add-ons (which were achieved in full).

Sadly I was to be disappointed – early on Stan limped off injured to be replaced by another ex-Shrimper, Jason 'Pineapple Head' Lee. Old Piney had been Southend's replacement for Stan and, after a less than impressive 22 games, someone must have joked to Frank that there was a new Stan at Roots Hall. He fell for it and gave Baddiel & Skinner something new to titter about with a series of a sadly comical 'out of his depth' displays. Forest were already two up so Piney's appearance evened things up a bit and Wolves drew level. But in the last throes of a pulsating match, tub-thumping Chumbawamba and punk wanna-be Stuart Pearce clenched his fist one more time and banged in the winner.

Back to the hotel bar, time for a whisky drink, or a lager drink, etc. Just 13 presentations left to do.

38/92 - ADAMS PARK, Wycombe Wanderers 4 Chelmsford City 0, FA Cup Round One, Saturday 12 November 1994

Rob told me that Chelmsford City were going to win the FA Cup and I needed to go to Wycombe to see the quest start. It seemed a little implausible, but with a new ground on offer I could not resist.

You can get to Wycombe quite quickly – it is well serviced by the motorway network. But then you have to get off the M40 to get to the ground – whoever built the Adams Park had no thought for access. It sits down the bottom of a long lane in an industrial estate – there is just the one road in and the same road out. Park down that lane and you might as well kiss goodbye to an hour of your life after the match trying to get out, park further away and you have a long walk. Adams Park is not an old ground – it was only built in 1990 – someone cocked up big time.

Get there and it's nice enough, it probably has more trees in its immediate surroundings than any other league ground, and has stands on all four sides, with some seated expansion since my 1994 visit. But access limits the capacity to 10,000 – when the main stand had an upper tier added in 1996 the increased capacity that investment brought meant that the capacity of another stand had to be cut to stick to the limit. How daft is that?

John Motson remembers Adams Park for famously giving a pre-match build-up report there during a blizzard. Traffic chaos aside, I remember Adams Park for reminding me that 90 minutes can make a big difference – on the way in the City fans were in ebullient mood and FA Cup scarfs were a fiver, on the way out Rob was sulking and I bagged a bargain for a quid.

39/92 - SIXFIELDS STADIUM, Northampton Town 1 Plymouth Argyle 0, Division Three, Tuesday 30 January 1996

What's the dullest thing you've ever done? Well, unless you attended one of my pension presentations there's a chance that a visit to Sixfields might be your answer. If the match you saw there was rubbish like Argyle's visit in 1996 then that increases the likelihood.

I'm sure Sixfields has its merits. It's clean, uniform (let's ignore the recent farce regarding the re-development of one side of the ground), you won't get wet, and access is easy enough. But the place has no soul. It is simply a low-capacity uniform concrete blob with faded maroon seats. The corners are open leaving gaps for the wind to whistle in, and for those not willing to part with hard cash, a limited view of the match from surrounding higher perches is provided. OK, its predecessor the old County Ground, with its sharing of out-dated facilities with the local cricket club, was far from ideal, but it did have some anarchic charm. Maybe Sixfields needs to build up a selection of

'I was there' memories. The County Ground has that George Best double-hatrick from 1970 to get all nostalgic about.

Despite the win, I suspect that even any Cobblers fan will struggle to remember the game on 30 January 1996. The only thing I recall was seeing the kids in the 'free seats' outside either giving up long before the end or preferring to amuse themselves with games of 'roly poly' down the hill.

On the plus side it wasn't it seems the most boring day of the 20th century. That accolade goes to 11 April 1954 when, according to one study, unlike any of the other 36,000 plus days in the 1900's, absolutely nothing of note happened. Or, according to BBC Radio, 18 April 1930 did not exactly set pulses racing either, as the newsreader opened and closed his bulletin at 6.30 pm with the no-bullshit statement "There is no news." He would never have made it as a football pundit.

HIGHFIELD ROAD, Coventry City 1 Wimbledon 1, Premier League, Monday 3 March 1997

An early start at a meeting in Birmingham the following day meant that an overnight stop could be justified, so the trip up just had to go via Highfield Road where a footie game was taking place. Good old Sky TV, renowned for screwing up the fixture list, had chosen 16th placed Coventry versus 5th placed Wimbledon as the match to make their ratings soar on a Monday night.

Coventry City is one of those clubs that most fans 'don't mind'. OK, there might be a bit of Midland rivalry from the likes of Birmingham and Villa, but the Sky Blues don't usually stir up any 'anti' feelings from further afield in the same way as say, Leeds, Manchester United or Millwall. Indeed, most neutral observers might think 'good on yer' for the 30 plus years they clung on to top flight soccer until relegation in 2001, that Houchen diving header that helped win the FA Cup in 1987, the inspirational lead that Jimmy Hill gave them as both manager and chairman, or even their often jazzy attempts at livening up football kit design. Yep, I decided I liked Coventry. But then I arrived at Highfield Road.

Concluding that a live match with Wimbledon as the opposition wouldn't exactly lead to excessive demand, Coventry had reduced the standard ticket price from £18 to £5. 'Result' I thought to myself, this wouldn't look quite so bad on the expenses claim form. I then saw a bit of a kerfuffle at the away turnstiles – Wimbledon fans were still being charged full price. There was nothing they could do, it was all perfectly legal (Oldham did it to Southend as recently as November 2015), they just had to cough up.

It gave me the feeling that the Wombles were just being picked on as, not being blessed with massive support, it was unlikely they would be too vocal about it– could you imagine the reaction if, say, it was done to Leeds? They would (quite rightly for once) tear the

163

place apart. It wasn't the fault of the Coventry fans, it was their club's doing, and looking at the programme I noticed that Jimmy Hill was not at the time on the list of Directors (he would surely never have permitted such a rip-off). In a rash moment of weird fan-solidarity I paid my £18 and sat with the small group of disconsolate Wombles.

Inside there was little further dissent, Wombles just quietly mumbled to each other, and anyway there was not really sufficient numbers in the away section to chant anything vocal enough to reach the Directors box. We just 'stewed' – one fan tried a solo "You can stick your fucking £18 up your arse" shortly after Wimbledon took a short-lived lead in the first half, but it didn't span too well and died after only getting a few chuckles from those within immediate earshot.

Now, the PR own-goal of ticket pricing aside, I have to say that Highfield Road looked good. Four different stands, all seated, relatively cosy despite two corners being open, compact yet still with capacity for well over 20,000, and all decked out in a 1960's disabled three-wheeler car blue.

Highfield Road was a ground that the home support could rightly feel proud of, and would be a ground which a great many clubs today would still love to have. Yet sadly it is no more, consigned to the bin of not being up to the job of modern needs of corporate comfort and kids' parties (a bit like those disabled cars which were banned from use on UK roads in 2003 due to an inconvenient tendency to fall over or catch fire).

I wonder whether the Coventry Board's thoughts turned to their old pad when they were squatting at Sixfields not too long ago.

40/92 - OLD TRAFFORD, Manchester United 5 Wimbledon 1, Premier League, Saturday 17 October 1998

Neville, Neville, Paul-Scholes, Keane, Beckham, Giggs. It was about time I paid a visit to The Theatre of Dreams to see the Trumpton fire crew.

If you are having a ground-hopping debate and someone is asking whether you have been to certain grounds, the more humble homes of Accrington Stanley (because it's in a different time zone) and Carlisle United (a geography thing) aside, you are perhaps most likely to be asked whether you have been yet to Old Trafford. It has always been the place to go to, it just has the lot – scale, history, structure, crowds, players ......

I'm not a Man U knocker – it is too easy to get on that boat and take a swipe at success when it maybe isn't all 100% perfect. What club is perfect? Man U get it right more times than not, and anyway they have Bobby Charlton, who deserves respect from everyone and that's enough for me. What is wrong with Man U is, in my humble opinion, what is wrong with the Premier

League as a whole – blind greed. Man U is no different to any club that is involved with that unsavoury gravy train or aspires to be. The only time I have really lost respect for Man U is when they ditched the FA Cup for a year – that was deplorable – but far worse things have happened elsewhere in football than that.

Anyway, at the risk of opening up a can of worms and waffling along a tangent far beyond the intention of this book, I'll get back to the subject in hand, a trip to Old Trafford. Back in 1998 it was not an easy place to get in to – Fergie had been collecting silverware for a good six years by then, and with capacity at the time 'only' 55,000, space was at a premium. To gain entry options were limited – join a season ticket waiting list and wait for 20,000 to die, persuade a friend with tickets that it would be good for the soul to let you go instead, take out a mortgage for a hospitality option, or travel away with a Wimbledon season ticket holder. I chose the latter, offering a Womble work client contact the chance for an all-expenses paid trip. Impressed with my show of solidarity at Coventry, he agreed and did his part by easily getting the match tickets.

I was in London with family that day close to where he lived so we met up without much effort and plundered up the M1/M6. Parking I was told required some careful thought, as whilst getting there could be pain free, getting out would often involve still being in traffic-hell around the ground whilst the 606 phone-in was in full swing.

Like many grounds these days – The Emirates and The Amex spring to mind – it leads to hordes missing the end as they sprint out to get a head start. How daft is that? You pay a princely sum to get your footie fix these days but many choose to throw away the ending. At the League Two 2015 Play Off final the cameras caught loads of Shrimpers running for the tube just as Piggot sent us into ecstasy. Complete numpties. I have a solution – just plan for the game to be three hours long. You then won't miss a thing and may then even get home 'early'. Anyway, on a tip-off from a work colleague who said he knew Old Trafford like the back of his hand, we went to a specific parking area on an industrial site with "great access", and then after the match spent over an hour waiting for someone blocking us in to come back from their corporate hospitality after-game piss-up.

At Highfield Road some 18 months before I had been with around 150 loyal Wombles. For Old Trafford the 2,000 allocation was sold out. As the goals flew in the Wimbledon net there seemed to be more than a few who looked quite pleased with what they were seeing, I suspected that they were not all genuine Orinoco's.

The Trumpton Crew all played and were completely dominant – Beckham scored a 35-yarder and Old Trafford (its 'library switch' turned to off) roared throughout at the near-misses, sublime passing and telling crosses. Fergie chewed his gum a little more

167

happily than he had at the mighty Roots Hall two years before.

41/92 - GRESTY ROAD, Crewe Alexandra 0 Blackburn Rovers 1, League Cup Round Three, Wednesday 28 October 1998

Crewe was only a short diversion on the way up to a business meeting in Liverpool, so it had to be done.

Arriving at Gresty Road back then was a completely different experience to what it is today – I got there early before the floodlights had been switched on and, unsure of my whereabouts, asked someone where the ground was. "It's o'er road, can't yer see" came the dismissive reply from a slightly rude local. Well, Gresty Road back in 1998 was not exactly imposing, but the season after my visit it had all changed as a massive stand (7,000 capacity – that's big by League One/Two standards) had been built to tower over everything else in the area. I suspect, and maybe with some justification, my unfriendly foe might be adding "..... yer blind twat" to his navigational instructions these days.

Pie and mushy peas repeating nicely as I went back to the ground for the match, with floodlights now showing me the way, I decided to be a Blackburn fan for the night. The reason was simple – I had seen five Southend home games so far that season and they had not won any (they had won most that I had missed) and when I had been with the Wombles they had lost.

So I needed to taste success and Blackburn as the Premiership big-bananas were the clear favourites.

It proved to be the right choice on two fronts and the wrong one on another. First, Blackburn won. Second, the atmosphere created by the small travelling group of Roverites in a low roofed stand was pretty good. However, being in the presence of the most foul-mouthed waster I've ever had the dis-pleasure to experience was not so great.

Now, we all know that the language at footie matches is not exactly all 'Joanna Lumley' and I've no issue with that – it is good to let off steam and a match can provide a useful release valve. It can also lead to some funny moments – once my youngest son Cameron, when he was of an age to be more amenable to going to games (if I pitched the bribery at the right level), asked me "Dad, why are they saying 'the referee's a waffle'?" The 'wanker' word must have not yet reached his corner of the nursery school playground. After recovering myself I just answered "'Because he is son" which gave Cameron the green light to join in to that popular Roots Hall Family Stand ditty at every opportunity he could.

But back to Sweary Spice. He was a small bespectacled middle aged man who looked as inoffensive as it was possible to be, but when he opened his mouth he turned from Jekyll to Hyde in an instant. The good acoustics just made it worse – he continually slated Chris Sutton (who scored the only goal of the game), was not too keen on anyone Scottish, and informed the poor old linesman at regular intervals that he had had intimate relations with his missus. Those were just the main themes that I can recall – the abuse was constant. He must have been a regular as everyone else around me just ignored him including the imported Blackburn stewards, but in a small stand I found it impossible to get out of earshot. What pleasure folk like that get from life with their continual vitriolic diarrhoea beats me. Maybe it's the only way they know how to spice up their life.

42/92 - BOUNDARY PARK, Oldham Athletic 4 Chelmsford City 0, FA Cup Round One, Saturday 30 October 1999

There are two comic lines I sometimes recall that somewhat obscurely make me think of Oldham.

The first is from a classic Jasper Carrot sketch on local radio when he talks about how they try and find someone to report from matches when Birmingham play away – "Oi you, wanna go to Oldham?" is the request from a radio man to a random man on the street. It's a line that probably wouldn't work if any other team was mentioned (bar maybe Macclesfield). Well, it tickles me anyway.

The other is a BBC football commentary at Boundary Park where the commentator (I believe it was Jonathan Pearce but I may be wrong – I can't find the clip now), whilst in full flow, hears a number plate being read out on the tanoy saying that a car will shortly be towed away if not moved. "That's my car!" Pearce shouts as his co-commentator pisses himself 'Agnew/Johnston style' in the background.

So I was hopeful of a few amusing moments when Chelmsford City drew Oldham away in the first round of the FA Cup. I didn't have long to wait. In preparation I decided that the event was worthy of a banner so Lizzie sewed two white sheets together and I laid them out on the garage floor. I then carefully spray-painted 'Chelmsford City FA Cup Tour 1999/2000' on it. Impressed with my handiwork, I kicked out the cat (which was looking intent on sabotage) and left the bold yet motivational message to dry overnight. The following morning all looked good as I lifted up the banner .... to reveal 'Chelmsford City FA Cup Tour 1999/2000' scribed in maroon on the concrete floor. We had around 20 viewers before we sold the house two years later – every time we had to explain why the message was there, and not one was a Chelmsford fan.

Anyway, off to Oldham – now a three-time Dad, the vehicle of 'choice' was a green Citroen Synergie (a square box with the aerodynamic qualities of a tank but with an insatiable ability to hold heaps of cargo). This meant that seven of us could make the five hour trip, via a Peak District pub respite, enjoying my 1980's soundtrack tapes in six-speaker splendour. On arrival Oldham was everything I had imagined it would be – desolate.

Look now at the shiny new North Stand with its three complimentary, but distinctly different blue all-seated cousins, and Boundary Park looks quite smart - somewhat rarely compared to the updated stadia of today it maintains a high degree of uniqueness. Back at the butt-end of the last century it was, well .... not quite as good. The driving rain lashing against us as we climbed out of the green box at England's third highest ground, we ran for shelter behind the away end. After a couple of minutes of recovery we joined the small squadron of Clarets in the deep-roofed terrace, stood at the back, and got wet again. The clouds were seemingly dive-bombing the place with bouncing buckets. I made a brave sortie to the front, lashed the banner to something stationary (I checked it wasn't a steward) and fled to the back again. An injury hit Chelmsford team must have been inspired as they only lost by four.

The trip home was much like the one on the way up – full of easy banter and my wonderful music mix. Travelling with friends to a game is all part of the event, as is the pre and post-match pub. Going to the footie is about more than football, it's a social with a goal, a meeting of common interests, a way to relax before getting hyped and then cooled down again, a time to put aside what else is going on in life, an excuse to pick up again with folks you last saw years ago, a time to hope, and a means by which you can discuss often elaborate plans to do it all again.

To date a re-run of the Oldham trip with my Claret cronies has yet to be repeated, but it is often quoted at regular get-togethers we have in the non-football world and spoken of with affection. We had spent ten hours in a car, saw our team pushed aside with ease and got soaked, but it was a great day out. A key desire is to revisit the return-journey watering hole stop somewhere near Leicester to see if the banner remains high in the car park tree where we left it. I am confident that it still flies proudly as a random curiosity and important tourist attraction.

NENE PARK, Rushden & Diamonds 0 Southend United 1, Division Two, Saturday September 22 2001

At a cost of over £50,000,000 (in today's terms), Nene Park was meant to bring in the dawn of a new era for the mighty Rushden & Diamonds of Northamptonshire. It's now abandoned and slowly decaying, a sad monument to over-inflated ambition built on 'air wair'.

Nene Park is not on its own. Darlington's 25,000 capacity Reynolds Arena (the original 'look at me' name given by its creator) now just plays host to a local rugby club in front of a few hundred Geordies every two weeks.

Most other disused old grounds have since been bulldozed to make way for the national obsession of supermarket shopping, but one real gem that remains is Cathkin Park. The former home of Third Lanark, it still exists today despite last seeing a game in 1967. After a fire or two and the odd bit of Glaswegian vandalism, the local Parks Department has since modified it into parkland but with significant chunks of the terracing remaining. Trees sprout up in groups on the old concrete steps beside cleared areas where the crash barriers stay intact. A pitch now also sits in the middle, and dreams exist for what would surely be the most romantic return to a spiritual home in history – imagine Paul Gascoigne rolling back the years and returning to Newcastle and you'll be near the gist of it. If you happen to visit now and stand on the terraces between the greenery, just close your eyes tight enough and you may well be transported back to crowds of 50,000 cloth-capped kilt-wearers watching early Scottish Cup Finals.

Scrolling forward to the more recent past from the start of this century, Nene Park in 2001 was bright, shiny and full of hope. Its development from the distinctly more modest abode that Irthlingborough Diamonds had bequeathed had only been completed in 1993 – twiddley bits had been added since, culminating with the ultimate stadium 'must have' in time for our arrival – a Nandos.

It all looked very pretty - adjoining training pitches, an orderly looking car park, a large club 'Doc' shop, exhibition centre and smart offices all added up to a tasty toy every self-respecting businessman should have. Mr Griggs was playing out a fantasy – but the foot-fall, which never averaged more than 4,500 and by the time of Rushden's demise was less than 1,500, was never going to match his ambitions or basic economics.

The visit to Nene Park was a landmark for my son Jim – at the age of eight he was attending his first Southend away match. Unlike my first such trip back in 1974, he witnessed our team keeping all of their men on the pitch and actually winning in front of some 1,500 Shrimpers who had come to take their first look at the future of modern stadia 'Northamptonshire-style'. We concluded it was better than neighbouring Sixfields, and went home to realistically recreate what we had seen with Subbuteo pitches and Lego. I was actually inspired – the following year, and with a newly acquired bit of rough ground adjoining our garden, we created our own mini pitch with a wooden stand behind one goal. Unlike the neat Nene Park, but in-keeping with Roots Hall, the stand sagged and leaked, but with a capacity of 48 it was good enough for us. Unlike Mr Griggs I did not over-stretch my budget, and with it doubling up as a compost container it was multi-purpose too.

Today all is not lost for dear old Rusty Dustbins. They had a go and must be given credit for that, but maybe now are back at a more natural level. The phoenix that has risen from the ashes of administration, AFC Rushden & Diamonds, now play in the Southern League Division One Central, ground-sharing with

Wellinborough Town at the Dog & Duck Stadium. It doesn't have a Nando's.

43/92 - KASSAM STADIUM, Oxford United 2 Southend United 0, Division Two, Saturday 22 September 2001

Ten years after Mr Maxwell was found temporarily causing sea levels to rise in the Atlantic, Oxford finally had the new home their former chairman had craved. Not though as some warped arranged marriage with an unwilling neighbour, but still as Oxford United FC.

The journey had not been easy. Financial and legal problems led to the build taking around five years to complete, and even then someone had forgotten to put up a stand behind one of the goals. But at least it was home, and though not as 'characterful' as the old Manor Ground, it can do what modern stadia are meant to, namely provide comfort for the corporate hospitality market. And if you are really lucky you might spot Timmy Mallett.

I did not spot any famous Southend fans there – we do boast Alison Moyet amongst our number and I have sat next to her at an away game before now (she kept pestering me for an autograph, it was so annoying) but it seemed she had decided to give our first visit to The Kassam in its inaugural season a miss. We did though have a few of our less savoury elements present and it seems they were intent on chalking up a new ground to get arrested in. After getting tired of pointing at the empty end and astutely chanting "There's no one there" for about twenty minutes, and with the home fans safely separated by about 50 yards of tarpaulin, a few got bored and started to wind each other up. This then broke into a skirmish and then into a full scale brawl. "Don't worry, football is safe these days" I had promised Lizzie as I put her eldest son in the car before driving to the game. We moved seats to get out of the way as the stewards waded in, but things simmered for the rest of the game which to some extent was an interesting diversion to what was a dull defeat on the pitch.

I have been back once since and it was oh so different. A meeting conveniently arranged in Oxford for the day after, I went to see Southend draw 3-3 AET in the Johnstone's Paint Trophy where, just seconds before the final whistle, manager Paul Sturrock pulled a psychological masterstroke I had not seen before or since. First choice keeper Paul Smith, distinctly miffed, was subbed, with rookie goalie Dan Bentley coming on to face the penalties. The Oxford players looked stunned, it seemed to affect their thinking and must have played heavy on their minds as they missed their kicks and Southend joyfully went through to the Southern Final.

The small group of united Shrimpers, this time refraining from beating each other up, celebrated as one. Hail Luggy - he got us to Wembley, with the reward for his tactical genius by the Chairman being

177

the sack before the final, but somewhat wonderfully Luggy turned up with the fans at the main pre-match Wembley pub where he was treated as a true gent should be (he was bought about 10,000 pints).

CAMP NOU, Barcelona 2 Real Sociedad 0, La Liga, Wednesday 6 February 2002

I'd first seen adverts for trips to European glamour clubs in copies of Shoot in the 70's but it always seemed to be a dream, which if not exactly out of reach, could not really be justified. However, patience paid off and, armed with an excuse and a cash windfall, a trip was sorted.

It was the year Dad would be 70 and me 40, and that seemed to be worth celebrating. Rather than opt for a package I booked everything separately and off we flew. Mum's parting words, in that concerned female tone which dared you not to disobey, were "Make sure you look after your Dad."

Barcelona proved to be a wonderful city – with a flaw. Yes it was packed with beautiful ancient monuments, inviting restaurants, charismatic walkways and sporting temples (we visited the Olympic Stadium as well as having a pre-match tour of Camp Nou), but we found to our cost it had an endemic darker side.

Whilst inside Barcelona Cathedral and looking up past towering pillars to its ornately carved ceiling, we suddenly heard right behind us the unlikely spiritual shout of "Shiiite, shiiite." We looked round to find two middle-aged locals pointing at the back of our jackets which it seemed were covered in some lovely brown stuff. In broken English one of them said that we must have rubbed against a wall covered in bird crap, and before we knew it they were helpfully leading us to a small enclave where there was a tap that would help with the wiping off of the mess. I refused an offer of assistance but in the confusion they were helping Dad, and then were quickly on their way with our profuse thanks for their kind help. A couple of hours later Dad tried to locate his wallet without success – a few calls limited the financial damage but all I could think of was what Mum's reaction would be on learning that I had unwittingly watched her husband get mugged and done nothing about it.

It did taint the trip somewhat but Camp Nou was equally unforgettable – the place is just immense and though not dissimilar in capacity to the new Wembley it somehow looks twice as big. Perhaps it was the lack of a roof around most of it that gave that impression; it certainly had the 'wow factor'. As the stadium was only half full the atmosphere was a little muted but we enjoyed watching Puyol, Cocu, Rivaldo et al put John Toshack's men to the sword in a game of football chess. I suspected that the big Welshman was a little bit out of his traditional comfort zone of 'hoof and shoot' coaching, though he has notched up a lengthy career as a Euro managerial nomad so must have sussed out something right.

179

Dad and I concluded from our brief experience that we preferred the 'English way' but I certainly rated Camp Nou above Sixfields (sorry Cobblers, I won't be rude to you again).

As a postscript though I would love to experience first-hand the wonderful mass orchestrated rhythmic chanting that occurs in Europe which the likes of Borussia Dortmund and others now have. Google 'Legia madness' to see just one captivating example – I wanna be the bald guy in that clip.

44/92 - VICTORIA ROAD, Dagenham & Redbridge 2 Plymouth Argyle 0, FA Cup Round Three Replay, Tuesday 14 January 2003

An open terrace in Dagenham on a wet night in January watching your team sleepwalk to defeat. What could be better?

Buried in London sprawl not far from Billy Bragg's A13, Dagenham is a bit of a mess. Day or night there are dark shadows – you just get the feeling that something is going on in every corner which would interest the police. It also gives the impression that everything purchased could be second-hand; it is a place where Private Walker would stock up before travelling to Warmington-on-Sea to sell Sergeant Wilson some nylons and Jonesy some risky sausage meat.

Dagenham does offer a range of local eateries. Not being one that favours football ground catering when you know the financial pressure is on to use up the remains from the last home match two weeks before, I have tried more than one of these non-Michelin star houses on my various visits over the years. The problem has been that the away support has always swamped the resource, which would do better if catering for a queue of one for a half-frozen pie and mushy chips. Take some sandwiches would be my tip.

So, you've battled through the traffic, avoided disturbing the locals and survived the catering – next stop Victoria Road. It's a basic non-league ground at the bottom of a cul-de-sac which, since my first visit, has gone against the grain by building its only decent facility for the enjoyment of the away fans. Back in 2003 the Argyle fans filled the crumbling terrace that preceded the shiny new stand which now sits there, in expectation that they would soon be making plans for a trip to Carrow Road in Round Four. But the Daggers dominated to complete the evening's woeful experiences, culminating in one of the most puerile chants you could ever wish to hear coming from the home support: "Digger Dagger Digger Dagger oi oi oi." It's not exactly one to make the hairs on the back of your neck stand up.

Sadly the Green Army responded with that line that fans always seem to like as a means of being scornful: "You only sing when you're winning." I count that as one of my pet hates, only beaten by folk claiming that they have given "110%" (when doing your utmost must surely be capped at 100%), and the number one all-time grater (akin to running finger nails down a blackboard) of someone using their hands to gesture speech marks when seeking to emphasise something. Come the glorious day these things will be banned, and Dagenham, and the rest of the world, will then be a better place for it.

Tilly Time

MILLENNIUM STADIUM, Blackpool 2 Southend United 0, League Trophy Final, Sunday 21 March 2004

Things were on the up on the Essex Riviera. That Col U infiltrator Steve Wignall had finally been sussed out and, after serving a backroom apprenticeship, Steve Tilson was appointed as caretaker manager in November 2003. Together with Paul Brush, it was the start of a seven year reign of glorious ups and, ultimately proving Mr Isaac Newton was right again, one big deflating down.

With relegation to the Conference a real possibility, Tilly and Brush masterminded an escape plan which had some gloss – a trip to a first ever national league final after 98 years of existence. OK, it was only the 'tin pot cup', but it was our big day out, and beating that other mob from Essex in the semi-final to get there made it so much sweeter. With Wembley out of action it was destination Cardiff, 20,000 Shrimpers paid money to get in to Wales, and with great pride I took Jim with me to be part of it.

We shook hands with Tangerines, joined in the city centre football sing-song, and made our way to the hugely impressive Millennium Stadium. Earlier that week Southend had played at Sincil Bank – the contrast was stark. With the sunroof open light filled the bowl, we waved our blue they waved their deep orange, noise filled the place albeit less than half full, and it was a truly moving experience despite the defeat. Jim clasped my hand as we made our way out and shed the odd tear, but there was an underlying feeling that the club was on the up and we looked forward to that.

With new found Shrimper friends (see Notts County next) we did it all again the year after, in a limo, the Essex vehicle of choice. The queue for the toll booths at the Severn Crossing was a sea of elongated white metal. This time the sun was in and the roof was shut, but the result the same. Despite the luxury travel it didn't quite match up to that first trip, and when Southend made it to the Millennium Stadium for the League Two Play-Off Final two months later I couldn't bear the prospect of defeat again so we went to the pub to watch and finally then had something to celebrate. But it was gut-wrenching not to be part of 'being there' and so I vowed not to miss out again, a decision which has since given me both disappointment and elation in the way only following your team through thick and thin can.

45/92 - MEADOW LANE, Notts County 1 Southend United 2, League Two, Saturday 18 September 2004

Surfing the net is now an established part of the footie experience – club sites, fanzones, news feeds, Facebook, Twitter, YouTube …… it's all there, part fact, part fiction, part rant. You can see it, watch it, say it and buy it.

Scan through Twitter and you might find 426 folk with nothing else to do other than participate in a debate on corner flags .... or a bit more usefully you could just find out that the place you were going to meet up next Saturday is closed and so you sort out a problem before its happened. Join Facebook and you can somewhat weirdly follow a group on football mascots .... or you can use it to track down friends from long ago and then meet up again at the footie as though the decades in between were just an interlude to accumulate grey hairs. Look on eBay and you will find someone who has been digging up his own lawn and passing it off as the hallowed turf that Robbie Fowler once sniffed ..... or you might just find that genuine one missing gem from your programme collection that you pick up at an absolute bargain (as the seller never really thought that anyone else in the world would ever be interested in acquiring the scribe on Workington Town versus Barrow from 1969).

From a personal perspective the use of a Southend United chat forum (Shrimperzone) has opened up a whole new community of folk who, yes, rant and moan a bit (there is a health warning to avoid it after a defeat if you have any suicidal tendencies), but who do really care about the club and will help their fellow fans. For the exile its use is almost essential – through kind fellow Shrimpers I previously didn't know I've

185

obtained tickets I otherwise could not get, found out about fan meeting places I would otherwise have missed, used it to sell items I could no longer use, received information that's helped make travel easier and cheaper, joined up with club events I'd otherwise never have heard about ...... the list is a long one. Above all though it's been a forum to chat with and meet others and, spotting there was another fan marooned like me in Suffolk, we made contact and agreed to meet up at Meadow Lane.

I took Jim with me (for protection) and did a quick tour of Nottingham's sporting trilogy before going to the game - Trent Bridge where we entered for free and briefly sampled Nottinghamshire versus the mighty Essex entertaining around 32 lost souls, and The City Ground where I attempted to explain to Jim just what a character Mr Clough was. It was then just a 275 yard walk round to our target for the day of Meadow Lane.

The home of the Magpies had been completely rebuilt during the preceding decade into a neat modern stadium, perhaps bringing in to question why clubs feel the need that only a new site will do to adequately build hospitality boxes and function rooms for focusing on everything bar football. Meadow Lane provides all a club could now want for widening the net to catch your pound, even something called the 'Celebration of Life', though when you delve further it is somewhat disappointingly a finger buffet for £7.95 + VAT.

Once inside you are faced with blocks of black seats on all four sides, each with large lettering displays or magpie emblems to leave you in no doubt where you are. It's smart yet a bit docile, like some kind of giant Hummer, only spoilt when fans start to gather with their multi coloured shirts and flags to rev the place up. Sitting amongst them was fellow Shrimperzoner Andy and we instantly struck up a supporter's rapport which would lead to many future trips to grounds far away. When you're driving to places like Morecambe it's good to have someone to distract from the endless motorway tarmac, and when you go 200 miles before you even think of turning on the radio it's a sign of a good conversational journey.

A double strike from our centre half and genuine love-the-badge thumper Adam Barrett put the seal on a very decent day.

46/92 - GLANFORD PARK, Scunthorpe United 3 Southend United 2, League Two, Tuesday 19 October 2004

My employer was on a bit of an expenses clampdown so no hotel this time; instead it was up at 4.30 am and on the road an hour later for the 225 miles to Wrexham. I get there at 9.30 am and the meeting is over by 2.00 pm. Great – now the day can begin.

Scunthorpe was only an approximate 100 mile diversion, almost on the way home in fact, so I set off for Glanford Park. I looked like being far too early, so go via the Snake Pass for a bit of interest, get lost, then stuck in a traffic jam on the M18 and arrive at my new ground destination around 7.15 pm feeling a little less relaxed than I'd hoped.

Just time for a quick read of the programme before kick-off, and inside Scunny Bunny was offering himself up to anyone having a party – it all looked a tad worrying. I do note that there was a subsequent campaign to get rid, with 'Iron Lion' being the proposed new fluffy suit to go clubbing with, but the over-sized cottontail won out albeit a tad more worrying was its subsequent picture with a lady rabbit. Southend's own mascot Sammy the Shrimp is just too scary to be allowed out of Essex, let alone multiply.

Glanford Park only opened in 1988, back then the newest build since Roots Hall in 1955, but it is so drab The Iron now want out. Low level stands mean a low capacity and minimal facilities – it is un-ambitious in the extreme and almost makes Sixfields look exciting. But it is saved from being totally dire by the low roofing and closed in corners creating a reasonable atmosphere, and 150 Shrimpers made themselves heard as we saw the new messiah Freddy Eastwood put us one up. It then all went a bit 'Pete Tong' and we lost by the odd goal in five, just the tonic needed for the trip home. I get back at 1.00 am – it had been a long day.

47/92 - THE MEMORIAL STADIUM, Bristol Rovers 1 Southend United 2, League Trophy Southern Area Final First Leg, Tuesday 15 February 2005

With a return to the Millennium Stadium the prize and a new ground the bonus ball, I had to go, but needed to make it cost-effective. The closest I could get was arranging a meeting in London for the day afterwards with a very early start, so requiring an overnight stop. It was good enough, game on.

Poor old Rovers, 12 years at Twerton, now at last back in Bristol though only at what is proving to be another long-term temporary fix. The Memorial Ground is for the oval ball game - Bristol Rugby Club had been there since 1921, it was their own cherished home sweet home, they had a new stand built in 1988 to celebrate their centenary, but in 1996 kindly invited the Pirates to share and so allow a Rovers return to the City. Improvements were made to increase capacity, though even some of these are temporary and look more like something you'd put up for a few days for a country fair.

The football club ended up getting a bit of a bargain. After agreeing a joint ownership deal with their new found rugger buddies they then secured the place outright thanks to a clause where whoever got in to financial difficulties gave up their share to the other for a nominal sum (so that they wouldn't then drag the other down the economic pit of despair with them). This ironically led to the rugby club becoming tenants

189

in their old home before finally having enough and getting in to bed with Rovers' friends at Ashton Gate where the locals biggest nightmare would be having Rovers to stay (I suspect the feeling is mutual). Neighbours eh? It's more like a soap opera.

The Memorial Ground is, well, different. Away fans who don't want to sit under the temporary canvass at one end can stand on the terrace to one side of the East Stand, itself a rather dilapidated looking affair which barely straddles the halfway line. The view opposite is of an odd looking structure which would be more at home at Lords, whilst the only bit that actually seems it should be there is the terraced stand at one end propped up by stanchion overload which the home fans seem to find comfortingly familiar and hence find it the more appealing place to congregate in. The whole place is so odd it's brilliant.

Anyway, a great night with Southend winning a ding-dong game unfortunately had as its stand-out memory a vile and drunken verbal attack by a couple of spectators on one Rovers player who at the time was having a bit of a brush with the law (he was subsequently acquitted). They launched into him every time he got close or touched the ball, and how he didn't jump over the wall and lump them one Cantona-style I'll never know. To his credit he just ignored them, played the whole match when at the time it must have been tempting to ask to be subbed, and walked off calmly at the end. Actions can speak louder than words.

BLUNDELL PARK, Grimsby Town 1 Southend United 1, League Two, Saturday 7 May 2005

Founded by Grim the Danish Viking and home of the inflatable cod, a day out at Grimsby can be a bit of a hard sell. But on the final day of the regular 2004/05 season, and with a promotion party in the offing, I managed to persuade my mate Paul (who generally succumbs to the Southend calling about twice a year) that he should join Jim and me for a day to remember.

If Southend won and did so by at least the same margin that Swansea could muster at Bury then we were up and could return to League One after seven woeful seasons in the basement. Grimsby had absolutely nothing to play for, had no one of any real note in their team, had only won once in their previous nine games, and were ready to go on holiday. There was surely only one outcome.

It's a long slog up to Blundell Park from Ipswich – you can opt for the direct route and travel through the monotonous flatlands of the Fens getting progressively more bored as each 37 mph mile is only relieved by avoiding the suicidal over-takers, or ignore the crow and go the easier motorway route with its wonderful array of healthy eating stops. We choose the latter but, seafront fish 'n chips waiting at the journey's end, we slogged up in expectant mood without stopping.

I remembered that Grimsby wasn't in Grimsby, so we parked up on the Cleethorpes esplanade. It was raining sideways and the whole place looked a bit, well, grim, but a plate full of splendidly proportioned cod at a window seat overlooking the beach was alright by us. I told Paul - thirsty for a pint - that it was beer-battered, which seemed to keep him happy for a bit. Mealtime entertainment was laid on too - a fight outside between local youths and a couple of Shrimpers (the latter appeared to lose, not a good omen).

With friendly looking pubs a bit thin on the ground we opted for early entry to Blundell Park. Inside the atmosphere was beginning to build – an all-ticketed 2,000 Shrimper contingent was starting to gather, a good number of them in traditional end-of-season fancy dress. A collection of Thunderbirds, a masculine looking Kylie Minogue, Pinocchio and Sylvester Stallone were in front of us in the queue for the bar, but we were served soon enough and took our seats to sup and enjoy the spectacle. Behind us Bob the Builder was venting his angst, some 1,000 of the 2,000 seats in the away end have a restricted view and he was enquiring if the proper planning consent had been obtained (or words to that effect). Slumped next to Paul was Oliver Reed, playing to character by sleeping off the effects of too much alcohol. I was beginning to feel a little out of the party – my traditional Russian Doll costume (four layers of Southend clothing) seemed inadequate. I did harbour a secret desire to dress up as Sponge Bob

Square Pants, but was not sure that the yellow bathing scrub was an appropriate role model for Jim.

Anyway, we sat there playing 'guess the celeb' and taking in the Blundell Park vista. As a footie ground it has its own unique charm – a grandstand paid for by fish finger profits which towers above everything else but, like a school kid still wearing last year's trousers, comes up a bit short length-wise. Opposite, held up by a good collection of rusty stanchions, is reputedly one of the oldest football stands left in the country, and at the home end under another supported roof is a modest collection of covered seats arranged in zebra camouflage. Blundell Park's connection with Roots Hall is that both belong to a small band of grounds left in the Football League (ok, let's assume Grimsby is still there) that have stand-alone floodlight pylons in each corner – I'll leave the desperate and the nerdy to spend a joyful evening guessing who the others are (less than ten - so I'm told).

Kick-off was minutes away, the Mighty Mariner (Grimsby's mascot – think Bayleaf the Gardener in a Newcastle top) was goading the away support and particularly upsetting Barbara Cartland who had to be held back by Tony Blair. Batman was practising his Dad-dancing moves (alone). A group of dwarfs led by Snow White were singing "You're gonna get your fucking head kicked in." It was building up nicely.

I'm sure you've been at games like this before – it all matters much too much; you are so tense you really can't enjoy it and just hope for the goals to go in to relieve the blood pressure a little. After an hour one did but it didn't help as Grimsby, who had clearly not read the script, scored and celebrated a little too joyfully for Yogi Bear's liking (he was arrested). Sir Fred equalised but it wasn't enough for promotion certainty – it now all depended on the result from Gigg Lane. Some twat put around the rumour that Bury had equalised so we all went mental, but the joy was short lived as we soon learned that Swansea had won. Margaret Thatcher flung her handbag on the pitch in disgust and we all went home. The party was well and truly pooped, those relaxing play-offs now awaited.

BELLE VUE, Doncaster Rovers 2 Southend United 0, League One, Saturday 15 October 2005

Southend had won their last eight games and were riding high on top of the Tilson tidal wave at the summit of League One. Having missed all six away games so far that season I thought it was about time to put in an appearance, so Jim and I travelled up to struggling Doncaster confident of victory. Football fans rarely learn from experience.

It was also an opportunity to visit Belle Vue before Donny upped sticks and moved in to their brand new stadium which was due to start being built the following Monday. With some football homes I have wondered why there was ever the need to move - Highfield Road and Maine Road immediately spring to mind. That was not the case with Belle Vue, it looked to be falling down all around us.

In many respects this was not surprising, recent history had seen both arson (by the Chairman) and subsidence (due to mining works), and it was not as if the place had been pretty to start with. The outside car park looked in parts as though it had been the victim of a strafe bomb attack, the two open end terraces were in need of some gardening work, one old and hence odd looking floodlight pylon had been left in place behind its new replacement to satisfy Doncaster's need for telecommunications, the main stand covering half of one side had several holes in its sides, and the narrow covered terrace opposite just had that woebegone feel.

The most outstanding feature though was saved for the 'home end' where eight portacabins had been fork-lifted on top of another eight to fulfil the Doncaster Rovers' dream solution to corporate hospitality. The price of one of these luxury pads was kept discreet – the match programme invited you to call to discuss costs ("A fiver sir, why thank-you, do you want change?"). Most looked unoccupied during the game, the shifters and shakers of Yorkshire's entrepreneurial world instead I surmised looking to the more opulent surroundings of the nearby racecourse for their chicken in the basket.

We went to the clubhouse for our pre-match meal where in sparse but welcoming surroundings we dined out on the 'Today's Special' of sausage roll and ketchup. It failed to satisfy, as did Southend on the pitch as two late goals put an end to the winning streak.

We bade farewell to Belle Vue - it was the first time I'd been to a ground where the time limit for its demise had been definitely set. It seemed sad for a ground with a long history (which had been home to Donny through mostly thin and more thin) to bite the bullet, but for the future health of the club and its catering options, the end could not come quick enough.

48/92 - HUISH PARK, Yeovil Town 0 Southend United 2, League One, Saturday 4 February 2006

After meeting my fellow Suffolk Shrimper, Shrimperzoner and namesake Andy some 18 months ago at Meadow Lane, I hooked up with him for a shared trip to Somerset. After another pick-up in North Essex his people carrier was filled with fellow Shrimpers and it made the trip down to Somerset pass very quickly. We were all dyed-in-the-wool Shrimpers, who had seen more bad than good during our decades of travelling, but now was a time to saviour as we went in to the match top of the league and, unbeaten in 11 games, were also playing with style. So the talk was all positive as we sped around the M25.

Google what Somerset is famous for and it will major on cider and cheese - football comes somewhat down the list. Yet it is a place where stories from long ago will tell of heroic cup battles which any John Motson wannabe will regale with relish. Such tales, with the passing of time, now firmly belong in a different era as more recent Yeovil success has been limited. One old news snippet did catch my eye though – for a cup replay in 1939 against Sheffield Wednesday a then record crowd of over 14,000 were packed inside the ground, but with thousands locked out a large number had climbed on to the roof of one of the stands which then split from one end to the other under the weight. I expect that caused a few hearts to miss a beat – thankfully no one was hurt and they all just got on with the game. They are made of more than cider and cheese these West Country folk.

That was at their previous ground Huish – patching up the old over many years and facing rising maintenance costs, the Glovers ultimately cut the chord with their famous slope and since 1990 have plied their trade at the sanitised but safer Huish Park. Neat in green and white, if one link with the past is its name, another is its away end facility – whilst the home support enjoys covered comfort those who travel get to endure those prevailing south-westerlies in traditional fashion to give the cosseted home support something to laugh at even if losing. There was an away seat allocation, though this was just four columns at one end of the main stand where the Perspex side prevented eye contact with friends on the terrace.

Thankfully for our visit the weather was kind, especially as we were blessed at that point with a couple of great old pro's from sunnier parts of the world. Firstly, and direct from Yeovil, we had secured an old Sodje, Efe, the oldest of four footballing brothers who was certainly striking in appearance with his colourful bandanas typically colour co-ordinated with the kit he was wearing. It was not a fashion that was ever going to catch on in south Essex, but he certainly made an impression in his short Shrimper sojourn with his whole-hearted displays. Another colourful character in our midst at the time was Sean Goater, revered in Moss Side Manchester, and like Efe an international. Somehow we had tempted him to play out his final season on the Essex Riviera (maybe he had misheard when being sold that one). Like Efe it was a case of 'play when the old bones allowed' and he did so in 33 games during his 2005/06 swansong, allowing us to chant 'Feed the Goat' 11 times including at Huish Park. Both men are true footballing gents.

Unbeaten in 12 now – things were warming up.

THE NATIONAL HOCKEY STADIUM, MK Dons 2 Southend United 1, League One, Saturday 18 March 2006

Mmmm, MK Dons. If anyone owning up to, or secretly harbouring feelings for, supporting MK Dons gets this far in the book then you know what's coming next, and somewhat predictably you might feel, it's not a rose-tinted tribute.

As nice a chap as the chirpy Mr Winkelman comes across on the TV screen, the charade played out which spawned his play-thing still sends shivers down the spine. Like a vast many others I do not hold with the idea that a town can, in effect, have a club bought for it. Yes, Wimbledon was in trouble, but they belonged to the borough or at least the general area that they were in, not a totally unconnected place some 80 miles away. If the only other option was for them to fold then that is what should have happened. If Winkelman wanted a club for Milton Keynes he should have set one up in the town and helped it to work its way through the league pyramid – he is a determined man and I'm sure he would have got there in the end and in doing so gained national respect for it.

If I lived in Milton Keynes I could not bring myself to support MK Dons – they have not earned the right to be where they are. I would feel 'false', it would be like following something manufactured or alien which had no soul. AFC Wimbledon on the other hand are the true spirit of football and deserve every plaudit that comes their way for doing it 'the right way' - what they have achieved since 2002 is wonderful and the one good thing to come out of the Dons debacle.

My views are nothing Mr Winkelman hasn't heard before and he has been unrepentant in defending what he did. For me though it is telling that, in order to gain official recognition for their supporters club, MK Dons agreed to return all of the memorabilia attributed to the old Wimbledon to AFC Wimbledon (albeit via the borough of Merton) – if they had truly believed that they were the old Wimbledon then they would surely have never given up something so precious as the replica FA Cup that the Crazy Gang won against all the odds in 1988?

I'll get off my soapbox now, things have to move forward and we have to visit Milton Keynes if we want to follow our team against them. The National Hockey Stadium was the initial bolt hole for the new creation and it had an odd history all of its own – built in 1995, home to England Hockey until 2003, buffed up a bit for the Winkelman show until MK Dons could move in to their new home in 2007, then as if tainted by the experience, no one wanted it so it was bulldozed in 2010. I suspect it will not be revered in the same way as, say, Highbury, Belle Vue or Somerton Park.

If you never went what did you miss? Well, it was all a bit weird. The main stand had a cantilever roof which looked as though it might move downwards at any moment to gobble up those inside like some giant Flintstones spare-rib (give yourself a pat on the head if you get that one). Opposite there was a small tiered block, open to the elements, which would have looked more at home at, say, behind Hole 12 at the Royal & Ancient Golf Club of St Andrews during the British Open. It was also along this side that a couple of life-sized plastic cows grazed to amuse the locals, not the usual stadium feature of choice. Both ends were temporary stands, Winkelman this time respecting tradition by giving the home fans cover whilst letting the away support at the other end enjoy the breeze.

There was no breeze though when we visited. It may have been on the cusp of Spring but there was no hint of anything remotely warming in the weather that day, it was raw-bollocking freezing. To make matters worse our team of table-toppers decided it was time for an off day. Early doors the Goat ran past the cows, got fed and put us one up. But thereafter nothing remotely of interest happened to enthuse the 2,000 Shrimpers, and slowly but surely signs of frostbite started to set in. Standing in the cold is one thing – sitting in it for two hours is another. Requests to start fires were denied by over-officious stewards, folk who hadn't smoked for years were blagging fags for the faint glow they gave off, gloves were being traded at extortionate prices, and a low rumbling gradually increased in volume as feet stamped up and down to keep the circulation going.

A day to forget at a place you somehow just can't eradicate from the memory despite wanting to.

49/52 - LIBERTY STADIUM, Swansea City 2 Southend United 2, League One, Saturday 29 April 2006

It all seemed to be a bit of a dream. Only two seasons before we had been pants and had been that way for some time. Then, the previous season, promotion had been secured at last via the play-offs, we had enjoyed two other (albeit losing) days out at the Millennium Stadium in national finals having been going since 1906 without any before, an ex-Premiership cult hero was our foil striker teaming up with a young protégé who was banging in 20 plus goals a season, we had a management duo who could do no wrong, and there was even the seemingly decent prospect of a fabulous new ground in the offing to take us into even higher stratospheres. You've read such build-ups in this book already that are then the cue for it all to go tits up – well sometimes, just sometimes, the tits stay in the right place.

With two games to go a point would secure only our second ever foray into the second tier. The first chance to do it would not be easy against a Swansea team needing points itself for a play-off spot, and it had been them who had put paid to our hopes of automatic promotion the year before. It was also on their new patch in front of a near-capacity crowd - they would be eager to please to justify the investment. Andy's people carrier was also at capacity as we joined 2,000 other Shrimpers making yet another trip to South Wales – we were in good mood.

The Swans old Vetch Field had been virtually decomposing around them. The contrast with the brand spanking new, pristine white Liberty Stadium could not have been greater – it positively gleamed and was best viewed with a decent pair of sunglasses to protect eyes from the glare. Coming to the end of its first season, the average attendance had increased by nearly 6,000 as Welshmen flocked to enjoy unrestricted views throughout, toilet facilities with hand basins, scoreboards that worked, TV sets everywhere to watch the footie news come in, spacious concourses with plentiful food - things that the previous digs just hadn't excelled at particularly well. Cyril the Swan was still around, but even he had been given a wash, some fresh feathers and I suspect been told to be less aggressive.

The one downside was the parking – away fans are very much encouraged to use a park and ride set up, an odd bit of isolated wasteland plastered with potholes and surrounded by a wire fence. The only thing missing was an armed guard patrolling the perimeter – it all looked a bit perturbing. Captive audience secured for making money, we happily parted with a fiver to escape, taking a punt that the bus was going to take us to the football rather than some interrogation complex.

It was not an occasion for messing about trying to find a pub, on arrival we did what Swansea wanted us to do and went straight in the stadium where we could buy their pies and beers before taking our seats to get warmed up for the big one. Strangely there was no mass fancy dress parade this time – it all just seemed too important. Nerves were quelled by adding to the gradual noise build-up as both sets of fans tried to out sing each other – the Liberty could certainly hold the noise in and the atmosphere was tremendous. 'Feed the Goat' got its last away trip airing.

A ding-dong match saw Sir Fred equalise for us twice and that proved to be enough – we had done it. The players, Tilly and Brush, a grinning Chairman, Dave the Kit Man and the rest celebrated wildly in front of us, almost as amazed as we were that we had out-performed a league containing former European Champions, Division One treble champs and FA Cup winners (ok, none of them that recent, but still all considered bigger than what is really just a small club in a town with a very long pier).

The tits had stayed where we wanted them to be, and in a memorable finale at Roots Hall the week after, the championship trophy was secured for skipper Kevin Maher, a very proud cup holder, to hold up.

GELSENKIRCHEN FANZONE, England v Portugal, Quarter Final World Cup Germany 2006, 30 June to 2 July 2006

"Me and Paul and Jon and Darren, we're off to Gelsenkirchen, me and Paul and Jon and Darren, it's better than going to Burton."

World Cup fever had taken hold in the office, folk were going down with it around early afternoon from mid-June onwards and seeking cures in pubs. Sven the Scandinavian Forehead and the WAG army were on the march, the flag of St George was flying everywhere, and we had a man who could dance The Robot leading our forward line. It was intoxicating.

England annihilated Paraguay with an own goal, saw off the mighty Trinidad & Tobago with two late strikes, drew with Sven's real team, and then stuffed Ecuador 1-0. An urgent meeting was held – England were on course to win the World Cup and we needed to be there for the quarter final. Plans were made, the ferry was booked, a camp site sorted and passports found – with three work colleagues I was off to the World Cup.

I volunteered to drive – it gave me a chance to test the old people carrier on the Autobahn. The Harwich to Hook of Holland ferry was rammed with expectant Englishmen, the ferry bar ran dry four hours out and, on reaching the Netherlands, a mass Wacky Races ensemble sped off towards Germany. The Citroen Synergie strained its way to 119 mph before I concluded that another 15 minutes of trying to get to 120 mph might not be too wise, so we slowed down at which point the German Federal Police pulled us in to enquire where we were going. The flags and scarves hanging from the car windows seemed to be a bit of a giveaway but, not wanting to risk any acts of retribution for 1966, appropriate monotone answers were given, documents shown, I proudly pointed to my brand new regulation triangle and fire extinguisher, and we were let on our way.

The Gelsenkirchen Fanzone campsite was not the height of luxury but did provide all of the essentials for life: rows and rows of tent pitches broken up by portaloo islands, and at the site's hub a bar area with TV screens surrounded by the high flying flags of the 32 nations who had qualified (so, not Scotland). Entertainment was immediate – Germany v Argentina on the screens in the first quarter final, but a bit of a tricky one for deciding who to support. It was just a great place to be – beers were sunk whilst watching Germans losing their sense of humour as the game got more and more tense, Argentines getting melodramatic, Italians (next up that evening) getting nervous, and Irish (not in the World Cup but they had sniffed out there was a party going on) just dancing. It was a late night.

A hungover tented version of the United Nations rose slowly on an already scorching morning - I could hear a slightly undiplomatic rendition of 'Dambusters' in the distance and, with the tent getting hotter by the minute, forced myself up and out for breakfast. Jon and Paul were already up having a pint. We made our plans for the day and, having agreed that tickets for the match were a bit of a non-starter, decided to head for the 'main fanzone' at the Trotting Racecourse. I'd not been to an event where I'd travelled to another country to watch the telly before.

Set in a hollow, the Racecourse was just bonkers – a bowl full of some 40,000 Englishmen, a couple of Portuguese, a splattering of Irish, cart loads of beer, searing heat, two giant TV screens, and an army of

Germans with patrol dogs stalking the perimeter. Nervous tension was in the air.

Cliques of fans sprung up impromptu camps all around, staking territory with their club flags to attract fellow fans. Millwall set up next to Leeds, Tottenham next to Arsenal, Crewe next to Port Vale and so on, welcoming steady streams of new brothers whilst runners were sent out to replenish drink stocks. I hung up my 'Suffolk Shrimpers' flag – it attracted some mild amusement.

The whole atmosphere was confusing yet fascinating - choruses of Vindaloo and Jerusalem rang out, Englishman stared at Englishman, the Irish danced and the two Portuguese just kept moving as if in some kind of giant 'Where's Wally' game. The match was an anxious distraction, winding its way to the traditional penalty shoot-out debacle. In the end that defeat and the heat kept the lid on whatever may have been simmering, and a becalmed lull wafted over the bowl as we all filed out. At the exit gate I took a look behind me – littered on the grass below amongst a sea of plastic glasses were scores of comatosed bodies, one or two being poked by friends for signs of life, others just left to fry.

The trip home the following day was full of reflective mood – it had been an experience to remember and we even briefly flirted with the idea of a return as neutrals for the final, but common sense prevailed. "We're gonna score one more than you." Well, maybe next time.

50/92 - PRIDE PARK, Derby County 3 Southend United 0, Championship, Saturday 30 September 2006

We were now in the Championship with the Premiership pretenders, rubbing shoulders with clubs who played the role of Ronnie Barker aka the classic 'Class Sketch' from the 1960's Frost Report – Southend United were very much looked on as the Ronnie Corbet of the league.

You could imagine Derby folk playing the role convincingly: "I still look up to him (John Cleese, so think Manchester United or Liverpool) because although I have money I am vulgar. But I am not as vulgar as him (Southend United) so I still look down on him (Southend United)."

Whether of course Derby did/do have money is another question - the finances of a football club are a minefield and I'm not going to tie myself in knots trying to answer that one. But they do have a nice stadium.

Copying Middlesbrough's plans bar the bit on seat colours and a few other twiddley bits, what Derby have done with Pride Park is neat without exactly being inspiring. It certainly has all you could want – great views, a 'closed in' feel which generates a good atmosphere, a giant scoreboard, a PA system you can hear, clean toilets, pictures of Rams …. the list is endless, everything on the design wish list got put in. But it just doesn't have that 'je ne sais quoi' – maybe it should have floodlight pylons shaped like expectant ewes, or a statue of Barry Davies pointing at a grinning Franny Lee (think hard on that if you don't get it – I reckon it would be a sure-fire winner), or a giant moving mechanical Roy McFarland bringing down Stuart Parker just as he was about to score in 1976 (not that I'm bitter), or large plastic rams on the side of the pitch aka MK Dons. I don't know, maybe a poll on some key ideas should be held, but scrub that last one, it's a bit naff.

Lots of leg room, comfy seats, outclassed on the pitch although we tried, we all got a bit bored. The sketch was played out true to type: "I know my place …….. but while I am poor I am honest, industrious and trustworthy. Had I the inclination I could look down on them. But I don't."

51/92 - TURF MOOR, Burnley 0 Southend United 0, Championship, Tuesday 17 October 2006

An afternoon off for a little midweek jolly to Burnley – I joined my fellow Suffolk Shrimpers for the trip up.

You can expect the occasional hold up on England's motorway network. So when we came to a grinding holt on the M62 we were not too worried. When nothing had moved for 15 minutes we started to get a little concerned. On 30 minutes we were bored and concerned, people were walking about speaking to fellow travellers, not a good sign on a road we should have been travelling along at 70 (ish). To pass the time we got a game of 'penny against the wall' going against the central reservation. After 90 minutes and the loss of a few sheckles we were at last on our way again, so now the race was on to get to Turf Moor in time for kick-off.

We got there, just, and joined the couple of hundred or so Shrimpers equally mad enough to travel 'oop north' midweek. A shade over 10,000 were in attendance overall, not a massive number but still impressive given the population of Burnley is only around 70,000. These days Burnley average circa 15,000 – if, say, the Tyneside conurbation around Newcastle had a similar ratio wanting to turn up to St James's Park there would be over 190,000 wanting to get in.

What do you think of when someone mentions Turf Moor? The home-grown Division One championship team of 1959/60 gracing the hallowed turf? The flowing locks of Ralph Coates running down the wing during the 1960's? That emotional narrow win against Orient in 1987 to keep Burnley in the Football League? The welcoming stares from the cosily named Suicide Squad Burnley fan group in the 1980's? The smart claret and blue facade of the James Hargreaves Stand? For me there is only one thing that has stood out for decades now – the wooden seats at what is currently known as the David Fishwick Stand. They looked dated when they were first installed, when any got worn out they were patched up to stand out from the rest, then some were coloured to make it look even more like a badly constructed patchwork. It was just a mess, drawing the eye in to detract from what otherwise is a decent little stadium. Now at least they've all been painted (in 2014) and look much better, funny how a club can readily spend millions on player transfers, agent fees and wages yet a few quid on some paint took years to find.

The match? In the 15 preceding fixtures dating back to 1915 there had been 6-0's, 3-5's and 1-4's with an overall average of almost four goals a game. We witnessed a 0-0 as Tilson decided to defend at all costs to try and stop the rot that was setting in on the season's form. Great entertainment for talking about on the 250 mile trip back home.

52/92 - RICOH ARENA, Coventry City 1 Southend United 1, Championship, Saturday 30 December 2006

I was born in a cross-fire hurricane. Well, not exactly, I've always thought it would've been cool to have been, but instead it was Billericay Hospital and I expect Mum was the happier for that (plus she would not be that flattered by the second verse of 'Jumping Jack Flash').

Arriving at Coventry we were caught in the mother of all storms – it was as though the rain was being poured from the sky in buckets. It was almost impossible to see where we were going and, turning off the M6, I just pulled in to the first place that said 'football parking'. Big mistake – the rain wasn't going to stop any time soon and, as we soon found out, the ground was a good mile away. It was not worth making a run for it, we were soaked as soon as we stepped outside the car, so Jim and I just trudged in, resigned to our sodden fate.

It did spoil the experience – we just sat in our puddles, admiring the way the pitch (sheltered by the Ricoh bowl) was standing up to the deluge and jealous of those who travelled by coach being dropped off immediately outside. One bloke came in, stripped off to his underpants and just wrung out his clothes in the December air. I had my son to think of so declined to follow – he always suffers enough when we score and I forget myself for a bit.

It was not only the pitch, the Ricoh looked good all round – three uniform sides faced up by something a little quirkier, with 'Ricoh' plastered everywhere (it will cost them a fortune to remove it all as and when their sponsorship deal ends). When less than half full though the sky blue décor tends to stand out and make it all look a little empty. With vast swathes of un-sat on seats glistening in the floodlights it looked a bit of an over-investment that to date has gambled unsuccessfully on hosting Premiership football to fill the gaps.

A dull game in a damp atmosphere ended level – Sir Fred came on as sub (a sub would have been useful a little earlier) but failed to ignite things. Three years later he did sparkle by scoring the first ever hatrick at the Ricoh (in Coventry colours) – 'it's all right now, in fact it's a gas' he might have mused.

53/92 - THE BRITANNIA STADIUM, Stoke City 1 Southend United 1, Championship, Saturday 3 February 2007

I never managed to get to the old Victoria Ground during its 119 years, something else was always happening. However, with only the once-mighty Leeds below us and the season ticking on, support was galvanising for the relegation fight, so I joined my fellow Suffolk Shrimpers for the trip up to the new Stoke abode.

A vision in red, the Britannia rightfully pays full homage to legend Sir Stanley Matthews. We drove up Sir Stanley Matthews Way, admired not one but three statues of the great man, surveyed the range of memorabilia in the club shop (there was a 'sold out' note in the space where the Sir Stan 'legend' birthday cards should have been – his popularity will never die) and wished that we had the cash to have splashed out on a lunch in the Sir Stanley Matthews Lounge. Sir Stan lived just long enough to have opened the place in 1997 – he must have been very humbled by it all.

One ad in the match programme did catch my eye. It was for a lap dancing club and featured a picture of a young lady covering her essentials with an opened bra boasting that she was on show until 4 am every Friday and Saturday night – I wonder what Sir Stan would have thought of that.

What has always impressed me about Stoke City is the noise generated by their fans both home and away. It helps of course to have a great song with lyrics that everyone can recall, and for years now the Potters have belted out Tom Jones's 1968 hit 'Delilah' all over the country. I vividly recall being impressed by hearing 10,000 or so Stoke fans bash it out and drown out the Kop when I visited Anfield for a cup tie back in 1994. It really made the hairs stand on end. The song has everything the footie fan could want – a chance to shout 'woooooahhhhhh', a deep-throated element when the word 'she' is sung, humour prevails with the 'ha ha ha ha' bit, and there's a simple chorus that everyone knows because it was a mega pop hit. You can even find a bit of controversy as the ditty is all about killing a woman. Perhaps with some justification it might be considered to be bad taste to 'glorify' that, though that never stops the BBC having it on their playlist and I sincerely doubt it's the reason Stoke fans have adopted it. Delilah is just a catchy tune, end of. Anyone protesting is just jealous.

Anyway, an equalising poacher's goal by Sir Fred in the second half earned us a point and we mustered a chorus or two of 'Sea Sea Seasiders' – it seemed a bit inadequate in comparison but we made some noise with it. To this day the Southend fans have never really landed on anything unique which we can truly call 'our song'. All power to whoever finally sorts that one out.

54/92 - ST MARY'S STADIUM, Southampton 4 Southend United 1, Championship, Sunday 6 May 2007

St Mary's for me will forever be a place to remember - it was the last place I went with my Dad to a match. It was May 2010, almost 40 years on from when he first took me to Roots Hall, and though I might have seen a few more trophies if we'd kept up the 1971 visits to Stamford Bridge, even if I could, I would never have swopped the choice he made for me, and I never will.

In 2010 Mum and Dad were living on the Isle of Wight so Jim and I picked Dad and one of his friends up at the Southampton hovercraft terminal. At that stage Dad was needing help to go to matches due to the onset of Parkinson's, something which today has sadly gripped him to the extent he can no longer contemplate going to a match. We managed to go for a quick drink and then rolled up at the away end with some 1,500 other Shrimpers. Southend had already been relegated (from League One) and Southampton had nothing to play for, but pride meant that both teams still 'went for it'. Despite losing 3-1, the Shrimpers sang throughout and I know Dad was impressed, especially with SpongeBob, Superman and Fred Flintstone jumping up and down on his row all game long. All those years ago it had been Dad driving me to games, making sure we met up with Barry and Harvey to complete our little Roots Hall group, installing me on my milk crate so I could see, buying me programmes, ensuring I was warm and safe enough, and after the match guiding me back to the car and home. I didn't let him see, but I had a tear in the eye as I supported him walking out at the end, I could sense we wouldn't be doing this together again.

The 2010 visit hadn't been my first trip to St Mary's, that had been three years earlier in circumstances which had many similarities. Again it was the last game of the season with Southend already relegated (this time from the Championship following a disastrous run of five defeats in six games). Shrimpers had also travelled in numbers, this time selling out our 3,100 allocation. There was also an emotional element. Alan Ball had died from a heart attack the week before aged just 61 and everyone in the full house, without exception, greeted the Ball family onto the pitch with a minute's applause and broke out with several spontaneous chants of his name throughout the game – it really sent shivers down the spine. SpongeBob was around too, dancing up and down the stairs with Squidward as we sang his theme "Who lives in a pineapple under the sea? SpongeBob Square Pants". It was deep and meaningful stuff to accompany the high emotion.

St Marys is slick with all the ingredients to be a money-making machine even if it is lacking a little in inspirational design (Kevin McCloud I suspect would be a bit non-plussed). Its closed-in structure certainly

216

facilitates a great atmosphere when there is a full house and I don't think I have ever experienced anything quite like that 32,008 'love-in' back in 2007 – Saints respected Shrimpers and vice-versa, we joined in each other's songs, encouraged each other to up the anti even further, and the noise was incessant. When Southampton scored their third and fourth goals there was no break in the away end chanting, if anything it just got louder, it really was quite something.

Two memorable days at a great venue. On the one hand I can't wait to go again, but on the other know it will be difficult to live up to the first two visits. Maybe next time though we might win instead of getting stuffed – that would make it memorable.

55/92 – BESCOT STADIUM, Walsall 0 Southend United 2, League One, Saturday 20 October 2007

What's the 'most looked at' ground in the country? I can only think it must be The Bescot Stadium. Not though I suspect for reasons of magnificence or iconic status, but simply because it sits alongside the M6 on which thousands travel every hour. True, not all will glance towards the romantically named Tile Choice Stand (let alone wish they were in it), but eyes will be drawn by the giant advertising hoardings behind the away end, which every time I've passed look to sell anything but Walsall FC.

Not every team can win silverware and Walsall are one of those clubs whose role it seems is destined to be a 'stocking filler' – bobbling along in the lower leagues not upsetting anyone and playing the essential role of providing opposition to play against. The Football League just wouldn't work without teams like Walsall. The Bescot fits the team – it won't win any awards for its beauty but you can get a seat (though beware the stanchions) and you won't get wet (unless there is a really big puddle on the M6).

One definite disappointment is the lack of drinking hostelries nearby – Walsall look to capitalise on this by charging you to drink in their 'Saddlers Club' which we thought was a bit cheeky. Maybe if it offered cheap beer or entertainment or a decent real ale selection it would be OK, but let's just say it was a bit underwhelming.

However, win at Walsall and you'll have a good day. A few hundred Shrimpers in the 2,000 capacity low-roofed away end made a hell of a racket. We celebrated with some fish n chips afterwards – we didn't need to pay to get in the chippy.

56/92 - THE KEEPMOAT STADIUM, Doncaster Rovers 3 Southend United 1, League One, Saturday 29 December 2007

Built in 2006 at a cost of some £21 million (a staggering £32 million if you count the wider complex it's situated within), The Keepmoat is a little more plush than the £4.5 million Bescot.

It is really just a 'mini-me' of Southampton's St Mary's. It is everything dear old Belle Vue wasn't – stand roofs don't leak, the paint isn't peeling, the car park has tarmac, stewards have been trained to smile …… though with a capacity of just 15,000 it must be one of the most expensive stadiums per bum on seat in the country. There is also corporate hospitality which doesn't involve climbing into a porta cabin, and for the more successful ladies team there is The Keepmoat's toy 'mini-me' just outside with its own 500 seat stand.

The match programme included a page of notes from the then Chairman John Ryan where he signed-off with 'Rovers till I die'. How good is that? Many chairmen might be more inclined to end with 'XYZ until I can flog it to a property company'. Not Mr Ryan, he was born in Donny, supported the club as a boy, saved it from oblivion, oversaw its move into The Keepmoat, is so 'Rovers through and through' that he once got the manager to bring him on as sub for the last three minutes of a reserve fixture (in so doing he became the oldest ever footballer to turn out for a British professional club), ploughed shed loads of dosh from his cosmetics fortune into the place, and then wrote off all of his debt when he resigned in 2015. You don't get many of those guys to the pound.

Another programme note caught my eye. There was a letter from some chap who wanted to surprise his girlfriend by getting her to be the club mascot (Donny Dog) for a day, his wishes having been duly granted for

219

the preceding match on Boxing Day. Take a bow that man - gifting your loved one the opportunity to dress up as a giant dog for a day is taking Christmas presents to a whole new level. I suspect I'd be filed with divorce papers if I surprised Lizzie with the opportunity to clamber into the sweaty Sammy Shrimp costume in front of a few thousand at Roots Hall. It is an idea though.

57/92 - VICTORIA PARK, Hartlepool 4 Southend United 3, League One, Tuesday 22 January 2008

Hartlepool away on a Tuesday night in January. Hmmm.

If you were running a vote on the 'least glamorous away trip' then a visit to Victoria Park would surely poll well. To me the very name 'Hartlepool' just conjures up a depressing image of 23rd place in the old Fourth Division – there may well have been a poorer team in any one given year, but 'having another duff season' just seems to have been life's remit for Hartlepool. They applied for re-election 14 times between 1924 and 1986 - more than any other club - but never actually got voted out. Somehow they have also dodged the bullet of automatic relegation since the re-election voting charade was abandoned.

If a history of poor football isn't enough to discourage a visit, Hartlepool's 'Monkey Hangers' nickname hardly does much to endear – the local population concluded during the Napoleonic Wars that the only survivor from a French shipwreck, a monkey, was a spy and promptly swung the thing from a rope on the beach. This tale also does little to advance views on the intelligence or hospitality of Hartlepool folk, yet despite this the town's football club chooses to promote the event, not least via its giant furry ape mascot H'Angus.

Then there is the local climate. Biting winds frequently thrash their way off the North Sea into the town, or in the calm a sea mist descends. Arrive in January and, well, it won't be tropical.

Victoria Park itself does little to 'warm'. Low stands on all four sides provide minimal shelter, with each open corner specially designed to funnel in the cold air, and all of it painted in an icy blue and white. The away end is seated, but with less than 150 Shrimpers hardly getting in each other's way the stewards on our visit decided it would be fun to make us stay sitting in our plastic buckets so we could not even jump up and down to stave off frostbite.

In 1916 one of those Kaiser Wilhelm II giant balloon thingies, not the most robust of vessels, made it all the way across the North Sea to bomb Victoria Park. What threat the old Prussian slug-balancer thought could come from the home of Hartlepool United is anyone's guess – maybe he was after H'Angus thinking the weird furry was a challenge to his plans to dominate Europe. The main stand he destroyed instead was replaced by a temporary wooden affair (which stayed for over 70 years until the club finally realised that the German government would not give in to their claims for compensation).

All in all it seems to be a bit of a sorry tale, but any sympathy you might have goes when the home team score the winner in the 90th minute, H'Angus runs down the touchline in jubilation to give the away support a view of his arse, and you have 270 miles to get home with an ETA of 2.45 am.

58/92 - THE GALPHARM STADIUM, Huddersfield Town 1 Southend United 2, League One, Saturday 15 March 2008

Now, this is a 'new' stadium that shows a bit of invention. When originally built in 1994 it did only have three stands, but unlike Oxford they soon realised the oversight and added a fourth. It now looks splendid, like four blue half-moons with seats. There are even four stand-alone floodlight pylons, a real throwback rarity to satisfy the nerdy ground-spotter yearning for something from the steam age.

OK, it misses out on perfection for not having the corners filled in, but once inside that is forgotten as you admire the curved white steel tubing acting as supports for the stands each of which has its own identity. Catch it right on a sunny day and, if the game gets a tad dull, there is the bonus of watching the shadows of the steel supports weave patterns across the pitch. Then look up towards the Kilner Bank Stand

and, in a town not exactly famed for its beauty, a stunning backdrop is provided by a large wood. Eh bah gum it's a reet bobby dazzler.

Well, if you've got this far in the book (without cheating or being a Huddersfield fan looking forlornly for reference to your beloved old Leeds Road) you'll think it's about time that I dished out some praise. However, The Galpharm (or McAlpine, or John Smith's, or whatever you want to call it) does have a downside, namely the lack of atmosphere it creates. The open nature of the place just lets any noise created fly off in to the woods rather than hang in the ground to encourage yet more volume. Yes, about 400 Shrimpers might struggle anywhere in a stand that sits 4,000, but it did make me think that the away end at the more modest Bescot was a little more enjoyable. Still, I'll take a win anywhere – onwards and upwards, a relegation bounce-back was now looking a real possibility for my yo-yo team.

59/92 - BRUNTON PARK, Carlisle United 1 Southend United 2, League One, Saturday 19 April 2008

Carlisle is a bit of a haul from Ipswich for a day trip, so with the weather improving and Southend's fortunes on the up I thought it was time for a 'father and son thing'.

Jim and I set off early on the Friday and made our way to a camp site just outside Keswick, spent far too long remembering how to pitch the tent, and then walked in to town. Thinking the pencil museum might be a tad too exciting, we settled for a visit to a pasty shop and then a walk back to a comfy looking hotel situated just outside the camp site. In the bar we found another Shrimper sitting alone slowly working his way through the hotel's solitary barrel of real ale, and five hours later we had made a good dent in its capacity between us. Jim sat there wondering how two strangers could not stop talking for a whole evening as we found plenty in common, not least the football club and having been to the same school – 'tis a small world.

I always find camping a bit of a trial, not least when the bladder is full, but it's cheap and the lack of comfort encourages getting up early to make the most of the beautiful surroundings. Stopping off en route a couple of times to Carlisle to take in the view and have a leisurely breakfast was a wonderful way to start to the day, and made a change to the usual match day motorway mile-crunching. We briefly thought of the 500 or so fellow Shrimpers on their 650 mile round day trip, before having another slice of toast and then a quick walk up a hill by Bassenthwaite Lake to enjoy once more the serene landscape.

We arrived at the Football League's most northerly outpost (ok, maybe it ties with Newcastle) in a relaxed mood and in need of a bit of 'tension' to get up for the match. An air-sea rescue helicopter did its best to shake everyone up in the 9,000 crowd by delivering the match ball, maybe in a precautionary practice run should the place flood during the game. Shrimpers were situated in one corner of the impressive but unfinished 12 year old East Stand, slightly annoyed by the insistence of the stewards that one of our two seating blocks was to the rear of the touchline when there was still plenty of room elsewhere. I agree with 'building for the future', but putting a stand where one day the pitch might be does seem to be a slightly hopeful approach when we all know that football is a far from certain pastime. Also odd is the small block of seats on the otherwise terraced Waterworks End, though they did at least provide a good anchor for the Suffolk Shrimper flag to lie on.

All around, Brunton Park oozes individualistic character. The Warwick Road End housing the home fans has a hatrick of corrugated triangles providing cover for the home fans against the rains that occasionally land on Carlisle. The main stand is an old fashioned seating/terrace mix so often favoured by clubs in days gone by, made more unique by two extensions on its wings added later as the £12,500 the club received from Liverpool for Geoff Twentyman in 1953 wasn't quite enough to finish the job in one go. Brunton Park remains for now the largest English ground which is not all-seated, and it is sad that its future is often talked of as being limited as it doesn't quite have the ready-made facilities to make money outside of the often forgotten basic requirement of hosting a football match.

Anyway, reward on the day for plundering the long way up was gifted to the Shrimper fans with one of those oh-so-sweet last minute winners, and with two games to go it virtually assured that both clubs would end up in the play-offs where they would fail at the semi-final stage. We did not know that then of course, and another enjoyable evening was spent with Jim and my new-found fellow Shrimper pal in the same hotel bar from the night before, making promotion plans and sinking the remaining contents of the hotel's beer barrel. 'Must do again' noted in the diary against the football-weekender idea.

60/92 - WALKERS STADIUM, Leicester City 3 Southend United 0, League One, Saturday 6 December 2008

Writing this part of the book in February 2016 at a time when Leicester City were five points clear at the top of the Premiership, it seems strange that when I visited their ground back in 2008 it was for a League One fixture. I suppose it just reflects how rapidly fortunes can change and is why football fans rarely jump ship for another club – once bitten you're in for life anyway but to change would be like jumping queues in the supermarket when the one you leave then starts to move faster.

My cousin Derek has stuck with Leicester throughout the years. All too often in a large dispersed family a meet up with relatives only occurs at specific events such as weddings and funerals, so it was great to see him at what was then known as the 'Crisp Bowl' and catch up on family stuff and footie chat. Football does that – it lends an environment for folk to meet up to share a common interest and create new memories. It happens at every match across the land, seeing friends you last saw at the last game or like with Derek and me giving an excuse to say hello after some five years or so. When Jim was young enough we had a season ticket at Roots Hall in the Family Stand where, again just like for others everywhere else, we would exchange nods of welcome with folk we saw every home match and chat with others we sat around who we'd never otherwise meet. When at the start of a new season someone new showed up in a nearby seat it wouldn't usually take long before the 'knowing nod' turned into 'hello's' and then discussions on the state of play. Equally, when someone doesn't show up again you worry what's happened and are often left to ponder without ever finding out – becoming 'ground pals' is often restricted to being within your seating block, not the outside world.

One of our pre-match pub discussions was which celebrities you'd like to spend an evening in a pub with – I can't recall Derek's choices but my top three (which I still stand by today) are Boris Johnson (for his buffoonery wit), Jeremy Clarkson (to spark a debate if not to agree with) and Danny Baker (because he tends to have a funny tale about anything). Even if they wouldn't get on I think those three would keep anyone amused over a beer session – not a footballer amongst them, though Danny would provide the feed for reminiscing on what the game used to be like if the other two would let him.

Anyway, I digress (sort of – footie is all about banter), Derek and I bade our farewells, him off to his group of season ticket pals and me to the away end where I duly nodded to familiar faces before catching up with my fellow Suffolk Shrimper cronies. Away fans are accommodated in one corner of the ground which looked the same as the rest of the place, all very neat, blue and efficient. The wide roof does help to keep in the noise and that is where the one non-uniform feature exists as one-half of the ground has part of its covering in clear Perspex to let in the light to aid pitch growth - Archibald Leitch would never have thought of that one. Not that we made much noise on the day - Leicester's crisp (sorry) passing game left Southend chasing shadows and we hardly had a kick as Matty Fryatt bagged a hatrick.

I looked back at the ground on the way out, the view before me resembled an office block, it didn't look much like a football stadium (even a modern new one). But it's a meeting place, and that I've come to realise is more important than any concrete (or Perspex) feature.

61/92 - STADIUM:MK, MK Dons 2 Southend United 0, League One, Thursday 1 January 2009

Winkleman's play-thing finally got its permanent home in 2007, the hairy one even finding a celebrity (QE II) to cut the ribbon - I hope she redeems herself by offering to open the new AFC Wimbledon home as and when it ever gets built.

I'll concede that the place looks good, even though when we visited at the start of 2009 the upper tier had no seats. Foresight has been shown in making the roof high enough to allow a third tier to be added at a later stage to increase capacity from 30,000 to 45,000, though it is stretching the imagination somewhat to think that even the current capacity will be regularly tested. But imagination is not something Mr Winkleman is short of, and his obsession with growing something no one really wants extended to his match day programme notes for my visit. His musings were all about attendance figures and selling tickets, and when I read that he referred to work on Southend's stadium already being underway I can only surmise that he must truly be in fantasy land (or taking the piss) – we haven't even seen as much as a garden spade on the Fossets Farm site ever since plans for a new ground there were first submitted at the beginning of the century.

Around 1,000 or so Shrimpers made the trip up to boost the crowd to just over 10,000, but the place looked empty and we could still make out the irksome letters 'MK Dons' amongst the home support area. But the seats were comfy, I mean really comfy, it was like going to sit down on what you would normally expect to be the bum aching seat of a racing bike and finding yourself sinking in to a black leather armchair. Whether that helps the atmosphere much is debateable – in another sorry defeat I felt more inclined to doze off rather than encourage my team, I was too comfortable. And the leg room, well wow, folk could pass by without the usual squeeze against flesh you'd rather avoid. It was just so luxurious.

But will the place ever take-off in the way Winkleman craves? I don't think so. No matter how good the present you need a history to build on for folk to take up with pride when success starts to come and importantly cling on to and stay with it when times get tougher. Milton Keynes now has a very nice and expensive new stadium – it will be interesting to see what is happening in it in ten years' time. My bet is that it will be a rugby ground.

EDGELEY PARK, Stockport County 3 Southend United 1, League One, Saturday 17 January 2009

Another League One fixture I am not likely to see again for some time. But whilst Leicester have only since gone upwards, Stockport's exit ended up being out of the arse end of the division, and as we all know from what has happened since in falling all the way down to the National League North, they really did get a touch of the trots.

Stockport's tale is, to my over-simplistic 'outsider observer' eye, summed up in four 'easy bite' chunks: 1900 to 1990 – bumbled along quite happily in the lower league tiers; 1991 to 2000 – had a great time, reached the second tier, eyes maybe got too big; 2001 to 2010 – debt and disaster; 2011 to date – non-league struggle. It is not an unfamiliar story, a period of success can often be the prelude to bad stuff for a smaller club, but it's a lesson that not unnaturally few fail to learn. One of my other cousins, Mark, knows more than most about the Stockport saga and back in 2013, and as a real Hatters diehard, he landed his dream job – Club Secretary at Stockport County FC. It's a role many of us might aspire to, but speak to Mark for five minutes about the 80 plus hours a week spent doing anything from dealing with a blocked gents toilet in the away end to trying to raise funds just to ensure that week's wages are met, and you might think again.

For the match in 2009 I travelled up with my fellow Suffolk Shrimpers – having a couple of hours to kill we went in search of food along Edgeley's nearby Castle Street. Mmmm, vast swathes were boarded up and the rest was dominated by the obligatory charity shops with the odd 'Best Kebab' shop breaking up the monotony. A 2011 survey showed Stockport as having the highest high street vacancy rate in the country – it certainly was a bit grim. We retreated to the ground for sustenance.

Stockport County have lived at Edgeley Park for 114 years, an impressive residency time-span even if like many lower league clubs home is no longer owned by the user. With low level stands running along both sides, key interest is in the (all too predictable) contrast between the home and away ends. The double-tiered Cheadle (home) End is the impressive reminder of when the club was riding the high-life in the 1990's, full of banqueting and hospitality suites as well as some 5,000 seats. The open-to- the elements Railway (away) End is a terrace with just over 1,000 seats bolted on, a no-frills facility complete with a scoreboard that doesn't work (well, it wasn't when we were there).

The Railway End is often remembered for one of the best own goals ever seen. Just type 'Ian Dowie own goal' in to your search engine and up will pop a 30 second video delight of a jaw-dropping effort which left Mr Dowie holding his head in shame and the half-drowned West Ham fans in the background looking so pleased that they had travelled up in the pouring rain mid-week to witness it.

On our visit, however, we were afforded the comparative luxury of sitting in one corner of the Popular Side, where we were treated to a show of strength by some over-zealous stewards. One admittedly 'vociferous' Shrimper, claiming that standing helped with the stanchion-dodging for a view of the game, took exception to being told to place his bum on a seat. This developed in to a full scale row involving several fans and stewards which rumbled on for most of the match.

It's the kind of pointless-in-the-extreme event most of us have seen many times before – unless you are a Leeds fan. Having been to a few Leeds away fixtures I've yet to see any group of stewards dare take on 3,000 'White's', none of whom seem to like the feel of cold plastic. At least though it was a distraction from another away defeat which I can recall nothing of bar the 'seat debate'. It's funny how the oddest things can make you remember an otherwise forgettable day.

62/92 - COMMUNITY STADIUM, Colchester United 0 Southend United 1, League One, Saturday 21 February 2009

Built on the edge of a business park surrounded by wasteland and miles from the city centre. Doesn't sound great does it? I'll try again. Viewed from the A12, the four small similar looking stands sit apart from each other with the wind whistling through each corner. Mmmm, hardly welcoming, I'll have one more go. Once parked up, the ground is reached by risking life dashing across the busy slip roads to the A12, hurdling a crash barrier, sliding down a muddy embankment, walking through sodden grass, and clambering up a weed-infested slope. Yep, that I think does it.

Colchester's home since the start of the 2008/09 season hardly inspires – it has all of the function room stuff to host the tribute acts it regularly attempts to distract passing A12 motorists with on a shiny neon sign, has leg room a plenty, and unrestricted views of the pitch, but soul was left at Layer Road. If the wind and rain sweep in, the Community Stadium is a desolate place.

Thankfully I've only visited on Essex Derby Day so, with a couple of thousand Shrimpers, the atmosphere is then cranked up somewhat. Experience there for me has been mixed, though oddly one of the funniest moments I've ever witnessed at a ground came during a defeat the year after our 2009 inaugural visit win. At half-time a disparate mix of mascots from local stores, charities and the two clubs assembled on the touchline for a race around the perimeter. Right from the start the Colchester fans pin-up, Eddie the Eagle, streaked ahead like a true Olympian, going as fast as his furry brown legs and worryingly tight blue shorts would let him. Looking pleased as punch, he puffed out his chest on the back straight, well satisfied with the lead he had built up over a sorry looking monkey of indeterminate origin.

The two Southend mascots had no designs on race glory, instead Sammy the Shrimp (our coned head Ku Klux Klan look-a-like) and Elvis J Eel (don't ask, his relevance to anything is a complete mystery) had made their way to the penultimate corner flag intent on mischief. As Eddie rounded the bend Sammy took him out with a head butt and Elvis waded in to make sure he stayed down, as assorted primates, birds and a white thing chugged past to steal Eddie's moment of magic in the lime light that he had been craving for years for. Sammy and Elvis duly took bows from the ecstatic travelling Shrimpers as Eddie, intent on vengeance, grabbed a corner flag and made his way towards our two hero's, but perhaps mindful of the need not to invalidate his DBS certificate he just ended up trooping off head down in shame.

Derby days anywhere can certainly be feisty and this was true of the last match between Southend and Colchester at a packed Roots Hall in February 2016. Amid all of the mayhem on and off the pitch, one thing stood out head and shoulders above the rest, namely the courage of one Colchester fan. With his son desperately ill, Tom needed to raise money for the expensive treatment and care his son's condition required, and to raise some funds had chosen to run on match day the 39 miles from the Community Stadium to Roots Hall. He made it just in time for kick-off and, to rapturous applause, was introduced to the crowd before taking a lap of honour with his collecting bucket. Fans poured to the front to pat him on the back and put money his way, and you could see the tears welling up in his eyes with the emotion of it all. His lap was taking so long it had to be completed during the half-time break and his courage, and the reaction of the Roots

Hall faithful, will live long in the memory. All the very best Tom.

63/92 - KC STADIUM, Hull City 3 Southend United 1, Carling Cup Round Two, Tuesday 25 August 2009

The KC is no DIY flat pack basic model – it is a curvy bowl full of treats that any fan waiting on their club to sort themselves out with a new home would be happy to look forward to (subtle hint Mr Southend Chairman). It's comfy, light, close to the pitch, atmospheric, has pubs nearby, ample parking, is easy to get to (when the Humber Bridge is working) and basically just looks cool. No surprise that its won loads of awards and has a four out of five rating on Trip Adviser (that was even the rating from a fan who saw his team get beat 6-0 there).

Oh yes, and Elton John has had a concert at the KC – is he doing the 92 as well? It seems every ground I research has had the Rocket Man plonk his ivories there (bar maybe just Roots Hall who to date have been restricted to a half-time squawk from Chico, Chesney Hawkes and the Cheeky Girls – thankfully not all at the same time).

The KC is so good it's difficult to know what else to say about the place. OK, I wouldn't have minded seeing us win but that's not Hull's fault, and even then it was when they were managed by Shrimper-elect Phil Brown. The tangoed one must find his current surroundings a little less plush, though I'm sure he considers posing with a Shrimp mascot rather than a Tiger one a more street-cred experience.

That will do – it was Southend's last visit to date to a Premier League ground, a small indication of the dire period that was just around the corner.

Basement Patience

64/92 - VALLEY PARADE, Bradford City 0 Southend United 2, League Two, Friday 27 August 2010

With Jim earning some cash at his holiday job it was time for son number three, Cameron, to step up to the mark. Footie was not really his thing so some form of inducement was required to secure his attendance. An elaborate weekender was hatched - then aged just 10 he was a bit more susceptible to bribery than he is now.

With the game on a Friday night a mid-morning set-off ensured we got to our camp site just north of Bradford in good time. Our three-man tent pitched (two made it seem more than two-thirds full), we looked enviously at the caravans with their electricity, plumbing and satellite dishes. We were definitely the Ronnie Corbetts of the camp site. However, we hadn't come all this way to plug in the vacuum, do the washing up and watch the tele – how daft would that be? We had more vital things in mind - we were in search of League Two soccer at a new pasture (well, I was).

We stopped off en-route at a bikers rally, attracted by the sound of a band playing from the back of a truck on the side of the road. Four hairy pot-bellies were thrashing out ACDC numbers to a large bearded ensemble surrounded by chrome super-chargers, all centred on an ancient pub doing a roaring trade. It all seemed a little surreal, and looking to the hills beyond the picture-postcard village we were in, I kept expecting to see James Herriot's little black Austin roaring around the bends to the All Creatures Great and Small theme tune. Instead, we got 'Highway to Hell' and other welcoming melodies wafting through the early summer's evening air.

Pre-match entertainment needs satisfied, it was off to Valley Parade. Floodlit, the place shone out like a warm beacon across the landscape it dominates, its situation amongst rows of terraced housing providing a real throw-back image to savour. Imaginary strains of the James Herriot theme turned to echoes of the Hovis ad in my clichéd mind, and in its own 'dark-brick chimney pot' way I thought it all looked beautiful. I must have been just standing still staring as Cameron nudged me out from my dreamy slumbers, him wanting to get the match over and done with so we might then catch some more ACDC on the way back.

Like Hillsborough, reference to Valley Parade cannot be made without mention of the tragedy of the past. I was living in Bristol when that awful fire swept through the main stand on that end of season May Day back in '85. The first I knew of what had happened was a call from Mum – "Oh thank goodness you're there, I know you have the tendency to go to some odd matches and I was worried you'd gone to Bradford" was her opening line. She was right, and with little else

239

to do I had even contemplated it given the promotion party the game against Lincoln had been set up to be, but lack of cash and the hope that I might see Southend there one day had kept me from making any serious plans about going. The YouTube video with John Helm's commentary makes for horrific viewing, and Martin Fletcher's recent book on the tragic events raises some searching questions to which I expect there will never be any definitive answers. 1985 was not that long ago yet it seems to be a different world to where we are now. But when I sit in the old wooden East Stand with its narrow gangways at Roots Hall today, without fail it always makes me think for a fleeting moment of the Bradford 56 and I make sure I know where our nearest exit points are. We paid homage to those that lost their lives some 25 years before at the memorial behind the main stand and I tried to explain to Cameron what had happened. "Why did those poor people not get out?" he asked. There was no satisfactory answer I could give.

We made our way to the corner of the East Stand where away fans were housed and looked out on a part-impressive, part hotchpotch vista. Valley Parade is now a stadium-in-waiting, holding itself in readiness for the day, whenever that might be, that a consistent enough period of success will attract someone with deep pockets to take the current North/West structure around the rest of the ground.

Before the match we were treated to Billy Bantam parading around the pitch, who, unlike any other club mascot I've seen elsewhere, declined to hide behind some furry façade and instead donned an ill-fitting Bradford kit and bowler hat. The result was not pretty, the late-middle aged gent before us looking rather sad, and then also a tad aggressive when the sweets he threw into the crowd came back at him with more venom and in greater quantity. Dress up like that though and you perhaps are asking for a bit of abuse – I can only imagine the verbal exchanges he would have had over the years with the Leeds ensemble. I note he was sacked in 2013 for losing some seven stone (due to diabetes) and no longer being fat enough for the role Bradford City wanted him to play – shame. Who ate all the pies? He didn't.

The match proved to be the Antony Grant show, our midfielder for once coming to the fore and putting on a display which showed what a talented player he was including capping things off with a goal. It is not often you see a player put his foot on the ball in League Two and create the time to find a searching pass without getting his legs put in plaster.

The ACDC wannabes were nowhere to be seen on the way back, I suspected that the local population had put a time constraint on their vocal excesses. But we had plenty left to do, and at the risk of turning into a tour guide do not dismiss a weekend sortie to the Bradford area without giving it some serious thought. Weather permitting, the surrounding countryside, if not perhaps Bradford itself, is stunning, but we focused our Saturday on two attractions. First was a visit to the National Coal Mining Museum near Wakefield, where you get shown underground by an ex-miner. Then we visited the National Media Museum in Bradford where, amongst lots of hands-on stuff, you can pick out your own archive films to watch in a private viewing booth (we settled on an old Thunderbirds episode as a compromise lying somewhere between an episode of Tomorrow's World and a Pokémon film). Both attractions were free too, which always helps.

The Media Museum proved to be a bit of a safe haven from what else was happening in the city that afternoon - busloads of coppers were trying to herd a handful of British National Party enthusiasts who had also chosen Bradford to have a day out. From our high view-point outside it looked like the police were having trouble keeping track of them all as sirens were constantly wailing all across Bradford in what appeared to be an alternative version of One Man and His Dog. I wondered whether the hairy biker ACDC fans might have had more success in rounding them all up.

65/92 – b2net STADIUM, Chesterfield 2 Southend United 1, League Two, Saturday 9 October 2010

On the back of a great weekend in Bradford, Cameron happily agreed to come with me to Chesterfield. It was not a great day.

Too cold for tenting, this was a day-trip with no frills unless you count a glance at the crooked spire. I felt mean – I should have invested in a B&B and we then could have explored some of the beautiful Derbyshire countryside. Instead, we had a quick look around the town centre market, a bite to eat and then it was off to the terribly dull b2net Stadium. Yes it's trim, but the only non-standard Lego bricks are the curved ones that form the roof lines of the two stands running along the length of the pitch. The rest conforms to a basic build plan which does little to enthuse or keep in that mysterious 'atmosphere' stuff us footie fans crave. As ever, filling in the corners would help, though I accept that new build budgets cannot always stretch that far and, as another one of those vital 'stocking-filler' clubs, Chesterfield are not necessarily going to have the cash to splash.

At the time, Chesterfield's new home was called the rather un-snappy 'b2net' (it is now known as the equally zesty 'Proact') – try creating a football chant about that and maintain some credibility. I understand the need to maximise revenue, and selling naming rights is one way of securing much-needed readies, but why not be a bit more creative? The old pad 'Saltergate' had a name that was affectionately unique and made it stand out from the rest, surely putting the sponsor name before whatever you really wanted to call the place would be a better idea and still help to raise revenue? If just giving your stadium's handle to whoever comes up with the most dosh is the way forward, I look forward to the day when the 'Lick a Chick' poultry restaurant in Nova Scotia starts to show a decent profit and turns to the English football scene as a way of advertising their expansion towards worldwide dominance.

For our visit the b2net was certainly looking pristine – the Shrimpers were only its seventh visitors for a competitive match and there wasn't a seat out of alignment, even the gents failed to catch the air on the stiff breeze blowing. Part of the credit for maintaining appearance, the match programme boasted, was down to Wilfred the Harris Hawk. His job was to chase the pigeons out, taking care not to scare the shit out of them until they had flown away from the stadium. The Southend defence weren't worried about the wildlife but instead got spooked by Scott Boden in the 90th minute and we went home defeated to cap off a bit of a disappointing day. It would be a more difficult sell to get Cameron to come to the next away trip.

66/92 – THE GREENHOUS MEADOW, Shrewsbury Town 1 Southend United 1, League Two, Saturday 20 November 2010

"Another northern sky, another motorway parade. Another day like this, whatever will be will be, and we will be, in Shrewsbury."

Any hardened Shrimper, 'Playing the Field' aficionado, or Alison Moyet fan, will recognise those lyrics as being the opening verse from the song 'Blue', Alf's tribute to supporting her beloved Southend.

In short, my take on the song is that only the committed (either voluntary or mentally) will travel to places like Shrewsbury – a reference to Carlisle might have been more apt but it doesn't span as well. You go not because you expect to see a stylish victory but because it's what you do. It's certainly what we all do on the Suffolk Shrimper bus, the five of us swelling the away contingent to around 400 who were now starting to get used to the realisation that the club was on a downer and in reality doing well just to keep going. Stockport had slumped out of the league following a period of success, and with the Championship parachute dosh and more besides gambled away on trying to get back to the second tier, Southend were now in real danger of following suit.

New manager Paul Sturrock had started pre-season with four registered professionals and a budget of bog-all to get a team together. Luggy had risen to the challenge and assembled a team of rejects, lower league journeymen, the slightly demented, youth team hopefuls, and his son. Somehow they had managed to get in to the 'win one, draw one, lose one' groove required to avoid the bottom two trapdoor positions, all with a 'win the ball and punt it hard' style. Games were predominately boring, but at a time when the Chairman was on first name terms with the HMRC debt collection service, we just felt relieved we still had a team to support.

I did a bit of a 'double-take' on entering the Greenhous Meadow; it looked exactly like the b2net right down to the colour scheme, except that there were no curved roof bits. The 'STFC' lettering on the seats though made me realise I had not pressed the wrong button on the Satnav. My co-92 mate Elton turned up at the Greenhous in June 2011 and then the b2net a year later – I wonder if he opened the latter by announcing "Good evening Shrewsbury" and then plonked out Alf's ditty on his Joanna? I'm getting confused myself now.

"A late point and I'll be laughing". On cue Antony Grant popped up to equalise in the 87th minute to follow the lyrics script.

67/92 - BROADHALL WAY, Stevenage 1 Southend United 1, League Two, Tuesday 23 November 2010

Broadhall used to be home to Stevenage Town and then Stevenage Athletic. Stevenage Borough then moved in during 1980 and subsequently changed their name to just plain 'Stevenage'. It's a place used to change, though whether the vast majority of the football supporting public has noticed anything different over the years, or even gives a toss, is debateable.

But arriving at Broadhall is a joy – a massive free car park is just over the main road from the ground and provides good access in and then out subject to the proviso that your car survives the craters within. What awaits you across the thoroughfare is a modest red and white mix of terrace and seats, but at least the away fans have a roof and the Shrimpers filled the 1,400 seats made available to us to enjoy a stanchion-free view.

It remains though a non-league ground but, on a non-league budget, in their first season in the Football League Stevenage were faring better than Southend. They were making their way with careful steps, battering sides in an un-compromising style where few goals were scored but even fewer goals conceded. With Luggy's 'lump it forward and hope' solution to bargain basement soccer it was not a game for the squeamish. The home team's biggest concern was the number of balls needed to keep the game flowing, as a bucket full made their way over the low level stands.

I was impressed with the small band of home fans that had positioned themselves in the middle opposite the main stand and who never shut up throughout the game - they were quite annoying. Big Bad Barry Corr, our new lower league lump up front, did give us something to cheer with an equaliser near the end, though it ended sourly with our full back Peter Gilbert being sent off to cap a refereeing performance that had proved wanting.

I noted from the match programme that Graham Poll had been booked as a guest speaker at Broadhall for the following month – the game could have done with his authoritative refereeing style. It would also have given us the opportunity to sing my favourite match officials ditty that I once heard the Chelsea fans blast out to a Sky TV viewing public before the watershed at Molineux: "Graham Poll, Graham Poll, is a fucking arsehole, Graham Poll." Even the good ones don't escape a sledging, no matter how unwarranted.

68/92 - PIRELLI STADIUM, Burton Albion 3 Southend United 1, League Two, Saturday 11 December 2010

The Pirelli's stand-out feature is that it's terraced on three sides, but that's about it. Small and tidy, it serves for tier three and below, anything above that will be a challenge, and as I write (February 2016) it seems that could be arriving soon enough.

Burton Albion have certainly been punching above their weight for a while now, and to date their Football League history has only seen an upward trend. Another test will be for their small fan base when a spell of bad form comes their way, as Burton will then need every one of their 2,500 hard core to stay with it to contribute towards the higher salaries a step up in fortune brings with it. I hope that anyone picking this book off the shelf in, say, 2026 is not thinking 'Blimey, Burton used to be in the 92?'

My Pirelli visit for the first ever Brewers v Shrimpers (a kind of lunchtime pub refreshment combo) fixture saw me seeing Southend's third away game in a row. With the absence of any home games in between, the faithful were looking to the previous two draws as a sign of the start of an upward trend. "There's only one Paul Sturrock" we chorused with tentative optimism, thankful that we didn't have to get our tongues around the Brewers more challenging "There's only one Paul Pesschisolido." However, what was to prove the theme of the season unfolded in just a few minutes: Luke Prosser prodded in an own goal to put the home team 2-0 up, Luggy's son came on from the bench, puny ponytail flapping in the breeze as he pulled one back and kissed the badge that paid the family wages, then Burton quickly snuffed out any flicker of hope with a third. Keeping above the Conference trap door and holding the taxman at bay was going to be the priority for now.

69/92 - DW STADIUM, Wigan Athletic 1 Aston Villa 2, Premier League, Tuesday 25 January 2011

After my sustained period of basement drudgery I felt it was time for an injection of quality, and seized on a chance to visit the Manchester office as a cost-effective means of feeding the need. Not far away from Mancland, Wigan were hosting Villa in an early relegation six-pointer Premiership clash, so it was off to the DW for a bit of evening entertainment before work the following day.

I'm not usually a fan of the 'four separate stands approach', but on a larger scale as at the DW it seems to work. Each single-tiered with a curved roof, the largesse of the stands somehow holds in the sound, and with an impressive circa 4,000 Villans filling most of the away end a reasonable noise was created. I noted from the programme that, on eight out of 14 previous home games that season, the home fans had seen over 4,000 visitors. This made Wigan possibly the number one place to visit in the country that season (though I suspected this was due to the more restricted away end capacities elsewhere than whatever else Wigan has to offer on a winter's evening).

When attending a match as a neutral there is the dilemma to ponder of which fan group to sit with. Seeing the Villans pour up the DW concourses made me feel it might be more fun to be with them, and so it proved. They sang throughout and I struck up a rapport with a guy next to me who, on seeing the Southend badge on my jacket, recalled how he had ran on the pitch with the Villa fans at Roots Hall in 1971, a game which I had also been at and I duly reminded him who had won that day. He was a bit of a character and, when Villa went one up he performed a ritual he had no doubt done countless times before by kissing the bald head of his mate. It made me more thankful than ever for my full crop on top. When Ashley Young won and scored a penalty his chum's dome first earned a polish and this was followed by two kisses as the spot-kick went in. His mate seemed happy enough. When Wigan pulled one back his mate's slap head secured a lick, which still left him unperturbed. I was hoping for a sending-off to see what ritual would be performed then, but sadly that was the end of the meaningful action for the night.

I had a short trip back to my hotel – it had been a good evening out and a reminder that being part of a crowd can often be as entertaining, if not more so, than the match you have come to see.

70/92 - CITY OF MANCHESTER STADIUM, Manchester City 3 Aston Villa 0, FA Cup Round Four, Wednesday 2 March 2011

Another visit to the Manchester office with a match the night before – my boss was starting to get a tad suspicious. And with a throwback to 1981 I now found myself once more a temporary member of the Villans in again attending in close succession their away fixtures. This time though I thought it would be good to experience dancing the Poznan, and so I elected to sit with the City fans.

Turning up at the Etihad (I'll use the current sponsor's name – it's just easier) is a world away from the old Maine Road – despite being close to the city centre you get a feeling of space which the stadium dominates without entirely filling. Go to it at night as I did and you are treated to a soft blue and white light extravaganza, giving a whole new take on the stereotypical but comforting moth-like attraction of four standard floodlight pylons. It was flashy, but I liked it.

251

There's just nothing modest about the Etihad – it is surrounded by eight giant circular blobs which act as access ramps to top tier seating, on one side there now sits a 6,000 capacity athletics venue, whilst all around there are buildings of all shapes and sizes which do every football function imaginable for the match day experience. It was all on a different solar system from my recent League Two ground-hopping experiences (and I had not yet been to Accrington Stanley).

When you go through the turnstile at the Etihad you don't enter the ground as such – instead you enter a giant concourse which you can walk around to shop, eat and be amused. I personally liked the height chart where I could look down on the life-sized image of a snood-loving Carlos Tevez and stare a moody looking Patrick Vieira in the eye until the first man blinked (it was a draw).

Feeling dominant I strode Gallagher-style in to the footballing arena which competed equally with the outside for the 'wow factor' prize. The only problem was that the ground was less than half full – as a result it was all a bit flat and, with City strolling to a 3-0 win, there was never anything in the game to enthuse even a slow bounce let alone a Poznan. For all of the glitz on offer, the actual 90 minutes proved only one thing – you need a decent match, or a decent atmosphere, or preferably both, to make the match day experience a good one.

Doing the 92 certainly gives you an interest in who goes in and out of the league, and given the geography I'd have been quite happy for Morecambe to go back from whence they came. But after three respectable seasons it looked as though they were in the Football League to stay. So it was off on a 600 mile round trip with four of my fellow Suffolk Shrimpers for Southend's inaugural trip to the Globe Arena.

Driving to a match is never a problem – the banter flows and there are new experiences and the match to look forward to. On arrival at the Globe an impressive façade greets you and we gained entry to the supporters' bar which was a very friendly place. It's on entering the ground that you get a bit of a deflated feeling – all very basic stuff, one seated main stand, open corners, two basic covered terraced ends, and then, all along one side, an 'open-to-the-elements' narrow 600 capacity terrace with a break in the middle which prevents any hope of the place having a decent atmosphere. I read that it cost £12 million to build which seems a tad expensive for something so basic holding only 6,500. Although I was not overly impressed with Chesterfield's b2net, on reflection that seems a comparative bargain at £13 million for something completed in the same year.

There were just 1,917 present and around 400 of them were Shrimpers – both sides played 'Route One' and the home team were distinctly more successful at it. The wind whipped around the place making every long ball a lottery and, at the final whistle, I gave thanks that I'd never have the need to go again. The journey back took forever, at around the 100 mile mark I looked to my side and in the rear view mirror, to see four sleeping Suffolk Shrimpers – thanks lads. Following a refreshment stop-off and a detour via Cambridge to push the snorers out of the car, I got home around 11 pm. Never again.

I was back three years later for one of those away-day 'promotion parties' I had vowed not to miss again – over 2,000 Shrimpers made it all the way up to the Globe wanting a win to secure automatic promotion out of the bottom rung so they could finally stop having to play Morecambe.

The ending was predictably rubbish – it was the ninth league defeat out of ten games against Morecambe and the other game was a dull home draw; Shrimpers clearly can't get over the cannibalistic issue in dealing with Shrimps.

But the day did provide one memorable sight. Courtesy of a burnt out building with the top floor completely obliterated and burnt rafters on show, the one remaining advertising hoarding of the now clearly defunct 'Megazone' still proudly declared 'The ultimate laser adventure'. Now, that at least must have been one hell of a game.

SINCIL BANK, Lincoln City 2 Southend United 1, League Two, Saturday 12 March 2011

There are some times where the match is just a distraction to the main event. The 'Thames Valley Royals' protest match I attended at the Manor Ground back in '83 was one, and Lincoln v Southend in 2011 was another. True, at that time we still held deluded hopes of sneaking in the play-offs, and The Imps were worried about the Conference trap door, but neither seemed realistic issues so this game became all about two men – Tilly and Brush.

For seven years the pair had reigned supreme at Roots Hall, yes the end had been woeful but the club's finances had as much to do with that as anything. And there is a not un-reasoned line of thought that says, with a few rare exceptions, staying in one place for too long is not good for football management. After leaving the Essex Riviera the duo had ended up in the Fenland bolt-hole of Lincoln, a seemingly unlikely home for two men whose footballing careers had been solely camped in Essex and London.

Shrimpers' opinion had been divided about their departure, though most certainly held a deep affection for what they had achieved and this led to well over 1,000 more than would have ordinarily turned up making the trip to Sincil Bank. Old faces not seen for years put in an appearance, though without any fuss we had the odd scenario whereby a whole coachload were quietly escorted out of the ground at half-time and shown on their way. Maybe the police had opened their file on old fan friends to renew acquaintances with.

There was a presentation to Tilly & Brush by Southend fans before the game and they appeared on the pitch before us to acknowledge the recognition that rang out from the massed away contingent. Luggy looked on a little bemused and the home fans made some attempt to disrupt things, but nothing put paid to the 'love in' which continued throughout the game.

On the day honours went to the Imps to take them to the virtual safety of mid-table. However, in the 11 games of the season that remained Lincoln gained just two more points, and amazingly ended the season relegated back to non-league circles where they still remain today. Tilly and Brush were soon on their way out of Sincil Bank and, to date, there has been no return for the pair to anything remotely resembling the period when they were feted as heroes at Roots Hall (a year at Canvey Island aside of course). The old lesson that you should enjoy the minute certainly rings true in the footie world and I think Tilly and Brush did so with theirs – they are both old pro's and realise that, whilst there is always hope, things might just never be that good again.

72/92 – CROWN GROUND, Accrington Stanley 3 Southend United 1, League Two, Tuesday 5 April 2011

There's something special about a trip to see 'the club that wouldn't die'. With some of the smaller clubs you get a feeling that it's all a bit manufactured and that someone with a bit of spare dosh has come in to pay some inflated wages and lay down some uniform concrete to build a new shed or two for a spot of temporary excitement. There is none of that unsustainable dreaming at Accrington – what you get is a 'warts 'n all' experience where the love for the game shines through.

On a wet Saturday in February our bus of Suffolk Shrimpers entered the outskirts of Accrington in good mood. This was the Southend's first ever visit to the Crown Ground and the mystique of the town it lived in was unfolding before us. Disused grey mills and dark back-to-back housing created an urban scene in a rainy mist which looked as if it had all been captured in a grainy black and white still back at the time the old Stanley had bitten the dust in the 60's.

The rain turned into a deluge as we approached the tumbledown ground and parked up, with rumours on social media starting to question whether the game was actually going to be played. We walked up to the away end and went straight through the gates on to the terrace – never a good sign. Players and match officials were looking at the middle of the pitch, as if staring at it might actually help – we were even allowed to walk on it ourselves. The pitch was just a bog in the middle, the only way the match could take place would be if the two managers agreed to dispense with the midfield and just lob hopeful balls from end to end – Luggy wouldn't have had an issue with that, but ultimately the only sensible outcome was to call the game off. We retreated to the local pub for a beer before turning for home. Oh joy.

Postponement meant a return on a Tuesday night in April – this time we got to stand on the open Coppice End terrace and witness yet another away defeat. The floodlights did at least bring out the place in full colour, though a few more bulbs in the surrounding streetlamps would have helped.

The piece-de-résistance of the Crown Ground is certainly the narrow Whinney Hill Terrace sitting at the bottom of a grass slope and running along one side of the pitch. Built for the vertically challenged, it is a part-terraced part-seated roofed stand which is all of three rows deep and with stanchions in the way of the view. Not only that, but above it towers a precarious perch for a camera ('TV gantry' I think would be over-doing it a bit) which trebles the height of the stand in that one place - I would not want to be manning a camera up there in anything more than a force four. It all helps feed the image though of days before common sense exploded in to the world of football stadia - I just hope they don't sanitise the place too much.

A total of 1,010 miles over the two trips to see what turned out to be a lacklustre defeat, but we all viewed it as being an experience to savour.

73/92 – BROADFIELD STADIUM, Crawley Town 3 Southend United 0, League Two, Tuesday 16 August 2011

The Broadfield is one of that increasing band of newish 'ok for a National League ground' places that a number of League One and Two clubs have nowadays, a reflection of the success of the Football League's feeder system in pushing up teams up the ladder and who then find they have a head for heights.

Morecambe, Burton and Stevenage are a few examples of many all cut from a similar cloth, and the feeling of déjà vu grows as you hop around the lower reaches of the 92. But there again, if looking to push on within a sensible budget, you perhaps wouldn't start off with the distinctly impractical blue-prints that the good folk of Tranmere, Lincoln, Grimsby and Wrexham had from their yester-year league days. Variety is the spice of life – but it's easier to be uniform.

Anyway, to use a term I'm conscious of having mentioned more than once already, Broadfield is 'neat'. That doesn't mean it's boring, it's just a bit, well, safe ..... and OK maybe a smidgen on the dull side. I did quite like the way the two terraced (and covered) ends curve at the corners into the main West Stand, that shows a bit of thought lacking from the similar builds elsewhere. And like Burton etc., one nicety of the new breed of budget-grounds is that away fans are afforded equality with the home tribe, i.e. they have a roof. Put a thousand or so Shrimpers in a small covered stand and the noise level ratchets up a bit too, which with that early season August optimism made it all quite a good experience .... until the middle of the second half when Crawley banged in three in quick succession and gave us a reality-check on how far the club had gone (downwards) in the preceding 18 months or so.

After going one down Luggy had put on our resident fruit-cake Bilel Mohsni to try and recover things. He got booked within two minutes and ended up being a distraction for his team mates who became preoccupied in trying to prevent him getting sent off. A walking time-bomb, you stood no chance of predicting what Bilel would do during a match. A defender-come-emergency-striker who often ended up in midfield because he kept forgetting the role he had been given, Bilel was more than capable of scoring a 35 yarder, bagging a hatrick or putting in a last minute flying tackle to save the day, and he did all of that in his time as a Shrimper. However, he also stomped his feet, lost concentration to allow the opposition easy goals, and frequently got booked or sent off. His off-field antics were equally 'Jekyll and Hyde', and after rejecting bids for him in his 'good spells' he was ultimately released on a 'free' to end up at Ibrox where, by all accounts, a similar story unfolded.

Characters like Bilel are increasingly rare, but every club has one from time to time. In Crawley's case it was their manager Steve Evans who added that 'little something extra' – I've seen him rant and rave on the touchline to the extent that his deplorable language nearly caused a fan riot behind him. But on the other hand there is no denying he has the passion to drive a club forward. He just needs to rein things in and turn down the volume a bit (OK, quite a bit).

74/92 – EMIRATES STADIUM, Arsenal 2 Sunderland 1, Premier League, Sunday 16 October 2011

There is an advert for a certain brand of lager which claims that they '... don't do flatmates, but if they did ....' You know the one, it's where they walk through some French Doors on to a balcony overlooking a magnificent floodlit stadium. Well, Arsenal do stadiums like that.

My patience was running out waiting for Southend to get promoted to the Premier League so I could go to the Emirates. Also, we were usually out of the cup competitions by the time Arsenal entered the draw, so I needed to find another opportunity to visit. It came courtesy of a prized corporate hospitality invite to see the Gunners from the comfort of an Executive Box.

Over the years I've not been deluged with the corporate hostility stuff, and these days it seems there's a red-tape 'bribery question' to answer if you get offered something which makes it all feel a bit

261

'dirty'. It's all become rather silly - business contacts still need to be made to make the wheels go round. From what I have experienced, the corporate stuff works if there's a small group - the one-on-one stuff tends to be a bit heavy, and if it's too big a do folk can get side-lined. The quality of the venue is important too, but it's the company you are in that's key. For my trip to the Emirates everything was just perfect.

Meeting my host Steve outside by a statuesque Tony Adams, we made our way up to our area for the afternoon inside the stadium's glass façade via an escalator (at Roots Hall we are lucky if the stairs work), taking us through bar and restaurant facilities to our plush box with its own bar, plenty of room to move around, and sliding doors to our padded seats immediately outside. The food was great, the banter terrific and the views of the stadium just like the lager ad. It just needed a decent match between Wenger's League of Nations and Bruce's Bashers.

Cue Mr Robin Van Persie. The prolific Dutchman took less than a minute to slide one in from the edge of the box, dominated throughout, kept his tempo up, missed a hatful of other chances, and then curled in the winner from a free-kick as the game was coming to a close. At the time he was at the height of his game, he had everything including a fan base that adored him and a squad around him that was packed with skill and verve. RVP declared in the programme "I am committed to Arsenal, I am the captain." At the end of the season he was on his way – a big shame.

I was fortunate to repeat the experience twice more in the year that followed, including once for an evening game when the orchestrated bouncing of the Dortmund fans provided a show of their own which lit up the Emirates with their passion. If every ground and match experience was perfect it would be boring so I wouldn't want every ground to be like the Emirates ...... probably.

75/92 - DEEPDALE, Preston North End 0 Southend United 0, FA Cup Round One, Saturday 12 November 2011

A trip to Deepdale feels like it should be a trip back in time, and pre 1995 it was – vast swathes of terracing half-covered by roofing and an iconic West Stand running along one side of the pitch which had more supports than an OAP marathon.

It took 13 years to wipe out the past, and today on the same site is a modern ground providing unhindered views from every seat. Just like Notts County's Meadow Lane, Deepdale provides proof that a ground can be completely revamped without the need to up-sticks.

Bygone days have not totally been forgotten though – three of the stands are named after ex-hero's and the other pays homage to the whole of the 'Invincibles' team of 1888/89. Best of all is 'The Splash', a water feature sculpture of Sir Tom Finney which replicates with spectacular accuracy a 1956 Sports Photograph of the Year of Sir Tom sliding on a waterlogged Stamford Bridge pitch. It really is a breath-taking piece of work which helps to remind all visitors today of an era long gone, and fittingly Sir Tom himself unveiled it. For our FA Cup visit in 2011 I joined a queue of people wanting to have their picture taken there, something I wouldn't have bothered with had I visited Craven Cottage at the time they had their embarrassing monument to Michael Jackson in situ.

Sir Tom was famously a one-club man, notching up over 400 appearances from the age of 24 after he had more than 'done his bit' in WWII. It took a bit of research to come up with anyone who had achieved comparable 'one club' status at Southend – I could cheat and name a few who only lasted a handful of games before being turfed-out to end their career before it had started. But a true one-clubber must surely have done a regular first team 10 year plus stint to qualify. I suspect I will be corrected by some avid anorak, but the only one I can come up with is Sandy Anderson who notched up 483 appearances between 1950 and 1962. Sandy was a full back during Sir Tom's era – I wonder if he ever came up against the Preston Plumber?

76/92 - KINGSMEADOW, AFC Wimbledon 1 Southend United 4, League Two, Saturday 31 December 2011

They had finally done it. After the hijack by Winkleman in 2002, the real Dons were back in the Football League nine years later – a remarkable achievement.

Starting in tier nine, they slogged their way through the Combined Counties Premier Division, the Isthmian League First Division, the Isthmian League Premier Division, the Conference South and the Conference Premier before finally getting in to League Two thanks to a penalty shoot-out play-off win against Luton. I bet that was some celebration – I would love to have a play list for the songs they would have sung afterwards in the dressing room.

The match programme for the New Year's Eve match put the 1988 FA Cup win at the top of the honours list, harked back to 1897 for winning the Clapham League, had two pages on past Dons v Shrimpers matches, covered in depth the players common between the two clubs, looked back at events 20 years ago, and had a page on the recollections of a fan of some 40 years standing. These were not the ramblings of a club formed in 2002, it was all about a club who had a long and proud history.

Kingsmeadow, still the home of Kingstonian FC, is looked on by Wimbledon as a temporary residence. Oddly for a club who often struggled to get 4,000 in the

Premier League when the away support was thin, their current abode is not really big enough as it is at or near its 4,850 capacity for pretty much every match. It is not a palace, but for now it does as home, and the four tiny stands (half seated, half terraced) look good with the place brim full.

The away allocation is naturally limited but somehow thanks to the good folks of Shrimperzone I managed to accumulate four of the 700 tickets available, and a nephew and niece joined Jim and myself for a little jaunt from our New Year's Eve family stop-over in London. Coming back from an early Jack Midson strike, Southend hit four to give us a great end to the year and afforded my young relatives the opportunity to see their Uncle dance. It also put Luggy's lads up in to the automatic promotion spots - heady days indeed, albeit short lived. If Southend United ever ceased to exist and I lived in London then, maybe because of 2002, I think I'd be a Wimbledon fan. Long live the Wombles.

MUNICIPAL STADIUM POZNAN, Italy 2 Republic of Ireland 0, Euro 2012 Finals Group Stage, 18 June 2012

Most readers of this book will have experienced a shiver or two down their spine at some football event or other and I don't mean when freezing your nuts off at a League Two fixture in the January sleet. There are just some times when everything comes together in an often random moment of perfect emotion.

It was time for another overseas trip. Jon, Joe (replacing Paul from the German expedition six years before), Darren and I had plotted this one some months in advance. We quickly realised that Ukraine was a bit of a sod to get to and possibly not that hospitable, so the unanimous decision was to become honorary Irishmen for a five night trip to Poland with a stop-over in Dortmund on the way there and in Leipzig on the way back. I even bought a green shirt, my 1982 Argyle one proving to be a little tight around the waist with its clingy nylon some 30 years on.

Stressed by its previous autobahn experience my Citroen had long since given up on life so its replacement, a more robust Ford Galaxy, did the job instead. Dortmund via Calais proved to be a breeze, and we were impressed with the fanzone set up in the city centre (all very organised as you would expect). The run to Poznan was a bit harder – long roads with nothing to look at, relief was evident on reaching the Carlsberg Fan Camp in Poznan.

On arrival for our two day stay we collected our breakfast vouchers (for a ham roll and two pints of lager) and pitched tents. The place was heaving, hot and full of green – sleep wasn't going to be easy. We escaped to the first pub we could see as quickly as we could, had a curry and learned that, somewhat predictably, Poznan had already run out of Guinness but that the lager was plentiful (a self-interested key sponsor might have had something to do with that).

It was in the local fanzone that we came across a tout selling tickets – taking a bit of a risk we decided to go for it when he offered us four at face value, it seemed too good to be true but this was a one-off so we took a chance. Well, three of us were keen - Darren was not one to make a snap decision but that in a way made it more fun, the look on his face as he parted with a wedge of Euro's to a complete stranger who then just disappeared was priceless.

After several jars we returned late to the campsite - the whole place was just a green drinking fest, it was impossible to keep pace with it all so we turned in around 2 am with the place still partying at full volume. Two hours and no sleep later there was a crash at the tent next door as two Paddy's unsuccessfully tried to enter it, gave up and decided instead to do renditions of every ditty they knew from the Irish song book interspersed with re-enactments of scenes from Father Ted. I gave up, got up and paid a visit to one of the army of portaloos. Each was occupied, but finally when a door opened the Paddy coming out on seeing me held up his glass and said "Ah, 'oim was just 'aving a cheeky po'int". The whole place was a mad house.

A couple of hours later the sun rose and, like in Germany six years before, started to blast like a furnace. Deciding not even to look in to (or get close enough to smell) the communal wash area, I walked head down in to a local hotel and used their facilities to freshen up - it was going to be a long day and I needed to at least start it in reasonable shape.

We consumed our free 'breakfast' and settled down in a decent looking pub by around 10 am - it was already rammed but we got a table outside in the shade and spent a thoroughly enjoyable few hours eating and drinking to the accompaniment of Irish singing and dancing. From time to time different groups would wander in and get a few songs going, do a conga and then disappear. It was a happy place.

Around mid-afternoon we thought we should move on, so took the short walk to Poznan Square - it was just a heated sea of green again. I later heard that there were a reported 20,000 Irish in just that area alone, and to hear "The Fields of Athenry" blast out from that mellowed choir was my 'shiver down the spine' moment. They then broke out into "Roy Keane is a cabbage" just in case anyone got too tearful.

Via a couple more bars we then took the long walk to the stadium and at this point even spotted the odd Italian. There was never a hint of trouble throughout - one of the many reasons that made us think we had made the right choice in not going to Ukraine. Entry to the ground was via three different check-points, and though each time we held our breath, the tickets proved to be valid. We had great seats amongst our green friends and sang with them throughout – qualification for the next stage was a lost cause but that just didn't seem to matter.

A more conventional end to the night (less beer more sleep) set us up for the next stage - a bit of a departure from what had gone before but we were unanimous in thinking it wouldn't seem right in going to all the way to Poland, not an everyday destination, without visiting Auschwitz.

Our stop-off point before going to the camp the day after was Katowice, not on the tourist trail (as proved by the beer being 75% cheaper), but after the campsite the luxury of a clean bed in a hotel with a pool was something to savour - as was a more conventional breakfast the following morning.

Anything to describe the horrors of the concentration camp just seem inadequate, it was all harrowing but nevertheless an experience to remember for very different reasons to the rest of the trip. We were though at one point treated to the image of Darren, dragging behind a bit, running in the heat to get the coach as it was leaving one part of the concentration camp to go back to main area. I'm not sure if he has forgiven us for that yet. We then had an evening drive to a hotel stop-off at Leipzig and then a very long drive back home the following day.

It had all been another great experience centred around the 'excuse' of a football match. The chorus of the Fields of Athenry also seemed to be pertinent to what followed the football part:

Low lie the Fields of Athenry
Where once we watched the small free birds fly.
Our love was on the wing we had dreams and songs to
sing
It's so lonely 'round the Fields of Athenry.

WHADDON ROAD, Cheltenham Town 1 Southend United 3, League Two, Saturday 15 September 2012

This was my anorak visit. I'd been to Whaddon Road in the mid '80's to see a non-league match. However, would that count for the 92? A bit like painting behind a radiator even though you might never notice, I didn't want to risk the feeling of not completing the job, so it was off to Cheltenham for a day at the footie. It was also early enough in the season to still have some optimism that this could be our year.

Whaddon Road is another of those 'made for the lower leagues' homes with a circa 7,000 capacity. The early '60's main stand sticks out as a bit of an untidy link to the past whilst everything else is clean, low and red. Away fans are given the newest and seated stand at one end which has a clear Perspex roof – it was like being in a conservatory (with around 300 fans blowing hot air).

The match programme had a great picture of a packed main stand from 1934 - it clearly shows at least 200 smiling faces but the interesting thing was that over 98% looked as though they were over age 40 (and

271

most much older than that). Look around your team's ground today and you don't have to be in the Family Stand to see a much younger population. Just an isolated example maybe, but perhaps a positive sign that the future fan base of our clubs is in as good a shape as it has been for a long time.

We had in our little Suffolk Shrimper band for this game Andy's grandson, who was still back then a babe in arms – I'm not sure what he thought or whether he will ultimately come back at his own behest, but he certainly brought us some luck as we came back from an early Cheltenham strike to win and give us all a little bit of optimism for the season ahead.

A quick footnote: the trend as we all know is to sell the naming rights of your ground for sponsorship dosh. Cheltenham's home is currently known as the 'World of Smile Stadium' after signing a deal with a local furniture store. I don't know whether to smirk or grimace.

77/92 - NEW YORK STADIUM, Rotherham United 0 Southend United 3, League Two, Saturday 13 October 2012

It was time to see that nice man Mr Evans again. Except we couldn't and instead were very shocked to hear that Rotherham's new manager had been given a six match ban by the FA after they found him guilty of "using abusive and insulting words and behaviour" towards a female member of an opponent's staff (at a game where five players had been sent off after a post-match dressing room brawl). Nice.

Never mind, we parked up but then ran straight in to a march by the English Defence League. The rally passed by, surrounded by mounted police. There were coppers everywhere, there literally seemed to be hundreds, many in full riot gear, lurking in groups at various places in the town centre and sitting in vans up side streets; you'd have thought it was Leeds United in town. The overtime bill must have been horrendous.

With all the pubs closed due to the rally (bar one which did not look too hospitable) our little group of Suffolk Shrimpers instead decided to take a look at Rotherham's old pad, Millmoor. Bordered by scrapyards, wasteland and a railway track, the setting was not exactly idyllic. A passing steward on his way to the match warned us against spending too much time in the area which he added had been a 'hang out' place for those involved in a recent abuse scandal. We gave up on the Rotherham tourist trail and instead made for the sanctity of the New York Stadium.

Named after the area it was built on with an idea that this might then attract investors from the Big Apple (hmmm, I suspect if Donald Trump saw Rotherham he'd build a wall around it), Rotherham's new pad looked ....great. OK, it was bordered by a railway track and a bit of a scummy looking river, but from what we had seen (maybe we had missed the best bits)

Rotherham was not blessed with a wide choice of picturesque backdrops.

A red and grey bowl, it stood out like a shiny new penny challenging the grubby change all around it trying to scratch its surface. Inside it was, well, ideal. There was lots of club red bathed in sunlight let through by a partially clear roof. The 12,000 capacity meant it would not look too silly when only the hard core support turned up, but we were told there was also room for expansion if an American thinking he was really in New York ever wanted to throw some dollars at it.

A decent Shrimpers turnout (on the new ground hunt) found the acoustics good and for once a polished display saw us romp it. Luverly jubberly, time to get all excited about promotion, after all it was mid-October and we were 10th. But the most joyful moment? Finding the car still in one piece where we'd parked it.

78/92 - GIGG LANE, Bury 1 Southend United 1, FA Cup Round 2, FA Cup Round Two, Saturday 1 December 2012

Ah the FA Cup, source of foolish hope, days out to places not normally on the menu, balloons, inflatable bananas, last minute drama, and the annual chance, if you are quick enough, (i.e. before kick-off in the first round) to ironically sing "Que Sera Sera".

It's a competition for the away fan, a chance to galvanise the troops and pretend to be the Billy Big Boys at outposts like Harlow and Telford and look down on the Ronnie Corbetts, or queue in the club car park swapping stories of years gone by with your new found mates in front and behind you for the next five hours all for the chance of getting a ticket for a trip to Chelsea.

Days gone by have seen me suffer the whole range of emotions, big build-ups only for it all to go flat, fan convoys up north with streamers trailing, or last minute goals under snowy lights to grab the glory and go mental. The FA Cup has something that no other competition can provide in such quantity – memories. In 2012 the opportunity it conjured for me was the chance to lay a ghost to rest, or more accurately, skewer a regret.

Scroll back to the last away game of the season in 1991, and 1,500 Shrimpers minus me travelled up to Gigg Lane hoping for new history to be made and to end 85 years of lower league soccer. A man down in the first half, it all looked unlikely until Ian Benjamin, back to goal and in the box, turned and slotted one home to send us up into the second tier. Players and fans celebrated wildly together, clinging on to their respective sides of the security fence and embracing as one. An ordinary team with a bit of guile and a manager who stood firm when the going got tough had finally cut the cord, it was bye-bye Aldershot hello

Newcastle. For the following 20 years the "Who put the ball in the Bury net, Ian Benjamin" ditty had been sung at regular intervals by the Southend faithful. This just got progressively more annoying as it kept bringing to the surface a memory of not being there and instead of trying to unsuccessfully keep hold of a signal from the Essex Radio commentary from deepest Suffolk. It was arguably Southend's most historic ever moment, one which I had spent in our spare room with the radio held mid-way in the air near the window as that got the best of a wavering signal.

We had played at Bury since but I'd always avoided the place. However, getting close to the 92 meant it had to be done sometime and maybe the FA Cup provided that 'special moment' opportunity to create a new memory. Bury had last won the Cup in 1903 so were not exactly in a rich vein of form – could this be our year instead?

Gigg Lane is an 'OK' place to visit, a 'Taylor-report' patched-up ground that is showing some signs of wear and tear but which at least provides shelter for all from the Manc rain. We sat in the Manchester Road End; old boys out for a cup run away-day were out in force and celebrating their middle-aged day of freedom by having too many beers and Dad-dancing their way through the first-half. But the game itself never took-off in any meaningful way; the Dads got weary from their exertions and quietened down by nodding off and dreaming of carpet slippers. The match ended in a tame draw and, as the final whistle went, a chorus broke out from the back – "Who put the ball in the Bury net, Ian Benjamin." Bollocks.

79/92 – HIGHBURY STADIUM, Fleetwood 0 Southend United 0, League Two, Saturday 8 December 2012

Nearly three and a half decades had passed since my last club coach trip. Back in '78 it had been a ramshackled old shell stripped of any comfort that had puffed its way from Benfleet to Wimbledon to take a bus load of bomber-jackets on an afternoon out. In 2012, and mindful of the slog up to Morecambe, the Suffolk Shrimper clan decided to let the coach take the strain, 52 seats of air conditioned luxury with a TV and bog, full of men, women and children all on a well behaved day out.

Living in Suffolk there was a distinct disadvantage of taking this option, namely the hour long car dash to the glamour town of Pitsea to get to the coach in time for a 7.00 am departure time. It was also a bit of a plod – back in '78 regulations, if they existed, seemed, well, a bit lax, the objective being to get in as fast as possible and get back quicker with as many of those that had been on the journey out as possible. In 2012 we were seat-belted in, head-counted, reminded of safety procedures, told to put our gas canisters and flares in the receptacle provided, anyone with an ailment had to declare it to the co-ordinator, and the driver stuck to a 60 mph motorway maximum in fear of his spy in the cab. On the 275 mile trip up I think we overtook just four times and three of those were breakdowns on the hard shoulder. But it was a happy coach – crisps, sweets and sweaty cheese sarnies were regularly passed around, and the banter flowed.

My lift to Pitsea and the coach meant a beer or two was allowed, and on arrival we found a decent pub, also the focus of many of the healthy contingent of 500 plus Shrimpers on our virgin trip to another team with a cod fetish. The Fleetwood mascot has to be mentioned - it is the scariest thing on the football circuit outside of Scunthorpe.

With its gob permanently fixed open on the lookout for crustaceans, Captain Cod moved with an odd lopsided gait towards the away end with its heavy head sat on top of a shrugged-shouldered volunteer decked out in Fleetwood kit and with turquoise legs. Sammy the Shrimp had heeded advice to stay at home, the rest of us just watched in silence until it had safely passed by to go and worry a school party. When it was out of earshot at the other end of the curvy new main stand that dominates an otherwise distinctly tier-eight ground, we mustered a "What the fucking hell was that?" chorus just to show that we were hard southerners.

On the pitch, during the 90 minutes nothing of note happened as if to mock our marathon trip 'oop north'. However, one of our lady coach passengers was feted as a hero on the way back home for being kicked out of the ground for swearing.

After a services stop-off at around 8 pm, where we declined a fight with some Chelsea fans on the grounds of it being too late in the day, the coach settled down to a gentle snore all the way back to Essex. Andy dropped me off at home in Suffolk around midnight, no "hello dear it's time to switch Match of the Day on" for me, after a 19 hour day out at the footie it was straight to bed to dream of turquoise cod.

80/92 - BOOTHAM CRESCENT, York City 2 Southend United 1, League Two, Saturday 20 April 2013

The season had petered out in a series of mostly low-scoring dismal route-one draws, with 11th place being our final resting place. But before then the final away game offered up a chance to meet with old Uni mates for a weekender in York.

I suspect the prospect of Minster Men v Shrimpers wasn't the key attraction for Brian the Tranny fan and Craig the Sky Blue, indeed Brian holed up in the bookies whilst the match was on, but York is a good place for a few jars. Pubs of all sorts adorn Dickensian streets, and fellow Shrimpers with the same idea were found in various corners.

But Bootham Crescent was the reason we were there so Craig and I somewhat reluctantly left the comfort of a watering hole to soak up some sunshine on one of those lovely open-ended terraces that really come in to their own on oh, maybe two times a year. Indeed, it was quite warm - Biffo the Bear and Top Cat were looking distinctly uncomfortable in their traditional end of season fancy dress fur in the queue for the Grosvenor Road End. Biffo was also scratching far too much for my liking.

Bootham Crescent is the Maine Road of League Two – its approach takes you back to a bygone era where folk popped straight out of their front door, jollied along a neighbouring street or two and breezed up to the turnstile. Unlike the now defunct Maine Road though, it is not a place that has ever seen major investment. Charity appeals and sponsored marathon runs are just some of the many ways that has led to add this bit and that to the ground over the years, which will tell you that nothing too ambitious has ever been attempted. The whole place is stuck in a pre-Taylor Report time-warp, but is fascinating for it - even the latest key addition (now 25 years old), the David Longhurst Stand (the home end), has a low-budget feel about it made unique by the heavy advertising hoardings hanging from its low roof. I suspect our long high ball tactics of the day reduced viewing time significantly for those in it.

For some time now a new ground for York has been 'only a season away', but the date for the turning of the first sod keeps getting put back. Bootham Crescent was built in just four months in 1932, I would imagine it will take longer for the new home to be completed once the JCB's are finally fired up, but if you haven't yet been to 'BC' I suggest you do it soon to err on the side of caution. Once the place is gone I doubt you will ever see the like of it again. Oh, and if you do stand on the away terrace, keep an eye out for Biffo's costume, it got discarded as the temperature rose further and you might even be glad of it on a January night (but don't expect it to pass the sniff test, and examine it for wildlife first).

Upping the Anti

81/92 - MADEJESKI STADIUM, Reading 1 Leeds United 0, Championship, Wednesday 18 September 2013

This one was a bit of an operation and requires some explanation, which I only repeat to demonstrate the lengths we sometimes go to get a match in.

I 'needed' to go to Reading – well, as much as anyone ever really needs to I suppose. Elm Park had long since bitten the dust so a visit to their new (ish) 'ground for the Premiership' was required to tick it off the 92 list. However, Reading in their new abode were no longer 'really crap' so, unless I got lucky with a cup draw, they were never going to play Southend. A trip to the Madejeski to see a match as a neutral on my tod didn't appeal, but 40 plus years of footie following has given me one ability - it has made me proficient in finding an excuse to be anywhere in England in circumstances that suit.

One of my work clients had recently given up the world of finance in his mid-50's and opted for a life of doing, well, very little it seems. Apart that is from following Leeds United and, as a side-line, completing the 92 (which he did just before me in March 2016 at, of all places, Roots Hall). This hedonistic lifestyle has also allowed David to write a book each year about his

Leeds-watching which, with every season (he is now on book number five), paints an increasingly dejected picture of his team's failure to get to the league he feels they belong (our opinions are divided on which one that is). Anyway, for a trustee interview procedure (I promise to spare you the details on that) I needed someone to join me on the interview panel with relevant experience - David fitted the bill. I had to provide him with an incentive though, and came up with the idea of a fully expensed night's stay in London before the interviews which would allow him to see his team at Reading without a long trip back oop North immediately after the match. He bought it.

That was just one part of the puzzle - I now needed the four trustee candidates and two other interviewers to agree to hold the sessions the day after the Reading game. As all were from different parts of the country and different walks of life it wasn't going to be easy, but I got lucky and with a bit of 'fixing' here and there I set everything up. All in all I had organised seven people's lives for a day, reserved hotels, arranged travel, booked a meeting room and sorted catering, just so I could have someone to go to Reading with me. I suspect that's a bit sad really, but hey-ho.

I had also arranged a meeting for the morning of the match so I would already be in London for onward travel to Berkshire. For once I cut my waffling to the bone so the meeting ended by early afternoon. I then dumped my bags in the hotel and caught the train to meet David.

A wander through darkest Reading saw us roll up to a pub full of Leeds fans; David was more experienced at handling such crowds than me and quickly returned from the bar with two pints each to cut down on bar queuing time, and we then settled down with his Leeds mates. The time passed quickly - footie banter is the same whoever you support, either hopelessly optimistic or full of gloom. There was though that hint of 'we are a Premier League club so why are we not in it?' feel to the conversational mood - a question Leeds have now been asking since 2004. Having arrived at Reading Railway Station at around 4.30 pm we didn't get to the ground until kick-off. Like most of the Leeds fans I found it difficult to leave the pub.

For a mid-week match over 200 miles from Leeds, I was impressed - the away end was packed. I was also impressed with the Madejeski – curvy, closed-in, close to the pitch and very blue; it looked good and sounded good. The Leeds fans dominated with deep-voiced simple stuff that all 3,268 joined in with - the home fans appeared just to listen, knowing they couldn't really compete. Well, not until the sixth minute of injury time when those still left in the stadium finally did spark into life as Le Fondre nodded home the only goal of the game. That quietened the away fans, though David's talk on the train back to London was still of plans for the Premier League .... I now needed to get him equally enthusiastic for the long day of pensions meetings to follow.

82/92 - AMEX STADIUM, Brighton & Hove Albion 1 Leeds United 0, Championship, Tuesday 11 February 2014

It had been a good run and the Amex made it a round dozen, but this was to be the last on my 92 list that just 'happened' to fit in with work - a year later I resigned from office life after 31 years to tick the biggest one yet off my bucket list, namely to become a self-employed gardener. No corporate hospitality or trips to foreign towns oop north in the world of digging and mowing, though on the plus side no red tape to wade through to organise a trip whenever I wanted.

The Goldstone had been my first ever away trip back in '74 but since then I'd avoided seeing the Seagulls in their temporary homes at Priestfield (on the basis that I didn't like it much) and The Withdean (as I never had strong enough binoculars to view the match from the away end). But by 2008 Brighton had saved enough for a deposit on a home of their own, and in 2011 finally celebrated moving out of the rental sector to become owner-occupiers once more.

I had enjoyed my Reading meet-up with my new-found Leeds pals and, given the need for a work meeting not far away, saw the opportunity to do it again for an evening match at the Amex. The advice was to park up in the town and then catch a train to the ground – in a world where car is king Brighton discourages vehicle use except for the chairman, a few other cronies, and anyone willing to pay £15 to park 10 minutes away at the nearby university; stuff that. In between parking and train there was the obligatory pub meet-up, David sourcing one off the beaten track away from the Leeds masses who this time had a 520 mile round mid-week trip and so only numbered 2,000 or so.

Letting the train take the strain for the four miles from Brighton Central is, actually, a bit of a pain. We had left plenty of time, but the concourse was packed and it took far too long to finally get a rammed-to-the-rafters carriage. I thought of the chairman driving to his car bay down clear streets where no one else could afford to be.

Once there though you can't help but be impressed by the place – it nestles in a valley all bright and shiny, the floodlit oval blue and white bowl seemingly shouting out to the Seagulls 'This was worth waiting for wasn't it?' The flying variety though isn't allowed to get anywhere near – like their feathered mates at the b2net they are regularly scared shitless by a hawk on the club's payroll.

Clubs today seem to think they need to conjure up ever-increasing ways of providing something different for their fans. A new one on me was something I noticed from the club programme which proclaimed "We are now taking bookings for memorial internments at the Amex Stadium". Blimey, I had thought things were on the up for the Albion.

The Amex, like the Madejeski, is a vision in blue but takes it all to a higher level - a bigger capacity (having already been expanded since its 2011 birth), more curvy white bits, better lit, a bigger roof ...... Brighton fans must think that all of their play-offs have come at once. They just need to avoid getting too hyped up and so dodge a premature entry in to the memorial garden.

The match was almost a mirror image of the one at the Madejeski; Leeds fans stood up, out-sang the home fans throughout, their team did bog-all, and they lost 1-0. The slight difference was that the goal came after only 64 minutes, but for a match at the Amex this is almost full-time. Hordes of Brighton fans started to leave not long after and for once the "Is there a fire drill?" chant from the Leeds tribe seemed to be a genuine question. I then twigged what was happening - to avoid the massive queue for the train that a 27,000 crowd would cause the locals were exiting early to ensure they got home before it was time to get up and go to work.

Getting progressively more nervous about it and with the match hardly setting any pulses racing, after 80 minutes I decided to join them. I spoke to some locals at the station - they were adamant that leaving early was the only sensible option. The Amex is great, but investing in adequate transport for those who do not have a reserved car bay in front of the main stand must surely be high on the 'needs list' for this otherwise top-notch stadium.

83/92 - SPOTLAND, Rochdale 0 Southend United 3, League Two, Friday 18 April 2014

In an un-predictable world it is reassuring to know that some things can be relied upon. Buy a '90's compilation album and "Sit Down" by James will be on the track list, watch a man fishing on the beach and you will never see him catch anything, see a child with a cut knee and you'll know the scab will be picked well before it should fall off, buy a sledge based on the weather forecast and it will rain. Rochdale FC is equally reassuring – they never win anything.

You know that no matter how bad a run your team are on it can't be as bad as that suffered by Dale fans in the basement division from 1921 to 1969 and then from 1974 to 2010. It's comforting to have such thoughts to fall back on.

But just think about how they would feel when something finally does go right - they would surely go ballistic, dance naked 'til they drop, and shout 'eureka' from the top of the highest mill. When the Suffolk Shrimper bus arrived in Greater Manchester on Good Friday 2014, the locals were daring to dream (thankfully still fully clothed).

With four games to go, Rochdale were a mere point behind chart-toppers Scunthorpe (it was a heady season for glamour) and just a win away from securing automatic promotion. However, their fear of silverware was starting to bite - two goalless draws and a three goal spanking by moribund Mansfield had seen them fall from the top spot just as the end was in sight. The visit of Brown's Barmy Army still though saw the second highest league home crowd of the season gather at Spotland in anticipation of a party – 3,884. Club mascot, Desmond the Dragon, was positively hyper-ventilating at the thought of glory, and his son Dale (his mother surely couldn't have been a dragon) was spending most of the time shaking in a corner. It was nervy out there.

Spotland does not live up to its image – the place is actually pretty good. Three smart single-tiered seated stands in soft blue tones and a covered terrace for the home fans to practice their trophy-winning dance on, you don't need it to be packed to hear some noise. The travelling Shrimpers made the most of the good acoustics and were not there just to be dragon-fodder. Tango Brown, who had replaced Luggy a year ago, meant business so he could then 'stick one' to all who had not even responded to his application forms since leaving PNE, and we were looking a good bet for the play-offs. A win was needed and was duly delivered - it somehow though seemed cruel.

Rochdale got their promotion in the end but they had to settle for the non-trophy cabinet disturbing third spot. One day I'm sure they will win a pot - I would love to be there.

84/92 - MACRON STADIUM, Bolton Wanderers 1 Leeds United 1, Championship, Saturday 10 January 2015

A confession: every other game I'd seen over the previous 42 plus years I had wanted to be there. I had gone because I was supporting my team, or was intrigued about the place I was about to visit, or excited about the match awaiting me, or sometimes even all three. For my trip to Bolton it was different - it was cold, I was tired, I had plenty of other things I could be doing, and above all I would have preferred to have been at Roots Hall for the visit of my old Green Army brethren.

However, Bolton was on the 'to do' list and a match appeared on the fixture schedule which would make it a little less of a chore. Edward needed to get back to university at Huddersfield after the Xmas break and the AA route-finder said that the Macron would then only be 35 miles away. Furthermore, my mate David would be there watching his beloved Leeds huff and puff. It was an opportunity I decided to take.

I met David at the obligatory pub and collected the ticket he had sorted for me. The Leeds tribe as usual was out in force and their dire league position (one point off the relegation zone) meant that even the most blinkered were beginning to think an automatic promotion spot might be a challenge too far. Their fans have certainly suffered from backroom shenanigans at Elland Road for a long time now, yet despite all that remain intensely loyal. However, no club has a 'right' to success and personally I think it is great that the traditional big guns get out-seated at the top table by the likes of Bournemouth from time to time. It gives supporters of Crewe, Rochdale, and even Southend, the hope needed to keep the faith.

On the surface, Bolton fans appeared to have all they could want to help in their quest to re-join the feast at the summit - a manager with excellent credentials (albeit Scottish League ones), a large squad which included players I'd even heard of (Kenny, Heskey, Gudjohnsen) and a stadium which looked superb. The Macron is simply stunning – a blue and white temple to be proud of. But the Trotters, like their visitors, were not having the best of times, and despite all of their proud history, of late their fans had not been that enthused to turn up in numbers - possibly they were all hibernating in the bedrooms that overlook the pitch in the adjoining hotel waiting for the sun to come out over Bolton. I fear their hotel bill may be a big one.

The away contingent of almost 4,000 predictably out-sang the homers. Equally predictably they all had doctors notes to show the stewards that their painful piles prevented them from sitting down, frustrating the orange ones in their usual quest for a hospital atmosphere. In the end the match finished in a dull draw, but life following Leeds and indeed in just being with their fans is never dull. I had enjoyed my little trilogy amongst their number and have struck up fan friendships that I know will continue in meet-ups into the future .... though if there's a 50-50 in an old Chopper v Bremner clip to be viewed I know who I'd be wanting to win it.

85/92 - ST JAMES' PARK, Newcastle United 1 Watford 2, Premier League, Saturday 19 September 2015

Football is a time to meet up with friends and enjoy a common passion, but it can also provide an opportunity to do something you need to do. Jim had been living up in Newcastle for a year and we had seen little of him - I had missed my footballing father and son trips and he had too. Things oop north had also recently not quite been going as he would have wanted and we needed to see him. An afternoon out at the 'other' St James' Park came to the rescue.

Edward also needed to get to Huddersfield again, this time for the start of his second year (this parent taxi thing can get a little mile-heavy). So it was an early start to get to his Uni halls at 10.00 am, a quick breakfast in a nearby café, and me then hot-footing it to Newcastle to get to Jim's flat just after mid-day. It was then a long walk to the station, a 20 minute metro ride and another walk through the town centre to a pub. Phew.

The Geordies have one of those traditional great town centre grounds, and in regularly attracting 50,000 to pay homage, match-day is a glorious parade of black n' white to the focal point through Iceland, Poundland and other lands I'd pay to avoid spending an afternoon in. We had a good catch up in the pub, considered a plan for Jim's return to Suffolk, and supped the brown stuff. It was a small hostelry in view of the ground and oozed Newcastle United, but the locals seemed to be in pessimistic mood. Two points out of 15 was not a good start, and even the 'Umbrella Model' in his programme notes was recognising that backward steps would be experienced. The programme also reflected on "... external negativity that has been building ...", had a picture of Mitrovic being sent off, and in the manager's notes section had three pictures of the boss showing him alternately head down, dishevelled and grimacing. The mood was set.

Newcastle's version of St James' Park is a tad more ambitious than its Devon namesake. Peering down on its surroundings, the outside view is of a large-scale engineering tribute to steel girders, but it is inside which provides the wow-factor: two substantial stands that would do any ground proud which are then dwarfed by two others with four tiers stretching up to meet the clouds. At some point no doubt the two smaller brothers will grow to rise up to their giant siblings and change an already imposing venue into something for vertigo sufferers to truly fear.

Pictures of the old place in the '60s with mass swaying terraces are iconic and it must have been some place back then, but if we move beyond romanticising for the past (I'll try I promise) then the seated super-structure of today really is the dog's bollocks. We had our pictures taken with the Milburn Stand dominating the background and took our seats for the match in its Leazes Stand brother.

All around us were tense Geordies whilst above us 2,000 Hornets were buzzing with piss-taking singing such as that old favourite "You're gonna be sacked in the morning". Some of those in black 'n white looked as though they wanted to join in. And then the game kicked-off.

'Seen it all before' faces gave resigned looks as Ighalo slotted one home after 10 minutes and Watford could have bagged more before the Nigerian doubled his tally not long after. Cue more Geordie head-shaking, with some of them getting really angry, making their way to the front of our concourse and shaking their fists in the direction of the bench in an expletive frenzy. The Watford fans were loving it and didn't shut up, they were just having a great day out and from their lofty perch their happy tones rang around the ground. It was a fascinating environment for the neutral, and Jim and I tried not to look as though we were enjoying ourselves by putting on our best Poundland shopping faces. Getting decked by an irate Geordie for wrongly being identified as a Hornet is not the way I would choose for any day to pan out.

Why Newcastle put the away fans up in the gods is a mystery to me. Visitors know it's probably the tallest peak they'll get to in the 92 unless Chelsea opt to play their home games at the Nou Camp when Stamford Bridge is finally re-developed, and fans rise to the challenge. Plus the sound they make seems to bounce off the roof just above their heads to deflect down to those below. Then, if the visitors have something to celebrate, the players always seem to make a special effort to acknowledge their friends from high up. Time for a tactical re-think I'd say.

Newcastle did pick up in the second-half and for a brief few moments the Geordie roar impressed – I wanted more but things just petered out into a swearing fest. 'A ground to go back to when times are a little better' noted in the diary – I suspect it will be an even more imposing place then.

I left Jim at his flat with a date fixed for his home-coming to focus on, and plotted on the long drive back how to get the 92 done once and for all. It was all becoming a bit of an ongoing sore with no end game in sight - time to cure it. I set Blackpool as the final destination in April, and at an A1 refuelling stop devised a plan for Jim and me to fit in the six others left before then.

86/92 - RIVERSIDE STADIUM, Middlesbrough 3 Charlton Athletic 0, Championship, Saturday 31 October 2015

You'll note that I had neglected the North East somewhat over the previous four decades. From wherever I had lived it was hardly 'around the corner' – indeed, until my visit to see the monkey assassins in 2008 I had not ventured any further north than Scarborough (which Mum and Dad had chosen as our holiday destination for the two weeks it pissed down in the middle of the '76 heatwave). But six weeks after Newcastle I found myself again renewing acquaintance with the A1.

Jim's return trip home and a need for the parent removal service coincided with a home game for the Smoggies, a term of endearment conceived by their red and white friends from up the coast in reference to pollution on Teeside. In turn their neighbours preferred nickname now is the 'Black Cats', a badge originating from a wailing old pussy at a local gun battery in 1805. Inventive folk these North Easterners – some southern clubs could surely do better. 'Plague Rats' I suggest is an affectionate reference to the past that some London club is missing out on.

Anyway, we packed up Jim's flat, handed in the key, collected back most of the deposit and made our way one last time past that rusty old roadside hand glider to drive down to the Riverside. We did take a slight wrong turn on the way - some plonker had decided to name a sports arena near Durham the 'Riverside Leisure Complex'; we fell for it. However, less spectator activity than a Dagenham home game, and a façade which was not living up to expectations, led us to stop doing the 'I'm sure it's easy to find' bloke-thing. I consulted the Satnav and we were then soon on the right track guided by its scolding female tones.

Close to the ground we met a friendly Smoggy/Monkey Hanger dual season ticket holder (how many of them are there?) who showed us some wasteland where we could park for free right next to a car park offering the same for a fiver. The free space looked less dodgy so we took our new pal's advice. On the walk to the ground he advised us which burger vans to avoid (useful), gave us a potted history of watching Hartlepool (less useful), and informed us about his autograph collecting (slightly worrying). We made our excuses at the Ayresome Gates and went on a circuit of the impressive arena now before us.

The Riverside - a more apt name would be difficult to find. Right by the Tees, its backdrop is stunning. With the Transporter Bridge and docklands in the background, moored up a stone's throw from the North Stand is the rusting hulk of the 'North Sea Producer', a massive oil field service vessel. It really is a unique sight – Roots Hall has the more traditional English surroundings of a kebab shop and pizza takeaway.

I just warmed to the whole place – vista aside, the stadium has an eye-catching main entrance fronted by the gates from the old pad, and impressive statues to former legends. Inside, the larger main stand gives variety and the club makes every effort with its pre-match music to get the locals psyched up. Fresh from making Louis van Gaal seem less chipper than normal with a mid-week penalty shoot-out League Cup win, Middlesbrough were hyped too and thrashed poor old Charlton 1-0 (it should have been 10). The whole place just seemed to be in a good mood and I felt myself getting carried along with it. I wondered whether a "Smoggy Smoggy Smoggy oi oi oi" chant would go down well, but Jim wisely urged me to be cautious.

Yep, the Riverside gets a thumbs-up. I'm just not sure of having a season ticket for Victoria Road at the same time.

87/92 - THE HIVE, Barnet 2 Blackpool 0, FA Cup Round One, Saturday 7 November 2015

Like many clubs, Barnet's story of why they are where they are is a complicated weave of money, hearts, facilities, red tape and management. Mix it all up, spit it out and see where you end up – suburban Edgware is where the gob has now landed for the Bees.

It's not quite as far away as Milton Keynes, but you can't help but feel that the omens are not good. Underhill to the Hive is 6.7 miles, that's 20 minutes according to the internet route planner which assumes that every one of the 4,000 or so traffic lights (rough estimate) on the streets in between are on green and that every family in North London has parked-up each of their five cars and taken their Boris Bike's on a ride into the country. In the real world, on a Saturday it takes about an hour in time and several more off your life. It's enough to turn bees in to wasps.

Barnet have never been blessed with a massive fan base – maybe 2,000 or so. For the 2015/16 season, up until our visit, the home fans flocking down choked streets from East Barnet, New Barnet, Borehamwood, Pinner, Stanmore and maybe a couple from even as far as Elstree, had dropped to around 1,600. A couple of years on, the appeal of Edgware (if there ever was any) is starting to wear off.

Anyway, for a while yet at least attendances will be boosted by a few ground-hoppers, and when Jim and I did finally get there to increase the crowd by just over 0.1%, the heavens opened. Fearing a Ricoh-style bath we waited for the deluge to reduce to a storm and legged-it to the Hive where shelter on the outside was hard to come by. We took refuge in the club shop, a distinctly modest affair selling a few orange garments, a pen and a mug. If Man City ever come to town their fans will be disappointed by the lack of essential Barnet monogrammed nightwear, sunglasses, dog leads, glow sticks and Nicky Bailey masks (take five minutes out to recover from that last thought).

Eight seconds later we had finished browsing and dashed to the away fan area – fancying a bit of a FA Cup party we had decided to show solidarity with Phil

Brown and become Tangerines for the day. This turned out to be a mistake – Blackpool's travelling army was reluctant to break silence (or even wind) all afternoon for fear perhaps of coming out of camouflage from their orange seats, and remained in a coma throughout. We were not impressed, ok your team may be cack and the ownership of your club not to your liking, but the FA Cup is a deluded once-a-season opportunity for glory and should be an excuse to have a bit of non-serious fun. I wondered why our chosen match-buddies had even bothered to turn up (surely they weren't all on the 92 trail?). Mind you, I think the closest their team got all match was when Barnet's goalie took a back pass - their team didn't seem too fussed either.

Seated in the half-decent West Stand, we had a good view, though immediately opposite was certainly the weirdest 'stand' I have seen, namely the arse end of an office block with what looked like someone's shed roof bolted on to half cover a few seats below. Any place in a storm I suppose, though no one was sitting there due to the rain, the roof proving inadequate for sheltering anything but a few pigeons.

We watched Barnet sleep-walk to an easy victory but did at least have the novelty to our left of watching trains on the underground-over-ground (Mike Batt – I've acknowledged your greatness). Sadly the matches on the other park pitches nearby were just out of view.

I do hope Barnet survive this move – they are a team that has provided a lot of colour over their hokey-cokey league history, but I think (and I suspect they know) that they need to get out of Edgware - quickly (traffic permitting).

88/92 - BRAMALL LANE, Sheffield United 2 Southend United 2, League One, Saturday 14 November 2015

Three new grounds three Saturdays running – Jim and I were becoming more prolific than roadworks on the A12 Colchester bypass.

This visit though had been on the menu since the fixtures first came out - a historic big ground for what still is a famous old club is always one to appeal and provide relief from the standard diet of out-of-town functional concrete blobs. Well over 1,000 Shrimpers (maybe double the average away following especially for a long trip) thought the same. It is a fact well known but worth repeating – starting in 1889, Bramall Lane is the oldest major stadium in the world to still be hosting professional footie. A footie fan likes a bit of tradition - just ask AFC Wimbledon.

Making it a weekender so we could sample student life with Edward for an evening of low-grade nosh and cheap beer, we arrived in the Steel City nice and early and promptly got lost in the one way system, venturing into a bus lane to boost funds for the local council. These blatant money-making schemes which put warning signs on tarmac full of traffic are just legalised fraud. You do get a nice picture with the fine demand, mine showing two cars following me to the same fate. It is accompanied by a note stating that if you pay early you get a 50% reduction - ever one for a bargain I opted for doing just that. I couldn't help feeling though that I'd just been mugged. May all their buses break down. Rant over.

Shrimpers were everywhere around wandering from pub to pub in the pouring rain which hadn't stopped since the previous weekend. Unlike the Hive, Bramall Lane had plenty of shelter on offer and we made sure we got there reasonably quickly to give this footballing monument the time it deserved.

This was nearly a match that wasn't - in the weeks leading up to it there was the possibility that Sheffield could have called the game off due to having at least three international call-ups, but thankfully that never happened. The amount of planning that would have had to have been un-done, and no doubt monies lost on train fares and hotels booked, would have been, well, annoying for the travelling Shrimpers. It was not until 10 days before the game that we could be certain it was on, yet another example of how the authorities treat fans as second-rate. Another rant over.

Big but cosy, all red yet still tasteful, enclosed yet light, Bramall Lane is the business. You can almost feel the history running from its pores: that jinking run from Tony Currie with Motson eulogising "A quality goal by a quality player," in the same era Tony Field going on a mazy run past three Ipswich defenders who each tried to put him in hospital but he rode them all to score, or even Dean Saunders directing a throw against the Port Vale goalie in the late 90's and curling the rebound past him before he could get back between the sticks. Mind you, ask a Blade about their top three goals and they will probably come up with a hatrick of tap-ins against Wednesday - any win against your closest rivals is one to savour no matter how it comes about.

Back to the present day, we did like the 'SUFC' lettering on the seats of Sheffield's Kop before the home fans started to arrive in number and spoil the Southend United FC tribute. The match when it came was great and the atmosphere from a ground only half-full was surprisingly decent. Southend's two scorchers went in at our end too which always makes the celebrations better – none of that 'Did it?' time delay that can occur before you realise that you've scored at the other end hence explaining why your team is bundling on top of one another.

The Blades did pull two goals back to spoil things a little but we were happy with a point and enjoyed the final-whistle prolonged acknowledgement that our team gave to our support. A bit of mutual badge-thumping at the end of a hard game at a difficult place to usually get anything from is always good for the soul.

If you can avoid the bus lanes, Bramall Lane is a place to go back to.

89/92 – RODNEY PARADE, Newport County 1 Plymouth Argyle 2, League Two, Monday 28 December 2015

In the final run-in the two Welsh trips were always going to be a challenge (ok, a pain). Setting aside the annoyance that I'd already seen both clubs at their old home grounds, from Suffolk the trip to Wales is a decent stretch. There is also the joy of the M25 in the way plus that long run of the M4 where, east to west, the junctions get further and further apart as you approach Bristol to make the drive seem endless. But a fixture-switch for Cardiff had at least presented the prospect of doing them both in one trip on consecutive days, with the added bonus of a re-kindling of past away days with the Green Army. Sorted.

Newport was our initial destination and, after parking up, we went in search of liquid refreshment. Our first stop was the club house on the edge of the ground complex – it was one of those 'walk in and try not to make it too obvious that the folk in there know you immediately think it's crap by walking out of a different door out of view of the one you came in' moments. The pub we found close by wasn't much better, but the locals were friendly and I bored a few of them with my party talk winner of 'being a Southend fan at an Argyle match' story.

We had tickets for the sell-out away end, a small scale version of the Priestfield scaffold delight and, like its bigger brother, dependent on dry weather for a better and safer experience. We were lucky, for once it was just freezing, and we took our seats amongst the soothing West Country burr. It felt good to hear the complex words of the 'Wheelbarrow Song' again.

An old rugby ground, the Rodney Parade pitch takes a regular beating from the cauliflower ear brigade so their footie bedfellows have adapted style to suit - high and mighty heave-ho where the sight of the ball hitting the ground is discouraged. It also makes travelling to Newport just that bit more exciting – you don't know until just before kick-off whether the ref will take exception to the ploughed furrows and postpone or whether he'd remembered his wellies in which case it was 'game on'.

Newport's new home is an odd mix of the old and new. On the east side is the new, a structure which looks like a bigger version of the office-come-pigeon loft at The Hive but with 'curry splash' coloured seats. On the west you will find the old, a tribute to pre-fabricated roofing where, when County have possession, spectators in the seats above its terrace frontage peer through a narrow slot playing 'where the fuck has the ball gone now?' Assuming the away terrace scaffold is on loan from a local builder, a budding groom has the perfect ready-made 'something old, something new, something borrowed' day out gift for his bride.

305

Argyle scraped through a scrappy game, I got to sing "We are top of the league" for the first time in years, and we left behind a weird but interesting Rodney Parade. We travelled to Cardiff and our hotel with a big decision to make – hard or soft pillows? I wonder which Lenny prefers.

90/91 – CARDIFF CITY STADIUM, Cardiff City 1 Nottingham Forest 1, Championship, Tuesday 29 December 2015

Following on from use of a very efficient internet ticket purchasing facility, I had received an email from Cardiff's marketing manager sending a 'welcome pack' as part of their process for first time visitors. A nice touch, so I contacted Adam telling him about my 92 quest and we arranged to meet up pre-match.

A quick call on arrival and he was there to greet us, took us inside the concourse and showed us around - for someone who was undoubtedly busy on match days it was good of him to take the time, especially as it was clear we were not even an outside bet for attending again any time soon. It's things like that which can make you warm to a club - in my Uni days I had known a bit of an annoying Bluebird and often thought about tightening the yellow, blue and white scarf that he permanently wore, but Adam's efforts made me think about Cardiff in a completely different light.

The match was an evening kick-off and, even though both teams still had realistic play-off ambitions, the stadium was a bit desolate. Adam had said that, when in the Premiership, tickets were hard to come by, yet now just a league lower (and still doing ok-ish) over 50% of the interest had fallen away. I agree that the Championship is some way short of the next step up regarding quality (though they want to sample League Two), but dropping down a level has at least given Cardiff a much better chance of winning more than they lose. During their one season in the Premiership the Bluebirds seemed to be on a loser from the start, won only seven times and finished rock-bottom. I'd rather watch a decent game than a forgone conclusion, but the Cardiff public apparently didn't agree.

It all seemed a shame. The Cardiff City Stadium (the equally snappy 'Stadiwm Dinas Caerdydd' as it's known by the locals) looked superb and was trying hard. Inside the concourse, the walls were adorned with great pictures of yesteryear, and a band playing Stereophonics numbers tried their best to get folk going, but all around us it just seemed a bit empty and quiet - there was more life in a tramps vest. Inside the place at least looked sparkling, and if they can just put a lick of blue paint on those red seats in the recent stand extension (what was the guy thinking, it's such a colour clash) it will be fantastic.

Chosen a bit randomly (I had just gone for cheapest) our seats were in with the Cardiff hard core who did make an effort to get some noise going. They were aided by an excellent designated drum area built into

the back wall of the stand immediately behind them –
top marks for the designers on that one. Not least
because it means you then don't find yourself sitting
next to some deaf and tuneless skin basher (probably
wearing a yellow, blue and white scarf around his
neck) all game.

However, by half-time we'd had enough, every time a
Forest player moved forward the shout "scab" rang out
from a donkey coat next to us. I had to ask him why
and learned it was in reference to the Nottinghamshire
miners breaking the strike in 1984 (I interpret his
words politely for any sensitive soul making it this far
in the book). Not quite up there with Scottish fans
remembering a victory 700 years ago, but equally a
little dated - I wondered whether I should try my 'Free
Nelson Mandela' joke on him but in the end thought
there was a slight risk he might not appreciate my
ironic dig at his lack of contemporary politics. So we
moved to the corner for the second half and got a
better view of an average game before legging it to the
car for our late night motorway appointment.

In the December dark we could still just make out one
notable landmark on the way back which always
makes me chuckle. Coming off the M4 to travel
clockwise on the M25 you soon get to a railway bridge
with "Give Peas A Chance" emblazoned along its top in
now faded white paint – it has been there for years
now and has been seen by millions. Whether it's the
cry of a veggie, or a heart-felt appeal by an illiterate

pacifist, I don't really mind, but to me it's a humorous effort by some kind soul to help the weary travelling footie fan along their way. Top stuff.

91/92 – STADIUM OF LIGHT, Sunderland 1 Bournemouth 1, Premier League, Saturday January 16 2016

Another trip up the A1 to get to number 91, Jim and I did this as a day trip and it was good to get the chance to see AFC Bournemouth sparring at their new level. For decades they had been regular visitors to Roots Hall and frequently had been pants - one day they even turned up with an ageing George Best and managed to stifle the life out of the game in a way that the great man would surely have run away from had he been sober. But today, under the guidance of their youthful smiling assassin, they deliver a brand of football which is often sublime - aided of course by three ex-Shrimpers forming the backbone of their team.

At a stop on the way up the services were full of cheery red and black shirts – I suspected that six months in they still couldn't really believe what was happening. And how on earth are the Cherries going to spend the £81 million they will get from Sky TV in 2016/17 without spoiling the humble solidarity they stand for and have built their success on? I suggest they let their fans in for free all year and funnel the rest back down the leagues to stick one up to the over-blown greedy elements that populate a good part of the Premiership - the boost they would get from that would be priceless.

Anyway, we get to Sunderland, see a Black Cat crossing the road to park up on a piece of wasteland (it's clearly the canny thing to do in the North East), and after a quick word with him we do the same. This time it's only a brief acquaintance with no secret Monkey Hanger confession, and we make our way to a nearby pub with Norwich v Liverpool showing on their big screen. The whole pub is enthralled by this one, cheering for the Reds to put one over their relegation rivals. We leave at half-time with the pub a little subdued at the Canaries being 2-1 up, and make our way to the Stadium of Light to be greeted by a scary sight - Bob Stokoe.

Old Bob was 42 going on 82 when he did 'that run' to plant a smacker on Jim Montgomery. Forget your own loyalties for a moment - draw up a top 10 list of footie moments that make you go all tingly and surely Bob's 1973 beige mac sprint is in there, it's just joyful. The scene is now captured in bronze outside the stadium with Bob in full flight, jazz-hands style. It is certainly a unique portrait and we liked it, but on a dark evening there should probably be 'parental advisory note' signs up. Maybe a safer bet would have been Bob embracing Jim on the Wembley turf (shortly before Bobby Kerr swiped his Trilby).

We moved from the statue to the 'fanzone' - how cool is that? I thought they were only reserved for international tournaments, but the Black Cats have their very own 'fun fair' outside the stadium every match day - giant table football, penalty competitions, food and drink, merchandise stalls, picture opportunity scenes, a band playing ..... that's the way to treat and involve the fans. I stood in a queue of ankle-biters to have a go at whacking the ball as hard as I could to record the speed it went, and happy with my 38 mph turned to acknowledge greatness from a crowd of hard-staring dads who were less impressed. I think I had just won the under-10's competition.

We opted to move to the stadium where we were reacquainted with the Norwich v Liverpool game on the numerous screens in the concourse. It was packed, as not only was the game great, but the result was important. In injury time Bassong equalised for Norwich to make it 4-4 and all around us groans rang out - a valuable point would have put the Canaries six points ahead, and given Sunderland's form that would take some time to overhaul. But just as interest was starting to drift away Lallana bangs in the winner for Liverpool and the Black Cats celebrate wildly. It meant just one point less to find in the relegation scrap, but all watching knew it could be oh so important in the final reckoning.

Now, I do have a couple of beefs with Sunderland AFC. First, why can't they invest some of their Sky windfall in some new red plastic seats? The stadium will soon be approaching its 20th birthday and some of it is starting to wear a bit, but the sun-bleached seats on part of the lower tier look naff and stick out like a sore thumb on TV, especially as Black Cats start to vacate when full-time approaches (or earlier if they're getting stuffed). If Big Sam put the money aside he spends on beauty treatment each week they'd soon have enough to fund it all.

Second, our seats were at the front of the second tier in one corner, a nice view until we sat down and were confronted with a constant tide of folk walking to and fro, with trips to the bogs, burger top-up trips and frantic runs to the beer replenishment queues in the gangway right in front of us, all blocking our sight-lines. The tickets should have been marked 'restricted and very annoying view'; the home fans' need to shovel it in one end and funnel it out of the other end was insatiable. Why can't they just watch the game, or perhaps install commodes? My top tip for visiting the Stadium of Light would be to sit in the middle of a block - that way you will only be disturbed by those immediately around you rather than the 10,000 others in your stand.

But, faded seats and fan bladder weakness aside, the Stadium of Light lives up to its slightly pretentious name and was a worthy final ground stop before the last jigsaw piece was to be fitted in Blackpool. Time to return to the seaside.

Oh I Do Like To Be Beside The Seaside

92/92 – BLOOMFIELD ROAD, Blackpool 2 Southend United 0, League One, Saturday 2 April 2016

"..... Oh I do like to be beside the sea, with a bucket and a ...." The only time I can recall singing that at a match was on the sleepy shores of West Brom, but that was more for rhyming reasons than for any whiff of salty air.

Anyway, in a kind of long-winded version of Coast to Coast, 45 years on from Dad's Ford Anglia chugging along the A13 to the flickering floodlights of Roots Hall, I was now on my way to the flashing bright lights of Blackpool. It had been a long trip with one or two cul-de-sacs (Wycombe) along the way, but most had been experiences that had given me happy times.

Doing the 92 has provided memories I would never have otherwise had - I love the game and my team, but if not for the 92 quest would I have drunk the barrel dry with a fellow Shrimper in a Lake District hotel were it not for the 'need to do' Brunton Park? Unlikely. Or would I have had a wonderful weekend in Bradford with Cameron watching Keystone Cops being given the run-around were it not for the purpose of ticking Valley Parade off the list? Probably not. Or would I have hitched up to Prenton Park for a Friday night game with virtually no one else there? Definitely not.

Life has changed beyond belief in the last four and a half decades, much of it I must say for the good though that is from a personal perspective rather than any useless broad-brush statement on the world in general. Let's have a stab at that though: what was better in 1971 compared to now? Not being quite sure where to start, in a quick household poll on the best three pub topics (some abstentions on that so just Jim and me voting - it's a broad enough sample) we arrived at music, beer and football.

Music. A glance at the Top 10 from 26 March 1971 shows it populated by the likes of T Rex, Mungo Jerry, Paul McCartney, Perry Como, Neil Diamond and George Harrison. Scroll forward to 2 April 2016 and the only one I've heard of is Lukas Graham and that's simply because whenever his 'Seven Years' comes on the radio I immediately put a CD on to avoid that woeful dirge staying on my mind for the rest of the day (or worse, for seven years). Yes, I'm a middle-aged Dad who probably last tuned in to Radio 1 when Tony Blackburn used to speak to his mechanical dog Arnold, but IMHO (I am 'with it' on text shorthand) the songs of the '70's will live longer in the memory (especially if I keep turning the songs of today off). 1971 1 2016 0.

Beer. Hmmmm, a tricky one to judge given that in 1971 I was only eight. I do recall seeing that beer came in cans which contained seven pints and with no discernible way of being opened. CAMRA were founded that year to decide which sort they liked best - the red or the blue ones. Later on in the 70's I discovered the tinny water to be a bit 'Cold Blow Lane' (somewhat unwelcoming). Today we are light years ahead of that in both choice and quality, and any match-up with the past is unfair. A tasting session competition would be a bit like watching Man U stick nine past Ipswich. 1971 1 2016 1.

Football. On the pitch we all know that Jamie Vardy would get to the finishing line around 30 seconds before Franny Lee in a 100 metre race. But give Vardy a diet of pies and beer for a month to even out the fitness regime and I suspect the race would be closer. Off the pitch any contrast is equally nonsensical – would you now want to stand on a crumbling terrace where the presence of goalposts at each end ticks the box for the safety certificate? But when today each new stadium has the feeling of déjà vu, the call for some yester-year variety amongst all of the common sense is strong. You just cannot compare – the romantic in me will yearn for the past but I do like those seats (but only those seats) at Stadium:mk. Call it a draw and share the trophy. 1971 1½ 2016 1½.

So, it was off to Bloomfield Road to see what they'd done with the past there. I took a few to share it with me - 14 of us made a weekender of it and they all should get a name-check for making my 92nd so special: Adrian, Brian, Craig, Darren, Harvey, Jim, Joe, Jon,

Marcus, Nick, Paul, Simon and Steve. All had been to watch footie with me before over the years - Harvey right at the beginning with our Dads, up to Jim as he now follows my habit for all things shrimp-like. They presented me with a Southend '92' shirt, so on that one game a year it's too hot to cover it up I can declare to all that I'm a bit down the pecking order when they were handing out squad numbers.

There was another surprise too. In arranging the tickets I asked Blackpool if Derek Spence still worked at the club. I was told he did and that they would pass my number on to him - I was hoping we might briefly meet up on match day. We exchanged a couple of voicemails; Derek couldn't be there on Saturday but would make it to our designated pre-meal pub the night before if time permitted. Not really thinking he would come along, he did, and greeted us like an old friend even if he didn't recall me chairing him off the pitch at Plainmoor in '81. We spent a wonderful hour chatting through old memories and Derek recalling with great fondness his time at Roots Hall. As you will have seen, Derek kindly agreed to write a foreword for this book.

A little bit of luxury was demanded for this one so I had booked us in to Blackpool's 1953 Suite situated in the hotel that now adjoins Bloomfield Road. Very good it was too, they made our rag-bag group of Shrimpers, Trannies, Clarets, Reds, Sky Blues, Robins, Spurs, Saints and even the Tractor persons very welcome.

From the restaurant windows a tangerine explosion spread out before us, stewards in anti-camouflage lime green gathering in small groups to get gemmed up on how not to fall asleep for the next three hours. The vista was actually pretty good - a complete but pro-longed revamp since the turn of the century has seen the old place still keep its memories, but you now sit down to reminisce about that Mickey Walsh goal. Even the temporary East Stand adds a certain charm, using stanchions to block the view when the visiting fans come in sufficient numbers. A healthy 616 Shrimpers did not quite qualify for that honour, so we were housed in the Stan Mortensen Stand instead.

Though the weekend was all going to plan I might have known that Southend would decline to perform in line with a cheesy Hugh Grant script and bang in a last minute winner. Instead we got an inept defeat, which on the plus side saved me a celebratory run down the steps pointing thumbs towards the number on my back. The fellow Shrimpers in our group were typically un-phased by the result meaning any realistic end to our play-off hopes, it was just something we were used to. My band of temporary Shrimpers were a little more vexed, the game had interrupted the beer flow and had failed to ignite their interest, so post-match it was more pub and then a curry to round off a still terrific weekend.

Achieving the 92 passes without ceremony – no 24 gun salute nor is there a medal awarded to mark the end, but what you do get are great memories and experiences with both people and places. I would commend attempting it to anyone with patience sprinkled with a little bit of insanity.

As we all know it is a quest that never ends as the 92 mix is a shifting target, so next season I will no doubt be off to see West Ham in their new pad the public has kindly paid for.

For now though I've used it up and worn it out – time to go back to my Roots.

Ground List

The following lists the grounds visited (or in two cases, events) in the order they appear in this book under each chapter heading.

1. Second Home

Roots Hall – Southend United

2. Come To The Shed And We'll Welcome You
Stamford Bridge – Chelsea
The Goldstone Ground – Brighton & Hove Albion
The Baseball Ground – Derby County
Layer Road - Colchester United
Wembley Stadium
Plough Lane – Wimbledon
Griffin Park – Brentford
Upton Park – West Ham United
Vicarage Road – Watford
White Hart Lane – Tottenham Hotspur
Brisbane Road – Leyton Orient

3. Semper Fidelis
Home Park – Plymouth Argyle
Portman Road - Ipswich Town
St James Park – Exeter City
Plainmoor – Torquay United
Highbury – Arsenal
Fellows Park – Walsall

Recreation Ground – Chesterfield
Ashton Gate – Bristol City
Edgar Street – Hereford United
Fratton Park – Portsmouth
Eastville – Bristol Rovers
The Den – Millwall
Elm Park – Reading
Hillsborough – Sheffield Wednesday
Craven Cottage – Fulham
Maine Road – Manchester City
Somerton Park – Newport County
Anfield – Liverpool
Loftus Road – Queens Park Rangers
The Abbey Stadium – Cambridge United
New Writtle Street – Chelmsford City
The Manor Ground – Oxford United

4. She Had A Wheelbarrow The Front Wheel Went Round

Selhurst Park – Crystal Palace
The Valley – Charlton Athletic
The Hawthorns – West Bromwich Albion
The City Ground – Notts Forest
St Andrews – Birmingham City
The Priestfield Stadium – Gillingham
Kenilworth Road – Luton Town
The Recreation Ground – Aldershot
Vetch Field – Swansea City
Dean Court – AFC Bournemouth
Ninian Park – Cardiff City

The County Ground – Swindon Town
Prenton Park – Tranmere Rovers
Goodison Park – Everton
Field Mill – Mansfield
Villa Park – Aston Villa
Twerton Park – Bristol Rovers
Ewood Park – Blackburn Rovers
Gay Meadow – Shrewsbury Town
Oakwell – Barnsley

5. **Working It Out**
The Dell – Southampton
Carrow Road – Norwich City
Watling Street – Maidstone United
London Road – Peterborough United
Filbert Street – Leicester City
Underhill – Barnet
Vale Park – Port Vale
The New Den – Millwall
Elland Road – Leeds United
Molineux – Wolverhampton Wanderers
Adams Park – Wycombe Wanderers
Sixfields Stadium – Northampton Town
Highfield Road – Coventry City
Old Trafford – Manchester United
Gresty Road – Crewe Alexandra
Boundary Park – Oldham Athletic
Nene Park – Rushden & Diamonds
Kassam Stadium – Oxford United
Camp Nou – Barcelona

Victoria Road – Dagenham & Redbridge

6. **Tilly Time**
   Millennium Stadium
   Meadow Lane – Notts County
   Glanford Park – Scunthorpe United
   The Memorial Stadium – Bristol Rovers
   Blundell Park – Grimsby Town
   Belle Vue – Doncaster Rovers
   Huish Park – Yeovil Town
   The National Hockey Stadium – MK Dons
   The Liberty Stadium – Swansea City
   Gelsenkirchen Fanzone – Germany
   Pride Park – Derby County
   Turf Moor – Burnley
   The Ricoh Arena – Coventry City
   The Britannia Stadium – Stoke City
   St Mary's Stadium – Southampton
   Bescot Stadium – Walsall
   The Keepmoat Stadium – Doncaster Rovers
   Victoria Park – Hartlepool United
   The Galpharm Stadium – Huddersfield Town
   Brunton Park – Carlisle United
   Walkers Stadium – Leicester City
   Stadium:MK – MK Dons
   Edgeley Park – Stockport County
   Community Stadium – Colchester United
   KC Stadium – Hull City

7. Basement Patience

Valley Parade – Bradford City
b2net Stadium – Chesterfield
The Greenhous Meadow – Shrewsbury Town
Broadhall Way – Stevenage
Pirelli Stadium – Burton Albion
DW Stadium – Wigan Athletic
The City of Manchester Stadium – Manchester City
Globe Arena – Morecambe
Sincil Bank – Lincoln City
Crown Ground – Accrington Stanley
Broadfield Stadium – Crawley Town
Emirates Stadium – Arsenal
Deepdale – Preston North End
Kingsmeadow – AFC Wimbledon
Municipal Stadium Poznan
Whaddon Road – Cheltenham Town
New York Stadium – Rotherham
Gigg Lane – Bury Town
Highbury Stadium – Fleetwood Town
Bootham Crescent – York City

8. Upping The Anti

Madejeski Stadium – Reading
Amex Stadium – Brighton & Hove Albion
Spotland – Rochdale
Macron Stadium – Bolton Wanderers
St James' Park – Newcastle United
Riverside Stadium – Middlesbrough
The Hive – Barnet

Bramall Lane – Sheffield United
Rodney Parade – Newport County
Cardiff City Stadium – Cardiff City
Stadium of Light - Sunderland

9. **Oh I Do Like To Be Beside The Seaside**
Bloomfield Road - Blackpool

Lightning Source UK Ltd.
Milton Keynes UK
UKOW05f1334211116
288165UK00019B/1284/P

9 781849 149488